THE CORPOREAL IMAGE

THE CORPOREAL IMAGE

FILM, ETHNOGRAPHY,
AND THE SENSES

David MacDougall

PRINCETON UNIVERSITY PRESS

PRINCETON AND OXFORD

COPYRIGHT © 2006 BY PRINCETON UNIVERSITY PRESS

PUBLISHED BY PRINCETON UNIVERSITY PRESS, 41 WILLIAM STREET,

PRINCETON, NEW JERSEY 08540

IN THE UNITED KINGDOM: PRINCETON UNIVERSITY PRESS, 3 MARKET PLACE,

WOODSTOCK, OXFORDSHIRE OX20 1SY

ALL RIGHTS RESERVED

LIBRARY OF CONGRESS CATALOGING-IN-PUBLICATION DATA

MACDOUGALL, DAVID.

THE CORPOREAL IMAGE : FILM, ETHNOGRAPHY, AND THE SENSES / DAVID MACDOUGALL.

P. CM.

INCLUDES BIBLIOGRAPHICAL REFERENCES AND INDEX

ISBN-13: 978-0-691-12155-0 (ALK. PAPER)

ISBN-10: 0-691-12155-9 (ALK. PAPER)

ISBN-13: 978-0-691-12156-7 (PBK.: ALK. PAPER)

ISBN-10: 0-691-12156-7 (PBK. : ALK. PAPER)

1. VISUAL ANTHROPOLGY. 2. PHOTOGRAPHY IN ETHNOLOGY. 3. MOTION

PICTURES IN ETHNOLOGY. I. TITLE.

GN347.M32 2006

301—DC22   2004060754

BRITISH LIBRARY CATALOGING-INPUBLICATION DATA IS AVAILABLE

THIS BOOK HAS BEEN COMPOSED IN SABON

PRINTED ON ACID-FREE PAPER. ∞

PUP.PRINCETON.EDU

PRINTED IN THE UNITED STATES OF AMERICA

3 5 7 9 10 8 6 4 2

In Memory of
Jean Rouch 1917–2004
John Marshall 1932–2005

CONTENTS

ILLUSTRATIONS

ACKNOWLEDGMENTS

THIS BOOK was made possible by the support and hospitality of a number of institutions. The Centre for Cross-Cultural Research at the Australian National University has provided a collegial environment for my writing and filmmaking activities over the past eight years. I am grateful to the Australian Research Council for a Queen Elizabeth II Fellowship and an Australian Professorial Fellowship, under which much of this work was done. A part of the book was written at the Wissenschaftskolleg in Berlin, where I held a visiting fellowship in 2000–2001. I am grateful to the Kolleg and to the fellows for their support and interest. Among other institutions that have contributed directly or indirectly to the writing of these essays are The Doon School in India, the Humanities Research Centre at the Australian National University, the Istituto Superiore Regionale Etnografico in Sardinia, and the University of Tromsø in Norway.

I owe thanks to a number of friends and colleagues who have helped me with advice and encouragement during the writing of the book. Among them are Roger Benjamin, Dipesh Chakrabarty, Faye Ginsburg, Chris Gregory, Gary Kildea, Judith MacDougall, Howard Morphy, Nicolas Peterson, Rossella Ragazzi, Peter Read, John Shannon, Sanjay Srivastava, Lucien Taylor, and Salim Yusufji. Others not mentioned here have given me valuable comments and information on particular subjects. Their contributions are acknowledged in the notes for the essays concerned.

Several chapters in the book have appeared elsewhere in somewhat different versions. For permission to reprint them here, I should like to thank the original publishers of the following: "Social Aesthetics and The Doon School," reprinted from *Visual Anthropology Review*, vol. 15, no. 1: 3–20, with the permission of the American Anthropological Association, © 2000 American Anthropological Association; "Photo Hierarchicus: Signs and Mirrors in Indian Photography," © 1992 from *Visual Anthropology*, vol. 5, no. 2, reproduced by permission of Taylor & Francis, Inc., *http://www.routledge-ny.com*; and "The Visual in Anthropology," reprinted from *Rethinking Visual Anthropology*, edited by Marcus Banks and Howard Morphy, Yale University Press, © 1997 by Yale University.

THE CORPOREAL IMAGE

INTRODUCTION

MEANING AND BEING

T HE ESSAYS in this book address the corporeal aspects of images and image-making. This is not to say that they are indifferent to the meanings and associations that images awaken in us—far from it—but they are concerned with the moment at which those meanings emerge from experience, before they become separated from physical encounters. At that point thought is still undifferentiated and bound up with matter and feeling in a complex relation that it often later loses in abstraction. I am concerned with this microsecond of discovery, of knowledge at the birth of knowledge.

Our consciousness of our own being is not primarily an image, it is a feeling. But our consciousness of the being, the autonomous existence, of nearly everything else in the world involves vision. We assume that the things we see have the properties of being, but our grasp of this depends upon extending our own feeling of being into our seeing. In the process, something quintessential of what we are becomes generalized in the world. Seeing not only makes us alive to the appearance of things but to being itself.

One of the functions of art, and often of science, is to help us understand the being of others in the world. However, art and science are only part of this; it depends as much on how we go about the daily practice of seeing. In this, the meaning we find in what we see is always both a necessity and an obstacle. Meaning guides our seeing. Meaning allows us to categorize objects. Meaning is what imbues the image of a person with all we know about them. It is what makes them familiar, bringing them to life each time we see them. But meaning, when we force it on things, can also blind us, causing us to see only what we expect to see or distracting us from seeing very much at all.

My reasons for writing about this come from a background of trying to use images in an academic discipline. Images reflect thought, and they may lead to thought, but they are much more than thought. We are accustomed to regarding thought as something resembling language—the mind speaking to itself or, as dictionaries put it, a process of reasoning. But our conscious experience involves much more than this kind of thought. It is made up of ideas, emotions, sensory responses, and the pictures of our imagination. The way we use words all too often becomes a mistaken recipe for how to make, use, and understand visual images. By treating images—in paintings, photographs, and films—as a product of language, or even a language in themselves, we ally them to a concept of thought that neglects many of the ways in which they create our knowledge. It is important to recognize this, not in order to restrict images to nonlinguistic purposes—this merely subordinates them further to words—but in order to reexamine the relation between seeing, thinking, and knowing, and the complex nature of thought itself.

The chapters in this book are essays in the strict sense of the term—attempts to find words for observations that, in the present case, have resulted from varied experiences with photographs, films, and texts. Ultimately, all concern the human subject—as material presence, as thinking being, as child and adult; in still photographs, in ethnography, and in cinema. The book moves in part I from questions of embodiment, in and around film, to filmic representation itself; in part II to the representation of childhood, and my own attempts to film children's lives; in part III to photography in colonial and postcolonial settings; and lastly in part IV to the history and possible future of visual anthropology. If these essays have a common theme, it is that the encounter with visual images demands more of us than the mental facility that language has given us. There is a specificity and obduracy to images that defies our accustomed habits of translation and summation. In considering our use of images, it is no good simply insisting that we must do a better job of adapting them to the rules of scholarly writing. This will lead only to bad compromises. If we are to gain new knowledge from using images, it will come in other forms and by different means.

Our seeing is already deeply predetermined. Much of the knowledge we gain through vision and our other senses, and the way we direct our seeing, is highly organized. To a large extent this is not a matter of choice but of our cultural and even our neural conditioning.[1] We see conceptually, metaphorically, linguistically. But whatever our culture, we also see to some extent literally. There is always a tension between these two ways of seeing, and between our consciousness of meaning and of being. As we look at things, our perception is guided by cultural and personal interests, but perception is also the mechanism by which these interests are altered and added to. There is thus an interdependency between perception and meaning. Meaning shapes perception, but in the end perception can refigure meaning, so that at the next stage this may alter perception once again.

This applies as much to making images as to our seeing, and to seeing images made by others. Meaning is produced by our whole bodies, not just by conscious thought. We see with our bodies, and any image we make carries the imprint of our bodies; that is to say, of our being as well as the meanings we intend to convey. As a product of human vision, image-making might be regarded by some as little more than secondhand or surrogate seeing. But when we look purposefully, and when we think, we complicate the process of seeing enormously.[2] We invest it with desires and heightened responses. The images we make become artifacts of this. They are, in a sense, mirrors of our bodies, replicating the whole of the body's activity, with its physical movements, its shifting attention, and its conflicting impulses toward order and disorder. A complex construction such as a film or photograph has an animal origin. Corporeal images are not just the images of other bodies; they are also images of the body behind the camera and its relations with the world.

Photographic images are inherently reflexive, in that they refer back to the photographer at the moment of their creation, at the moment of an encounter. In films this is extended by a kind of triangulation, in which each successive scene further locates the author in relation to the subjects. There may be other signs of who and where the author is in the responses of the people being filmed. These signs are often difficult to interpret individually, but they gain direction and significance through the course of a film. Viewers cannot avoid interpreting these signs, however unconsciously, any more than they can in the exchanges of daily life.

Despite the parallels between seeing and image-making, looking with and without a camera can never be the same. However much it may be directed, a camera (or a photographic emulsion) produces an image that is independent of our bodies. This material image has not passed through us, even though the camera that produced it mimics many of the characteristics of human vision. There is thus an irreducible part of a photographic image that escapes from us. It is an intimation of something uncontrolled and uncontrollable. A literary view can take us only so far in understanding this. "Film is about something," Dai Vaughan once wrote, "whereas reality is not."[3] Despite the imprint of our minds and bodies, films and photographs remind us that in the end life is not "about" something—life is not like that.

Framing people, objects, and events with a camera is always "about" something. It is a way of pointing out, of describing, of judging. It domesticates and organizes vision. It both enlarges and diminishes. It diminishes by leaving out those connections in life to which the photographer is blind, as when it imposes an explanation on events that we know to be more complex. Or it does this as a deliberate sacrifice to some seemingly more important argument or dramatic effect. Framing enlarges through a similar process. It is what lifts something out of its background in order to look at it more closely, as we might pick up a leaf in the forest.

Through selection, framing also distills and concentrates experience. By isolating observations, it reveals commonalities and connections that may have gone unnoticed before. These may be the characteristic mannerisms of a person, or how a particular cultural theme emerges repeatedly in different contexts. Such intensifications and reinforcements of perception may make us, as viewers, more observant in our daily lives, but they can also dull our responses through overuse. Picture editors may wonder if there is much point in publishing yet another photograph of a maimed body or a starving child. Framing often reveals the sensibilities of the author by focusing on certain subjects or displaying a distinctive way of looking. Conversely, framing sometimes shows the author rebelling against framing, with a roughness that expresses impatience with all elegance, art, and artifice.[4] Successive generations of photographers and filmmakers have allowed accident and chance into their work in a calculated way. Framing thus has two intertwined impulses—to frame but also to show what lies beyond or in spite of framing.

Framing in a more general sense produces different modes of looking with a camera. One may, for example, distinguish between a purely responsive camera, an interactive camera, and a constructive camera. These approaches reflect different stances toward the subject. The differences are not so much a matter of degree as of kind. One approach is not necessarily more or less objective than another, or more or less personally engaged. They represent different temperaments and aims, not different moralities. In a single film, several approaches may be employed for separate purposes. Thus, a responsive camera observes and interprets its subject without provoking or disturbing it. It responds rather than interferes. An interactive camera, on the contrary, records its own interchanges with the subject. A constructive camera interprets its subject by breaking it down and reassembling it according to some external logic.

In making films, we are constantly advancing our own ideas about a world whose existence owes nothing to us. In fiction films as well as non-fiction films, we use "found" materials from this world. We fashion them into webs of signification, but within these webs are caught glimpses of being more unexpected and powerful than anything we could create. These may be qualities we discover in human beings or in the plenitude of the inanimate world. A good film reflects the interplay of meaning and being, and its meanings take into account the autonomy of being. Meaning can easily overpower being. We see this in the effect of the picturesque on portraiture and landscapes in nineteenth-century painting and photography. In making films, wise filmmakers create structures in which being is allowed to live, not only in isolated glimpses but in moments of revelation throughout the whole work. These form their own connections above and beyond our intentions as filmmakers. This is why knowing when to desist in our interpretations is so important, to allow these moments to connect and resonate.

In social science and the humanities, images have had an uneven career, depending upon the degree to which seeing has been accorded the status of knowledge. As photography has spread across the world, visual images have gone from being prized in the nineteenth century to being increasingly regarded as instruments rather than constituents of knowledge.

As writers, we articulate thoughts and experiences, but as photographers and filmmakers we articulate images of looking and being. What is thought is only implied, unless it is appended in writing or speech. Some would say that images, then, are not in any sense knowledge. They simply make knowledge possible, as data from observations. But in another sense they *are* what we know, or have known, prior to any comparison, judgment, or explanation. There is a perceptual as well as a conceptual kind of knowledge. This knowledge has no propositional status (of generality, of explanation) except the proposition of its own existence. It remains to a large extent inert, untapped. Only in the will to declare it do we detect the stirrings of thought.

A filmmaker's knowledge is often believed to lie in a film's conclusions, expressed through a visual rhetoric that juxtaposes shots and scenes, or at a more general level explains behavior through narratives of power, exchange, belief, and emotion. These are the "messages" that the film communicates. A kind of visual reasoning has taken place. Yet the filmmaker has seen and knows much more than can be communicated in this way. Is it possible to transmit this knowledge—which cannot be conceptualized—to others? In academic writing this question is generally dealt with by setting aside such knowledge as superfluous, or inaccessible, or outside the domain of the discipline or the problem at hand. But in films and photographs, it is far more difficult to cordon off statements about reality from the immediacy of the reality shown. The kinds of knowledge we gain from images and texts may have to be approached in quite different ways.

My image of you, or my many images of you in different situations, forms much of what I know about you. Appearance *is* knowledge, of a kind. Showing becomes a way of saying the unsayable. Visual knowledge (as well as other forms of sensory knowledge) provides one of our primary means of comprehending the experience of other people. Unlike the knowledge communicated by words, what we show in images has no transparency or volition—it is a different knowledge, stubborn and opaque, but with a capacity for the finest detail. How we reconcile this with other forms of knowledge—of explanation, metaphor, analogy—is one of the great themes of film itself, which more explicitly than writing pits being against meaning.

Through their stubbornness, photographic images dispute their consecrated meanings (what Barthes called the *studium*) or at least have the potential to undercut them. In films the complexity of people and objects implicitly resists the theories and explanations in which the film enlists them, sometimes suggesting other explanations or no explanations at all. In this sense, then, film is always a discourse of risk and indeterminacy. This puts it at odds with most academic writing, which, despite its caution and qualifications, is a discourse that advances always toward conclusions. For all the ways in which photographic images oversimplify and aggressively impose their messages (as they often do in advertising, for example), they are intrinsically tentative, oscillating between meaning and the self-sufficiency of their subjects.

In an effort to accommodate this alien knowledge, disciplines such as history and anthropology tend to find a place for it within the knowledge systems of the people they study rather than within the discipline itself. It can then be viewed through the filter of established principles, without challenging the premises of belief (of rational thought) from which these disciplines draw their authority. Seeing, hearing, and other forms of sensory knowledge are accordingly located in individual experience or in cultural and historical collectivities. They are seen as extending the reach of the discipline without fundamentally altering it. Methods that directly address the senses, such as photography and film, tend to be treated similarly—that is, chiefly as adjuncts to formulating knowledge at a higher level of abstraction. In accepting this, historians and anthropologists preserve the value of knowledge as meaning, but they miss an opportunity to embrace the knowledge of being.

Filmmakers compose images into a form for others to see and then are frequently asked, "What were you trying to say?" They have tried to say or mean certain things, but that is perhaps the least of their intentions. Most of their effort has gone into putting the viewer into a particular relation to a subject and creating a progression of images and scenes for understanding it, much as a musician produces a progression of notes and sequences. But before filmmakers can compose images in this way, they have had to film them, and this has required looking. Thus, before films are a form of representing or communicating, they are a form of looking.

Before they express ideas, they are a form of looking. Before they describe anything, they are a form of looking. In many respects filming, unlike writing, precedes thinking. It registers the process of looking with a certain interest, a certain will.

When we look, we are doing something more deliberate than seeing and yet more unguarded than thinking. We are putting ourselves in a sensory state that is at once one of vacancy and of heightened awareness. Our imitative faculties take precedence over judgment and categorization, preparing us for a different kind of knowledge. We learn to inhabit what we see. Conversely, thinking about what we see, projecting our ideas upon it, turns us back upon ourselves. So, simply to look, and look carefully, is a way of knowing that is different from thinking. This is not necessarily a matter of greater concentration, for often the more we concentrate, the more we see only ourselves. Concentration is not at all the same thing as being attentive and free of distractions. Sartre makes the point that consciousness cannot exist devoid of content; it is given shape by things-in-themselves in the world. But if the act of looking is what occupies our consciousness, we cannot be fully attentive to what we are seeing. Paying attention is not a matter of projecting oneself onto things-in-themselves but of freeing one's consciousness to perceive them.

It is therefore important to examine closely our own patterns of observation, undiverted by the conventions and interpretations that we receive from society and that constantly crowd upon us. This is particularly important for filmmakers, who are trained in a very restricted range of methods for seeing and recording experience. It is a difficult thing to do—to understand how one looks at things. It is made more difficult because it is apparently so simple, for we tend to forget how cursory looking can be. To look carefully requires strength, calmness, and affection. The affection cannot be in the abstract; it must be an affection of the senses.

A camera can be quite blind. Surveillance cameras in warehouses or apartment buildings are quite blind. Looking at the recordings they make, one can sense that there is no one behind these cameras. Or when, in a film, a camera pans over a landscape, again one can sense that no one is really looking. Anything that might be seen is in the process of disappearing off the screen. When young filmmakers start out, you often notice that they are looking at nothing but hoping that by moving the camera over the surface of a subject something will be gathered up. The camera never comes to rest, or if it should chance to do so for a moment it immediately moves away again. This is a camera that is hunting, searching for something to see and never finding it. It is constantly dissatisfied, as though nothing were worth looking at.

It is therefore quite possible to see without looking. Can one learn to look more attentively? From birth, some people seem to do so. You sometimes recognize this in the work of new photographers and filmmakers. Others, however intelligent and perceptive they may be, live in a world so dominated by concepts that they find it difficult to look at anything attentively. When they see a film they worry about what they are supposed to think about it. Their thinking keeps interfering with the process of looking. You may have known such people. They cannot give themselves to the images of a film, and afterward all that is left in their minds is a series of judgments, or a set of questions, or a list of items they believe have been left out. They may even find the images chaotic, as if they have been asked to follow an incomprehensible language.

This is not only a problem among viewers. Many filmmakers have little respect for images or for their audiences. One sign of this is that the images they use are wholly imitative, not valued in themselves but used as a cheap coinage. Another is that the images are changed as quickly as possible, out of a constant fear that we, the audience, will lose interest in the film. In the end, it is only the changes that keep us watching, since we are never allowed to pay attention to anything. There is perhaps a deeper fear as well. One has the impression that many filmmakers are afraid of looking. What is it in ordinary things that they fear to see? Is it a fear of their own feelings, that they should dare to engage so directly with the world? Is it the delicacy, fragility, and beauty of things that they fear—or the skull beneath the skin, the horror?

It is important to understand this fear, for none of us is completely free of it. It is the fear of giving ourselves unconditionally to what we see. It seems to me that this fear is allied to our fear of abandoning the protection of conceptual thought, which screens us from a world that might otherwise consume our consciousness. For to be fully attentive is to risk giving up something of ourselves. To lose this fear, we must examine it and try to understand it. If we are afraid to look honestly, and are afraid of our own responses, or of what others may think of us, our looking will always be evasive. It is this kind of dishonest looking that does immeasurable harm to others and to society. We see it everywhere around us. We have seen it in every age—that which may not be seen or be acknowledged to be seen. To overcome this fear we need to find our own kind of freedom. It is a freedom that we can only learn by accepting that we are alone, that no one will help us, that we must make it ourselves.

Notes

1. See Lakoff and Johnson 1999: 41–42, 49–56.
2. By the same token, mental images frequently complicate (and interrupt) the train of "linguistic" thought.

3. Vaughan 1999: 21.

4. Susan Sontag notes the equivalence of artistry and chance in producing memorable photographs: "Photography is the only major art in which professional training and years of experience do not confer an insuperable advantage over the untrained and inexperienced—this for many reasons, among them the large role that chance (or luck) plays in the taking of pictures, and the bias toward the spontaneous, the rough, the imperfect" (Sontag 2003: 28). This would seem to apply, however, only to the single photograph. The principle would not hold if one compared the collected works of either professionals or amateurs.

PART I

MATTER AND IMAGE

1

THE BODY IN CINEMA

I N A BRITISH "anthology" film of the 1950s made up of three separate ghost stories, a museum guide becomes obsessed with a painting that hangs in one of the museum galleries.[1] It shows a house on a hill and the lonely road leading up to it. One day the guide finds himself crossing the line between life and art as he is drawn into the painting, which proves to be another self-sufficient, three-dimensional world. There he discovers the artist, trapped in his own painting. Do they escape back to the real world? The answer to that forms the rest of the story.

This story is neither so eerie nor so silly as it might sound, for many of us have had the experience of being lost in a work of art. Indeed, it is the purpose of art to reach out and claim us. Music, pictures, and films do this again and again. Alfred Gell, in his last book, *Art and Agency*, argued that art is made to capture us—to fascinate and even confuse us. Our minds and bodies are not the passive receptors of art, they are the targets of it.

Films, like ghost stories, are littered with bodies, and although these bodies are in one sense ghostly and evanescent, they are also in many ways, to our senses, corporeal. In his book on cinema titled *The Material Ghost*, Gilberto Perez takes the view that "presence is not an illusion in the movies," but rather (adopting André Bazin's expression) a "hallucination that is true" in its effects.[2] There are always links between works of art and life, even if the worlds presented are imaginary, for, as Bazin suggests, art is a lifeline between the physical world and our physical selves. The technologies of art also ensure a connection between ourselves and something physical. Many works have a material basis—another work that inspired them, or a living subject, or simply the physical matter out of which they are made. Music is produced from pieces of wood and metal, or from human throats and mouths—what Roland Barthes called the body's animal "muzzle."[3] Films, for their part, testify to bodies that were present before the camera. These may be the bodies of movie stars or people on the street or decomposing bodies in a morgue.

What these bodies mean to us, and how they are linked to our own bodies, has been a matter of fascination since the invention of film, but all too often the disturbances they create become sidetracked in the byways of aesthetic, psychoanalytic, and political theory. It is important to

1.1. From *Le sang des bêtes* (1949). Courtesy of The British Film Isanstitute.
Copyright Estate of Georges Franju.

reclaim this disturbance if we are not to reduce films to signs, symbols, and other domesticated meanings. Some films do not allow us to do so. In Georges Franju's *Le sang des bêtes* (1949), the camera wanders not so innocently into a Paris abattoir, where it discovers bodies collapsing from life into death (figure 1.1). The audience is implicated as much by the photographed beauty of the animals as by the horror of what is being done to them. In Franju's later feature film *Les yeux sans visage* (1959), Dr Genessier peels off the faces of a succession of young women murdered for him by his assistant, Louise, in an attempt to graft these onto the face of his daughter, who has been disfigured in an accident (figure 1.2). The banality of everyday life surrounds these proceedings. Here the viewer is also implicated, drawn closer to the bodies by the doctor's fumbling attempts and failures. The agency of this film is like a contagion.

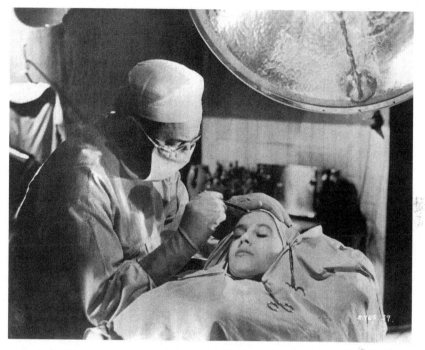

1.2. From *Les yeux sans visage* (1959). Courtesy of The British Film Institute.
Copyright Gaumont.

Documentary films add the authority of "found" objects to the artist's inventions. *Duka's Dilemma* (2001), by Jean Lydall and Kaira Strecker, shows the production of a human body in a manner quite unlike the fashionable childbirth films of the 1960s and 1970s, with their obstetric camera angles and shots of radiant parents. The birth—in this case of a Hamar child in southern Ethiopia—appears almost as a group effort by the mother, her co-wife, and other female relatives. Although there is pain and danger, there is also humor and an acceptance of the shared subjectivity of bodily experience. This same spirit infuses the rest of the film. Not only do the women seem close to one another physically but the images of the film bring us into a similar closeness to them. Through the birth the film crosses the threshold into a different sensory relationship between the film subjects and the film audience in which the human body is allowed to "speak" more eloquently.

These last two films lie at opposite ends of a spectrum of involvement, but they underline the centrality of the human body in almost all films. However, there are other bodies to be considered, as well—those of the spectator and the filmmaker, and even the body of the film itself.

The Body in the Film

The boundaries between our firsthand experiences and the ways in which we recall and recreate them are often unclear. These may be the boundaries between sensory perception and memory (or dreaming); between what we designate as life and art; or between the corporeal and incorporeal. In the end, these categories are so unreliable that we may be tempted to give them up. After all, a person seen in a dream or on television may be as vivid as a person seen across the room, and works of art may be as concrete as clumps of earth. Representations of experience immediately create new experiences in their own right.

Societies draw such boundaries at different points and endow them with different degrees of importance, but nearly everywhere some effort is made to maintain them. As Mary Douglas observes, the difference between spirit and matter continues to matter, but the ways in which the social body governs the corporeal body vary widely.[4] Changing circumstances such as the introduction of new fashions and new technologies constantly test this governance, and it is at the very borders of the borders, so to speak, that the principles regulating them stand revealed most clearly. Challenges to political authority may evoke fierce repression in a different quarter—in the area of morals, for example.

Film is among the newer technologies to create disturbances at the boundaries of art and everyday experience, along with its more recent and powerful offshoots of television, video recording, satellite transmission, and Internet streaming. Here, too, the extremes often reveal most clearly our fundamental biological and cultural responses. Linda Williams has taken a close look at the "body genres" of pornography, horror, and melodrama to see how their excesses challenge mechanisms of bodily control, and how they revive (but never actually close) the gaps between primal experiences and cinematically manufactured hallucinations of them.[5] In a similar vein, Klaus Theweleit discusses the excesses of brutality and torture as expressions of the psycho-sexual fantasies of the "armored" body engendered by German military training.[6] Barbara Creed sees the "body-monstrous" of horror films as at once the threatened body of the spectator, exploded or invaded or defiled by abject substances, and sometimes, too, as a reaffirmation of the spectator's purity and bodily integrity.[7] However, all films and not only these "gross" genres are potentially disturbing to the corporeal equanimity of the viewer, and indeed this is part of their appeal. Williams maintains that viewing other people's experiences in films is not simply a matter of sharing them but of discovering autonomous bodily responses in ourselves that may differ from those we witness.[8] Films allow us to go beyond culturally prescribed limits and glimpse the possibility of being more than we are. They stretch the boundaries of our consciousness and create affinities with bodies other than our own.

Conversely, the inability of art (or its technologies) to represent the body has often been noted. In 1556 Abu'l-Fazl, the chronicler of the Mughal emperor Akbar's reign, wrote of a charge of 1,500 military elephants, "How can the attributes of these rushing mountains be strung on the slender thread of words?"[9] In *Let Us Now Praise Famous Men*, James Agee laments the weakness of words and would substitute for them photographs and "fragments of cloth, bits of cotton, lumps of earth, records of speech, pieces of wood and iron, phials of odors, plates of food and excrement."[10] He nevertheless devotes hundreds of pages to the description of physical objects. A similar incommensurability of images and human bodies, and of film and history, is the theme of Bill Nichols's writing on "questions of magnitude."[11] Like Susan Stewart, he holds that films and other works of art are always the products of reduction and miniaturization.[12] Although one could argue, as Nichols in fact does, that it is precisely the inadequacies and gaps in works of art that serve to restore the mystery and plenitude of the real, I wish first to argue here for the enhanced material presence of film—sometimes expressed by early avant-garde writers of the last century as *photogénie*.

Among the many references to photogénie that concern magic, poetry, and the fantastic, at least two others are relevant here. The first is that photogénie is a technological phenomenon. Photogénie, wrote the French film critic Léon Moussinac, is "that which is revealed to us solely by the cinematograph."[13] What is extraordinary about it is not its transmission of reality but its creation of a new mechanical image of reality. If we simply wanted to see reality, it is all around us, but seeing a film presents us with a strange apparition, a photochemical imprint of the world.[14] Although this image may extend normal optical vision through magnification, slow motion, and so on, these are secondary effects. Its primary value is its triumph over actual, direct vision. The resulting image does not so much transcend reality as produce an alien perception of reality, sensitive to unknown qualities. The surrealism of the film image lies precisely in making us aware of a reality beyond our knowledge.

This view of photogenie, however, tends to ignore its other salient feature, the "blocked" responses of the spectator. Superimposed on the "empirical" view of photography—its photochemical precision—is what Edgar Morin calls the "oneiric" view, a private perspective suspended somewhere between privilege and paralysis, with all the power to see but an incapacity to act.[15] This may account for the horrific experience of seeing certain film images. People who have witnessed disturbing events often report that they find them much more disturbing when they see them on film. The mechanical vision of the camera is more inhuman, more unrelenting. Sensory deprivation in one area tends to isolate and heighten the other senses. Nichols notes that the absence of sound in the aptly titled *The Act of Seeing with one's own eyes* (Brakhage 1971) helps make that film (about autopsies in a Pittsburgh morgue) "one of the most unwatchable films ever made."[16] It leaves the viewer more helpless than usual, without an avenue of escape into the "realist" conventions of cinema. The notion of photogénie may also be seen as a heightening of cinematic "excess"—that physical residue in the image that resists absorption into symbol, narrative, or expository discourse. As excess, the by-products of mechanical vision defy the containment of the work and are more capable of touching the exposed sensibilities of the viewer.

More formal and melancholy than *The Act of Seeing* is the contemplation of bodies in Peter Greenaway's *Death in the Seine* (1988). In this fictional reconstruction, we see a succession of corpses fished out of the river Seine between 1796 and 1800 as they are registered and prepared for burial by two mortuary attendants. The camera passes gently over each body. In their naked state they form a catalogue of human types— male and female, weak and robust, fat and thin, adults, adolescents, children. We learn the few details recorded about them: a name, an occupation, sometimes the contents of their pockets. These people had witnessed the French Revolution and the events that followed. The film suggests that each body was the vessel of a largely private, unknown life, and even the little known about them was soon to be forgotten. The bodies seem cleansed of the pretensions and desires of the living. In viewing the film our experience is complicated by the knowledge that its "actors" are only pretending to be dead. They have entrusted their bodies to us with a kind of innocence. The film may be fiction, but the bodies are not.

Like Williams, Nichols cites various examples of human bodies in films at the extremes of exposure and destruction and their peculiar resonance with bodies outside it—in the Hindenberg disaster, the explosion of the NASA Challenger space vehicle, pornographic films, the exhumation of murder victims in El Salvador, the Pittsburgh morgue, and so on. Viewers are known to have strong physical responses to such images—of shock, flinching, faintness, sexual arousal, and even vomiting.[17] These responses underline Williams's point that in film viewing we do not necessarily feel for others, we feel for and in ourselves. It is also a fallacy to assume that vision is simply a way of possessing an "absent other" (as in much "gaze" theory) or to interpret the technologies of film as a one-way extension of the senses. This, in Williams's view, perpetuates the "lingering Cartesianism" of the disconnected voyeur, when in fact vision is much more directly connected to our own bodily processes.[18]

Well-mannered films, unlike the extreme genres of pornography and horror, mirror the kinds of bias and reticence about the body to be found in the social body more generally. Mary Douglas has described the ways in which societies view the human body and relate its functions to material and spiritual life.[19] These involve hierarchies based on the physical position of body parts (e.g., high and low), their perceived or metaphorical role in cognition and emotion (the head, the "heart," the "bowels"), and their organic function (sensation, respiration, excretion, etc.). Douglas observes that excretion, while it is sometimes viewed matter-of-factly and sometimes as impure and dangerous, is virtually never associated with spirituality. In the Judeo-Christian tradition "the organs of nutrition are never attributed to God; they are at once recognized as signs of imperfection."[20] In other traditions the gods are fed, but they are not considered to excrete. Douglas is less forthcoming about the connections between sexuality and spirituality, perhaps because these show a wider range of cultural variation.

Symbolic hierarchies reveal themselves in the cinema by regulating what can and cannot be seen. They may also chart cultural changes, as in the gradual introduction of kissing in Indian and Indonesian cinema. "Realism" is thus quite clearly a relative term, for some of the most familiar bodily experiences are either completely absent in the cinema or are treated with exaggerated caution. These include, as might be expected, nudity, excretion, and sexual relations, but also other commonplace bodily experiences such as menstruation and masturbation, and more mundane acts such as spitting, scratching, shaving, cutting the nails, bathing, and so on. Robert Gardner observes that fiction films, despite their frequent claims to realism, "never show anything as ordinary or as innocent as someone taking a pee."[21] In *Le fantôme de la liberté* (1974), Buñuel mocks this anomaly by inverting it, making eating the disgusting private act and excretion the open, sociable one. Nonfiction films are not immune to these taboos, despite their commitment to actuality. In many respects they are even more limited because they are more constrained by their portrayal of real people and the need to respect their privacy. Both fiction and nonfiction, however—even including pornography—steer well clear of the ordinariness of our actual daily experiences, particularly in relation to our own bodies. The most frank films often reveal these constraints more clearly (in the coyness of their filming and editing) than films that avoid the taboo areas entirely.

The experienced, functioning body is routinely countered and contradicted in films by the sanitized body, the heroic body, and the beautiful body, as determined by the culture and social practices of the societies in which they are made. However, the homogeneity of the audience cannot be taken for granted, and this is increasingly true as film producers aim for multicultural audiences. The sex or age or background of the viewer does not necessarily guarantee a predictable response. Moreover, the characteristics of the viewer's own body may have only a limited influence on how he or she sees the gendered, aging, or growing bodies of others in films. Assumptions about gendered ways of seeing, in particular, posit a polarized rather than a more complex and variable response, and they deny the possibility of both a nongendered sensibility and a more all-embracing sexuality. Attraction to (and identification with) the bodies of others in the cinema remains a more multi-faceted matter than one of gender, or even of age, physique, nationality, sexuality, or class. There are many gradations in how we respond, influenced as much by the narratives in which people appear as by their appearance. In the right context, the most loathsome character can be appealing and the plainest face beautiful.

The Body of the Spectator

Although Nichols's and Williams's extreme examples bring certain issues vividly (or morbidly) to light, it is important to remember that all films are designed to generate a continuous interplay of stimulus and bodily response between screen and spectator. This is exercised first at the dynamic and plastic levels of light, form, and editing, next at the level of representation, and finally in the imaginative spaces created by cinematic convention.

Williams characterizes the ideal response to the "gross" genres as jerks or spasms of various kinds—shudders, sobs, and orgasms.[22] It is no accident that Eisenstein chose the word "collision" to express the effect of juxtaposing two shots, and it is this concept of dynamic energy that permeates much of his writing on the various forms of montage—rhythmic, metric, graphic, planar, spatial, tonal, overtonal, contrapuntal, and so on. At one point he describes the "psycho-physiological" effect of a series of shots of farmers mowing with scythes, causing the audience to rock "from side to side."[23] Pudovkin, too, suggests that manipulating the editing tempo can affect the viewer physically and emotionally, although there is some confusion in his writing about whether this mimics or actually directs the viewer's psychological processes.[24] More generally in early Soviet cinema, editing is not a reflection of either the characters' or the viewer's psychology but a constant stream of authorial interventions designed to shock, make comparisons, and force complex connections.

The viewer's ability to recognize objects and persons is essential to most of these effects, which rely on conditioned responses. When we recognize an object we are, at the same time, attributing to it the physical qualities that we associate with it in our own lives. In viewing a person, or a face, we apply both our own prior experiences and the cultural associations prevalent in our society. There may also be a degree of idiosyncratic response to items with very personal associations—the triumph of the *punctum*, as it were, over the *studium*. Apart from these responses, further variations of response are likely whenever there is cultural ambiguity, unfamiliarity with the subject, or an excess that cannot easily be assimilated to prior experience. This is perhaps most apparent in the borderline cases of horror and pornography.

Neuroscientists, art theorists, and phenomenologists have all observed that we do not perceive objects in any complete or unitary way. We do not in fact see them as whole but (unless we move around them) only one face of them at a time, from one precise perspective. For the rest, we make inferences about them drawn from the probabilities involved, and from the fragmentary stimuli of shading, position, and size in relation to other objects.[25] This means we actively construct objects in a manner that suggests they are as much projections of our own bodies as independent of them. Thus, if other bodies influence ours, we also reach out and enrich them with our own responses.

In films the close-up creates a proximity to the faces and bodies of others that we experience much less commonly in daily life. The conventions of social distance normally restrict proximity except in moments of intimacy. The cinema thus combines the private view with the public spectacle, creating a sharp sense of intimate exposure of the film subject and a secondary sense in the film viewer of being personally exposed by witnessing the other's exposure. The face is for most of us the locus of another person's being, perhaps reflecting our own feelings of how we are constructed as a person in other people's eyes. The face has been one of the constant preoccupations of filmmakers and film theorists. In an essay published in 1923, Béla Balázs stated his belief that the cinema would restore to humanity a language of facial expression rendered "illegible" by literacy and the printed word.[26]

Attraction to the human face, so evident in films, can be traced back through European portraiture to the point at which it vanishes in the early classical period, when the whole body was the object of attention. In much Greek sculpture and vase painting the face was formulaic, the body less so. But by the late Roman period, portrait sculpture had reached a high point that remains unsurpassed today, and at about the same time the portraits painted in wax on Egyptian mummies gave astonishingly lifelike faces to the heavily wrapped bodies within. The reciprocal relationship of body and face reemerges in the unclothed body of High Renaissance Italian painting where, except in portraiture, the treatment of faces was often routine. Here the body continually "robs" the face of importance. In northern Europe, where the body remained more often clothed, clothing and faces were rendered in finer detail and the body remained at best a correct armature, at worst a lumpish form without articulation, movement, or grace.

Sculpture and photography give permanence to the human body and allow a perusal of it that film, with its closed time frame, denies the viewer. This is perhaps one of the reasons why the face has taken on such importance in the cinema. Although the camera can move around the body and show it in action (the ultimate promise of pornography), there is something unattainable and unsatisfying about its transience. The body's movements are glimpsed only in their passing, without the coherent framework that they have, for example, in dance. The film viewer is far more constrained than an observer in daily life, who can pause for as long as desired to watch workers at work, athletes practicing, children playing, or people sitting at a café. The face in films, although also seen in passing, becomes a more stable object of attention and a receptacle for many of our feelings about the body as a whole. As the most prominent part of the body not covered by clothing, it has tended to become this in any case.

Films linger on faces to such an extent that some (such as Dreyer's *Passion of Joan of Arc* [1928], Bergman's *Persona* [1966], and Johan van der Keuken's *Beppie* [1965]) become choreographed studies of facial expressions. The face becomes an extension of the lines and surfaces of the body as a whole. Filmmakers look for faces in which the sensitivities and tactile qualities of the body are concentrated in the eyes, the mouth, the cheekbones, the textures of hair and skin. The face thus serves as an emblem for the body, but also as its point of emergence from the clothed body. The revelatory power of human faces resembles the revelatory power of film itself, which successively reveals new surfaces. Like the uncovering of the body and the release from social constraints that often accompanies it, film provides a sense of liberation that is fundamental to the magic, photogénie, and underlying eroticism of the cinema.

In exaggerating proximity, the close-up brings to the cinema a quasi-tactility absent in ordinary human relations. When we meet others in day-to-day exchanges we do not explore their faces with our fingertips, but in the cinema we come close to doing this, becoming especially alive to the liquidity of the eyes and mouth and, at a more interpretive level, the flickering signs of emotions. Perez cites Ortega y Gasset's observation that proximity also emphasizes volume, or three-dimensionality. This applies as much to objects as to faces or other parts of the human body: "If we take up an object, an earthen jar, for example, and bring it near enough to the eyes, these converge on it . . . and seem to embrace it, to take possession of it, to emphasize its rotundity. Thus the object seen at close range acquires the indefinable corporeality and solidity of filled volume."[27] In this way, the cinema allows us to grasp the corporeality of inanimate objects with what might be called a "prehensile" vision. It alters our relation to the material world in terms of volume, weight, textures, colors, and detail. It allows us to incorporate objects into our own experience in ways that may reflect more directly the experience of those who handle them intimately, whether they be makers of pottery or farmers or industrial workers. Many films explore the possibilities of a special relationship to the material world. Shinsuke Ogawa's final (posthumous) film *Manzan Benigaki* (2001), for example, concerns a village's intensive involvement with growing, preparing, and packing the red persimmon. Clément Perron's *Day After Day* (1962) shows the way in which machines and products dominate the senses in a paper mill. Robert Gardner's films, such as *Rivers of Sand* (1975) and *Forest of Bliss* (1985), explore how human bodies and material objects oscillate between fluid life, dead matter, and symbol.

A related phenomenon is the involuntary mimicry involved in seeing others' bodies, a mimicry that may even extend to inanimate objects. This response is observable in earliest infancy, when babies imitate their mothers' facial expressions and cry upon hearing others cry, and it has probably evolved as part of the structuring of the human nervous system. It has both a motor and emotional dimension, affecting how we hold our bodies, often in a state of tension and unconsummated action. Merleau-Ponty described the experience as one of "a postural 'impregnation' of my own body by the conducts I witness."[28] The notion of impregnation suggests a deeper response than empathy, as if the body had been struck, or had taken on the physical qualities of the other body.

In discussing mimicry, the psychologist Martin Hoffman notes Adam Smith's observation of 1759 that spectators watching someone perform a high-wire act "naturally writhe and twist and balance their own bodies as they see him do."[29] A similar response can be observed in people watching a football match or even a game of snooker. Hoffman, citing an essay by Theodor Lipps of 1906, divides this response into two phases, the first a motor response, the second an emotional response, although the two occur in close succession. In the first, the spectator involuntarily and unconsciously imitates the expressions and postures of the other person and tends to move in synchrony with them. In the second, there is feedback from these expressions and postures to the emotions, creating feelings appropriate to them.[30] As evidence of this, if one artificially adopts a particular facial expression such as a smile, it tends to generate the related feelings of happiness. Darwin, who made a study of facial expressions, was the first to state the feedback hypothesis, and William James adopted it as a central tenet, writing that "we feel sorry because we cry."[31] Thus, at one level, the ability of filmmakers to create corporeal responses in viewers may be as basic as showing them certain facial expressions, and this may be transmitted across the technologies of recording and projection, as though by an actual personal contact. As Morin puts it, "the universal word of photography—'smile'—implies a subjective communication from person to person through the intermediacy of film, which becomes the bearer of a message of the soul."[32] Gell makes a related point when he says that we approach art objects as if they had "physiognomies." "When we see a picture of a smiling person, we attribute an attitude of friendliness to 'the person in the picture.' " We have access to a "depicted mind."[33]

Our relationship to images involves not only looking across boundaries but undergoing effects from across them, much as we undergo effects from looking at people in daily life and being looked at by them. In this sense, the artwork acquires a body, or as Gell puts it, "to all intents and purposes it becomes a person, or at least a partial person . . . a congealed residue of performance and agency in object-form."[34] Chris Pinney has described the "corpothetic" effect of Indian religious images, with which worshippers establish a relationship that differs markedly from the more disconnected perusal of images prevailing in Western and Westernized countries. Indeed, he regards this latter cooler, "Kantian" relationship with images as more the exception than the rule.[35] In India it was associated only with the new "naturalistic" school of art introduced from Europe, in which there was no direct address to the viewer. By contrast, in traditional Hindu iconography (as well as much modern religious and calendar art) the deity looks at the beholder and the beholder experiences this being-looked-at (or *darshan*) as *akarshan*. In some cases the image merges with a living person, as is the case with all photographs. (This is also the destiny of all movie stars.) Gell notes that in the custom of worshipping young girls as the goddess Durga in Nepal, the girl is perceived at once as the living goddess and the image of the goddess, or *murti*.[36] Such fluid interchanges can be perceived as dangerous. One might predict that disapproval of "corpothetic" responses to art would emanate from those authorities that, in Douglas's terms, seek to impose order through control of the body. And indeed, Indian popular movies, with their extravagant use of visual effects, color, and dance numbers, are often dismissed by critics and contrasted unfavorably with Satyajit Ray's "neorealist austerity" because of their "superfluity of corporeal affectivity."[37]

The cinema operates in yet another way to affect the spectator corporeally through its construction of imaginary spaces and its evocation of real ones. As we have seen, film viewing is far from a passive experience. Recognition of objects and persons involves a constant testing of hypotheses about what we see, drawn from our learned and automatic habits of perception (interpreting clues about shape, volume, arrangement in depth, etc.) and from our prior experience. Our sense of space in the cinema relies upon recognition, but also upon piecing together the shots into a larger imaginative structure. In participating in this construction, we are drawn further into the film in mind and body.

The earliest films, made from 1895 onward, tended to emphasize their own picturelike qualities—framed images to be regarded as objects—although occasionally, as in some of the Lumière brothers' films, this to-be-looked-at quality was overwhelmed by the unexpected autonomy of the images.[38] Exhibitors presented films as short, self-contained spectacles that created wonder and amusement but did not invite much audience identification. Recognition was essential to their effectiveness, and mimicry was often an element as well. Although these films sometimes addressed the spectator directly (as in the famous scene in *The Great Train Robbery* [1903] of a pistol fired at the audience), they did not attempt to construct a filmic space *around* the spectator.

With the further development of cinema, filmmakers discovered new ways of creating bodily sensations, exploiting the kinesthetic potential of images through camera work but even more profoundly through narrative. Another important discovery was that by means of editing the spectator could be made to "inhabit" the three-dimensional space of the characters. The formal and psychological principles involved in this have been explored in considerable detail from the time of Hugo Munsterberg's writings on film in 1916, to Pudovkin's in the 1920s, to later studies by Balázs, Arnheim, Burch, Oudart, Bordwell, Deleuze, and others. Whatever their particular bias—psychological, formalist, historicist—these theories all attempt to account for the way in which the consciousness of the spectator is altered and guided by the cinema, in both its perceptual and cognitive responses. Whether one characterizes the spectator as an ideologically determined subject, or an "imaginary observer," or the filmmaker's surrogate, it is clear that the cinema has powerful ways of "incorporating" the spectator into the film. As the word suggests, this involvement is as much corporeal as psychological. By providing a series of perceptual clues, films construct spaces analogous to those we experience in everyday life, as we sample visual and other sensory information and construct a seemingly smooth and complete picture of our surroundings. As in everyday life, this information is far from complete, and we fill in the gaps with suppositions. Films create the information and gaps in stylistically varied ways, and in film viewing this very stylistic nonconformity, or distinctiveness, acts as a further stimulus to our creative response. The cinematic account may in fact be far from "smooth"—it is often deliberately unsmooth and oblique—but we still feel the urgency of completion, even of abstract and "impossible" connections. As David Bordwell points out, "The act of filling in must then include our willingness to accept, in the name of perceptibility, very great violations of conventional or internally inconsistent space and time."[39]

This interpreting and filling in is the spectator's version of the cinematic imagination at work. It creates an almost continuous impetus toward convergence with the objects and bodies on the screen. In this and its withholding can be found the attraction and many of the "photogenic" qualities of film images. Films exceed normal observation and yet throw up huge barriers to it. They give us the privileged viewpoints of the close-up, the enclosing frame, the photographic "look" of things—their lighted textures, their extended focal lengths, their monochrome range in black and white—indeed, everything that heightens or defamiliarizes everyday perception—yet at the same time they confine us to limited frames, give us limited time to inspect them, and in other ways deprive us of our will. This becomes a gap on a larger scale, of a different order. It can create a compulsion to see, even to see something terrible.

The receptive, dreamlike state of film viewing adds a sense of inevitability to one's perceptions of how people behave on the screen, a sensation that seems to increase with the repeated viewing of a film. The mythic status of film stars derives partly from this accumulated exposure and redundancy. The effect may be better understood if one observes what happens when a filmmaker sees his or her own film. At various points along the way the filmmaker has actively controlled the images of the people in the film, but this disappears once the images have become fixed. Viewing the film can then become almost insupportable, for there is a renewed sense of responsibility for images that have by now assumed a life of their own, often in what seems an arbitrary fashion. A process that was thought to be completed returns with an intimation of its original indeterminacy, leaving the filmmaker powerless, with the sense of being stranded in the present.

The Body of the Filmmaker

Film viewing involves the conjunction of two acts of looking and two bodies, at the very least. The spectator views the objects on the screen—objects that have already been seen and selected with the camera. It thus goes without saying that whatever is seen has already been mediated by the filmmaker's vision, but this is more than a process of thought: it is as much a physical act. The presence of the filmmaker's body becomes a "residue" in the work of the kind alluded to by Gell. The human beings in the film create another residue that is not so different from the filmmaker's own, for both are imprinted in the film's images as equivalent facts. This is perhaps most evident when the filmmaker is holding the camera, for the camera then records the filmmaker's movements and those of the film's subjects in parallel. The image is affected as much by the body behind the camera as those before it.

Like other artists, filmmakers see many transient events that they would like to show to others. In effect, they want these events to repeat themselves for others to see. It seems an unattainable dream, and yet with a camera it is almost possible. The mimetic longings of the filmmaker are satisfied by the camera with an immediacy quite unprecedented in previous times in the production of poems, novels, and paintings.

Exactly why one should wish to show others what one has seen is another matter. Is it an affirmation of the thing itself, or of one's own vision, or a desire to command the consciousness of others? Or is it perhaps to transcend oneself, to overflow one's self-containment? Sometimes the descriptions of the filmmaking process sound rather like the last. For all the avant-gardists' descriptions of the camera's mechanical autonomy, they sound suspiciously like the experiencing body of the filmmaker. This begins historically with still photography and is not merely an expression of male *jouissance*. Julia Margaret Cameron, who began making photographs in 1863, wrote: "I longed to arrest all beauty that came before me, and at length the longing has been satisfied."[40] In Vertov's celebrations of the mobile camera, the camera is not so much anthropomorphized as that Vertov himself becomes a flying object. Basil Wright is mesmerized by the flight of kingfishers, the movements of a fisherman's arms, the legs of children in a dance. While filming, Rouch experiences *ciné-transe*. "Filmmaking for me is to write with one's eyes, one's ears, with one's body; it's to enter into something. . . . I am a ciné-Rouch in ciné-trance in the act of ciné-filming. . . . It's the joy of filming, the 'ciné-plaisir.' "[41] Rouch notes the synchrony of himself with his subject, the "harmony . . . which is in perfect balance with the movements of the subjects."[42] The ecstasy of the filming-body is captured in John Marshall's description: "You have this feeling, 'I'm on; I'm on.' You know, 'I'm getting it. It's happening; it's happening.' "[43] Here it is definitely Marshall who is "on," not the camera. The sensation, for Robert Gardner, is "as close to cinematic orgasm as I'll get."[44]

We must conclude that for many filmmakers there is an ecstatic, even erotic pleasure in filming others. This resembles the creative process in other arts but differs from it in its relation to its materials, which are almost always "found" objects, even if prepared to be discovered by the film. Perhaps a maker of collages or life-masks feels something equivalent, even though not responding so directly to the living human body and its fleeting expressions. The filmmaker "makes" nothing in an obvious sense but conducts an activity in conjunction with the living world. The pleasure of filming erodes the boundaries between filmmaker and subject, between the bodies filmmakers see and the images they make. Filming is fundamentally acquisitive in "incorporating" the bodies of others. The filmmaker's consciousness must also expand to accommodate these other bodies, but it cannot hold them all; they must be given to others—or at least returned to the world. In achieving this, the bodies of the subject, the filmmaker, and the viewer become interconnected and in some ways undifferentiated.

To speak of the dissolution of boundaries in this way is really to speak of the often fragile identity of the filmmaker at the moment of filming and, later, when viewing a film. Sometimes indifferent, sometimes obsessed, filmmakers experience a wide range of feelings toward their subjects. Occasionally another person's physical presence overpowers the filmmaker's consciousness. This results partly from the synchrony that Hoffman and Rouch both note, and from an internal mimicry of the other person's gestures, postures, voice, and emotional states. It can produce a sensation of power and expectancy, a willing of others to be precisely what they are, and to do precisely what they are doing, as they appear in the viewfinder. This becomes a spiritual synchrony, perhaps best expressed in Marshall's words: *It's happening. I'm on.*

The Body of the Film

The human body has often been pictured as a machine. Early in the twentieth century it began to be described as a factory consuming and processing raw materials.[45] Well before this, however, the dissection of bodies by Leonardo and Vesalius had established the mechanical principles governing the joints and the circulation of blood. In the sixteenth century, human vision was often equated with the *camera obscura*, the principle of which had been known since antiquity. As well, the camera obscura was taken to reflect the physical structure of the human eye and, at a more abstract level, the relation of the eye to the mind. Soon after its invention, the camera became a mechanical extension of the body, to be enlisted in surveillance, initially for police "mug shots" and later in prisons, banks, shopping malls, and offices.[46] The interplay of body and machine subsequently became a recurrent theme in discussions of films and what they do. As in the idea of photogénie, photographic images were held to transcend normal vision. For Louis Delluc, the camera took on the characteristics of a body, but a body liberated from previous physical, cultural, and psychological constraints. For Fernand Léger and the Futurists the film camera produced a new "machine aesthetic." Jean Epstein called it "a standardized metal brain, manufactured and sold in thousands of copies, which transforms the external world into art."[47] In Vertov's rapturous imagining, the camera was the "kino-eye," capable of a vision freed forever from "human immobility." Such conceptions of the camera as an autonomous body are partly signs of rebellion against academic art, but they are also a paradoxical way of acknowledging the camera's connection with the bodies it touches, including that of the filmmaker. Vertov went on to imagine the camera as a body fused with his own. "I am in constant motion. I draw near, then away, from objects. I crawl under, I climb onto them. I move apace with the muzzle of a galloping horse. I plunge full speed into a crowd."[48] Nineteenth-century novelists had already produced a mobile eye, sometimes anonymous, sometimes associated with an identifiable narrator. The focus on the senses, often dissociated from one another and yet creating a heightened sensory awareness, continued apace in the modern novel. Joyce conceived of *Ulysses* (1922) as an "encyclopaedia of the body," with fifteen of its eighteen chapters corresponding to separate bodily organs.[49] In novels and in many films (especially in the silent era), there is a shifting hypertrophy of one sense or another, brought about by their separation. As in *The Act of Seeing with one's own eyes*, lack of sound is capable of producing an almost unbearable acuity of vision. Equally, a dark or severely limited screen makes sounds more evocative, an effect explored as soon as the sound film was invented by Hitchock, Lang, and, later, Bresson.

Unlike Joyce's procedure in *Ulysses*, it is unusual for filmmakers to relate their films so closely to the human body and its organs, perhaps because a film is already so closely identified with the eye and ear. (A very few fiction films, such as *The Last Laugh* [1924], *Lady in the Lake* [1946], and *Sunset Boulevard* [1950], do, however, turn the camera into a living or dead character.) Yet filmmakers have inherited from classical thought certain notions about the body of the work as well as the "corpus" of works of an artist. Aristotle compared the plots of tragedies to living organisms compounded of specific parts. Similarly, filmmakers often conceive of a film as an organic whole with a beginning, middle, and end, corresponding roughly to exposition, conflict, and resolution. These, in turn, can be seen in a more corporeal light, corresponding first to cognition and sensory perception, then the muscle of action, and finally the emotional or organic processes of release. Filmmakers are known to refer to the skeleton and flesh of a film, its intellectual framework versus its "heart" or "guts," and so on. Films are also seen to have a life of their own in the public domain, a time span not unlike the stages of life of an organism. And although far in spirit from the mechanical-body notions of the avant-gardists, the psychoanalytical film criticism of the 1970s linked film to many of the attributes of the (mostly male) body—its desires, its "gaze," its self-reflection.

Films are thus seen in several different contexts as symbolic bodies— but to whose body do they correspond? Is it the body of the subject? Is it the body of the spectator or the filmmaker? Or is it an "open" body capable of receiving all of these?

Alfred Gell insisted that art was more a matter of agency than aesthetics, of power than of meaning. Art operates in a field of desires and conventions, as a technology of influence and "enchantment."[50] And yet, this potential of art has its own material being. It draws those around it to it—to its own body. It acquires a physical force of its own. A film's power is as much gravitational as outwardly directed—toward a place that W.J.T. Mitchell has described as a "black hole" in the discourses of verbal culture.[51] Much has been said about what the filmmaker and film viewer want. But one might ask, taking a cue from Sontag and, later, Mitchell, "What does a film want?"[52] Beyond influence or aesthetics or meaning, films are made to become objects in the world, to exist in their own right—as Sontag puts it, in the "luminousness of the thing in itself."[53] If a film wants anything, it is to preserve its immediacy each time it is seen, undimmed by age or fashion or reputation. In this, of course, it can never be satisfied. A film wants more power, more autonomy than it is ever granted by historians or critics or even by the filmmaker, whom everyone expects to know what "it is trying to say." A film knows its own weaknesses. At the height of its power, even the best film gives an intimation of what it has lost and what, if perfected, it might have been.

Notes

1. *Three Cases of Murder* (1953), Wendy Toye, David Eady, and George More O'Ferrall (directors), Wessex Films for British Lion Films, Ltd, 99 minutes. The segment referred to is "In the Picture" based on a story by Roderick Wilkinson, with a script by Donald B. Wilson, directed by Wendy Toye.
2. Perez 1998: 26–28, Bazin 1967: 16. Perez has somewhat modified Hugh Gray's translation, which is: "an hallucination that is also a fact."
3. Barthes 1975: 66–67.
4. Douglas 1973: 12.
5. Williams 1991.
6. Theweleit 1989.
7. Creed 1995.
8. Williams 1995: 15.
9. Keay 2000: 310.
10. Agee & Evans 1960: 13.
11. See Nichols 1986, 1991.
12. See Susan Stewart 1984.
13. Cited in Morin 1956: 23.
14. Garry Winogrand has said, "I photograph to find out what something will look like photographed" (Sontag 1977: 197).
15. Morin 1956: 24.

16. Nichols 1991: 144.

17. Nichols 1994: 76.

18. Williams 1995: 14–15.

19. See M. Douglas 1966, 1970.

20. M. Douglas 1973: 13.

21. Gardner & Östör 2001: 41.

22. Williams 1991: 4–5.

23. Eisenstein 1957: 80.

24. Pudovkin 1960: 73.

25. For an introduction to many of these principles, see E. H. Gombrich's classic *Art and Illusion* (1960). See also *The Perceptual World* (1990), edited by Irvin Rock.

26. Balázs 1952: 39–42.

27. Cited in Perez 1998: 135.

28. Merleau-Ponty 1964: 118.

29. Cited in Hoffman 2000: 37.

30. Ibid., pp. 39–45.

31. Ibid., p. 40.

32. "Le maître mot de la photographie 'Souriez' implique une communication subjective de personne à personne par le truchement de la pellicule, porteuse du message d'âme" (Morin 1956: 25–26).

33. Gell 1998: 15.

34. Ibid., p. 68.

35. Pinney 2001.

36. Gell 1998: 67.

37. Pinney 2000: 20.

38. Vaughan 1999: 3.

39. Bordwell 1985: 247.

40. Cited in Sontag 1977: 183.

41. Fulchignoni 1981: 7–8.

42. Rouch 1975: 94.

43. Anderson & Benson 1993: 144.

44. Gardner & Östör 2001: 37.

45. In an unpublished paper, Jakob Tanner has discussed in some detail the illustrations of "human machines" in Fritz Kahn's popular anatomy of the human body *Das Leben des Menschen*, which first appeared in the 1920s.

46. Tagg 1988.

47. Epstein 1974: 92.

48. Vertov 1984: 17.

49. Danius 2002: 150.

50. See Gell 1992, 1998.

51. Mitchell 1995: 543.

52. Sontag 1966; Mitchell 1996, in an essay entitled "What Do Pictures Really Want?"

53. Sontag 1966: 13.

2

VOICE AND VISION

The Cumulative and the Composite

SOCIAL SCIENTISTS speak in many voices and sometimes, but not always, try to make us see. In most of the classic British ethnographies you will find an introductory section giving an account of the material conditions of the people being described, often in a chapter called "The Setting," or something like it. These descriptions tend to be more factual than visually evocative, and if they evoke images it is due more to a vocabulary shared with the reader than any specific intention of the writer. Godfrey Lienhardt, for example, writes: "Dinkaland lies in a vast arc around the swamps of the central Nile basin in the Southern Sudan. It is a flat country of open savannah and savannah forest, intersected by many rivers and streams converging upon the central basin of the Nile. For part of each year heavy rains and river-flooding render much of the land uninhabitable and impassable."[1] A little later he presents, almost as a list, the typical contents of a home:

> The furnishings of such a home may be briefly mentioned. They include clay pots for cooking, water-carrying, and brewing; gourds of various shapes and sizes, some for serving the staple millet-porridge, some for storing oil and butter, and some for milking and drinking milk; plaited baskets in which grain is stored and plaited-grass winnowing-trays; wicker fish-traps and baskets, and perhaps a wicker cradle for carrying babies on long journeys; simple nets for scooping fish out of the river . . . [and so on for most of a page].[2]

This is matter-of-fact writing, in which words are treated like objects and an object's function is more important than its appearance. Occasionally, however, ethnographic writing produces paragraphs like this:

> In the dry season the landscape appears harsh and bare, and its general drab hue is hardly relieved by the shade trees in front of the native homesteads or the remnants of vegetation along the dry watercourses. The mud walls and thatched roofs of the homesteads seem to blend indistinguishably with the dusty country-side. In the middle of the wet season, when every footpath becomes a rivulet and every depression a bog, the homesteads are hidden

behind ramparts of luxuriant grain, and the whole country-side is resplendent with the green of flourishing vegetation.[3]

Scenes like this have a sun-drenched clarity. This is ethnographic realism of the sort Clifford Geertz has called "transparencies" because it is so intensely visual. Sounds and smells, heat and cold make an appearance, but only subliminally. But ethnographic writing cannot proceed like this forever, nor should it, and soon the anthropologist gets down to other business. The following passage is taken from later in the same book. Here matters are discussed that could never be expressed in photograph-like images.

> Clanship operates on the same level of relations as the lineage system, within the limits of common agnatic descent. It implies the notion of convergent patrilineal ascent; but in actual fact its range is extended by modifications of the strict rule of patriliny. The lineage system is the core of clanship, but not the whole of it. Lineally discrete groups are linked together by ties of clanship, so that the clan organization as a whole consists of a series of interlocked chains of linked maximal lineages.[4]

One may say that the earlier description has a novelistic or cinematic quality, while this one typifies the prose in which most expository and scientific writing has been couched since the Enlightenment.[5] Recent descriptive writing has borrowed some of its techniques from the cinema, but in fact many protocinematic techniques were already present in nineteenth-century poetry and novels. Italo Calvino observes that "visibility in the novel begins with Stendhal and Balzac, and reaches in Flaubert the ideal rapport between word and image. . . . The crisis of visibility in the novel will begin about half a century later, coinciding with the advent of the cinema."[6] At that point, novel writing takes a plunge back into the mind with the interior monologues of Virginia Woolf and James Joyce. But in fact novels like *Ulysses* are not any less visual; it is just that their vision becomes fragmented, visual perception is often detached from meaning, and the evidence of one's eyes is often called into doubt.[7]

At about the same time, theater directors began to feel they had stretched the confinement of the theater to the limit. Although the bare boards of Shakespeare's theater had been sufficient to yield a variety of settings, from bedchambers to tavern yards to battlefields, stages had become increasingly cramped and crowded. Meyerhold created fantastic constructivist sets using materials from the real world, and Eisenstein moved out of the theater altogether, staging a play in a gas factory.[8] When cinema arrived, and then the sound film, the theater was to become the whipping boy of the critics. The talkies were considered the death knell of the new film art, a return to the static qualities of "filmed theater."

In the theater we are thought to see a single space, without ever changing our angle of vision or our distance from the stage, whereas in the
cinema we see a succession of different images from a multiplicity of
angles. Provocatively, Edgar Morin shows how these ideas can be reversed. When we watch a play, our attention keeps shifting like a camera
from one character to another, from watching the whole to watching particular details. In short, we deconstruct the scene psychologically, creating
a succession of mental long shots, pans, and close-ups. By contrast, when
we watch the separate shots of a film, we reconstruct these into a single
mental image of the filmic world as a whole. "There is, therefore, a secret
cinema in the theater, just as a great theatricality enfolds all the shots of
cinema. In the first case, our psychological vision cinematizes the theater;
in the second, a rationalizing and objectifying vision theatricalizes the
cinema."[9]

Theater and cinema have at least in common their linearity, each unfolding in time sequentially. Writing and cinema share a less temporal
linearity—what might more properly be called a *directionality*—with cinema, compared to writing (but like the theater), more constrained by time.
In each the author is the guide to what should be seen or thought next, and
although we escape from this control in a hundred ways, like passengers
choosing different views from a train's windows, it provides the track
along which we run. The question then becomes what we see from those
windows, and how we see it.

One feature that descriptive writing and film have in common is their
lacunae. They rely upon a few sharp sense impressions, generally favoring
vision, and leave the rest to our imagination. If a writer attempted to
sketch in more than the barest details of a scene, it would go on forever
(although for novelists from Proust to Robbe-Grillet, observation of detail becomes close to an end in itself). Despite the dreams of some social
scientists for a panoptic film record providing a comprehensive account
of an event, the camera can record only a single perspective at any one
time. As in writing, the filmmaker must therefore proceed analytically,
constructing a new reality out of fragments, seeing it as much with the
mind as with the eye. At every moment a hundred alternatives are rejected
in the interests of a specific, often idiosyncratic understanding. The images
chosen by Rouch are unimaginable in the cinema of Flaherty, just as the
images of Kafka would be unimaginable in the novels of Thomas Mann.
The choices made leave huge gaps of time, space, and detail, and these
become as eloquent as what is actually shown. Apart from the absurdity
of attempting to replicate the world in all its perspectives and details,
these gaps give the reader or viewer a creative role in fusing together the
fragments that the author has chosen to represent the scene.

Readers are able to piece together even widely scattered events, provided they have a common denominator such as a central fictional or historical character. David Burton relates the life of the Compte de Boigne in a few terse sentences, any one of which contains enough material for a whole novel:

> Born in 1751 at Chambéry, he was forced into exile at the age of seventeen after having killed a Piedmontese noble in a duel. At one time he was a lover of Catherine the Great of Russia, who tired of him after a while and sent him off to the Turkish war. He was captured at Tenedos and sold as a slave in Istanbul, later freed only to be recaptured by Arabs when his ship foundered off the coast of Palestine. Having charmed his captors sufficiently to get them to pay his passage to Alexandria, he proceeded to India. Scindia, the effective Regent of the Mogul Empire, made him head of some forces with which he scattered the Rajput armies and made Scindia the most powerful ruler in India. De Boigne lived at a remote spot called Alighar with his Persian princess wife, and entertained any passing Europeans in great style.[10]

Most descriptive writing is far more fine-grained than this, but the lacunae are no less important. Here is the opening paragraph of one of Georges Simenon's Inspector Maigret novels of the 1950s:

> The chicken was on the stove, a fine red carrot, a big onion and a bunch of parsley, with the stems sticking out, surrounding it. Madame Maigret bent over to make sure there was no risk of the gas, which she had turned down as low as possible, going out. Then she closed the windows, except for the one in the bedroom, checked that she hadn't forgotten anything, glanced at the mirror and, satisfied, left the flat, locked the door and put the key in her purse.[11]

The writing is plain. It lacks apparent artistry, or at any rate the artistry of the high art novel. Simenon, like his contemporary Chandler, was often considered a "commercial" writer and here is writing in his most commercial vein. Moreover, I have purposely chosen a text in translation, to look at the bare bones, so to speak, and reduce the effect of any stylistic flourishes. But Simenon is in fact a master of this form and establishes the scene and mood with his customary economy. The paragraph is highly visual, highly concrete, and yet it contains only fifteen concrete nouns. It seems to capture everything—the food cooking (perhaps with the steam rising over it), the kitchen (perhaps with the sun streaming through the window), the confined flat, the little actions of checking the gas, the busy purposefulness of Mme Maigret. It does what an opening paragraph ideally should do, in picturing a place, introducing a character, initiating an action, and projecting a state of mind. Above all, it gives us the coordinates of the world we are entering, which in this case will not be epic or probably tragic, but domestic, conversational, and immersed in the concerns of daily life.

Between the chicken and the carrot, between the kitchen (never mentioned) and the bedroom (never entered) stretches a coherent world. The window is open, so it must be warm enough for that—therefore not winter, and it is not raining. Mme Maigret bends over to check the gas—we see the woman's body but can also feel this action in our own bodies, and the slight apprehension that goes with a low gas flame, whose tiny blue and yellow plumes are as vivid as if Simenon had bothered to describe them. As Mme Maigret prepares to leave the flat, an enlarged vision of this domestic space is sketched in, and then comes the close-up of the key dropped into the purse.

And yet we know almost nothing about the flat, or the woman. She glances into the mirror, but we know nothing of her face, its age, her hair. What kind of stove? Vaguely white enamel? But this is only a guess. The fine red carrot and the big onion are all very well, but on closer inspection this is the most banal description. Nor do we know anything about the furnishings, or whether Mme Maigret steps into a hallway or a street or a courtyard. Some of these things will become clearer, and perhaps we already know them from previous Maigret novels, but here Simenon has performed a magic trick, creating an integrated world out of almost nothing.

Not only have these very few objects been chosen for their precise effects, but like notes in a melody they have been presented to us in a certain order. Sensibly, Simenon starts with the food, the object of Mme Maigret's attention, rather than with Mme Maigret herself, thus binding us to her point of view. That fine red carrot now—it is Mme Maigret's pride speaking. The contents of the pot appear in a certain order, with the stems of the parsley last, and although it could be said that we finally "see" the whole ensemble, I believe the order makes a difference, for we could not have seen each object so much in isolation if this were a photograph. As for Mme Maigret's actions, they are arranged one after the other, so that we are obliged to follow her about the flat, which is a little different from standing in one spot observing her. As well, the details of her movements—checking the gas, closing the windows, glancing in the mirror— serve a double function, not only of painting the scene but also suggesting Mme Maigret's nervousness and the idea that she is girding herself up for something.

One could go on in this way, but the point is that although Simenon's style is highly "cinematic," this is not at all the same as cinema. It would be possible to shoot the scene he describes in several different ways, from the *découpage classique* of Hollywood to the more open frames of a Jean Renoir or Vittorio de Sica film. In the first, there would be many shots, constructing the scene analytically in much the way that Simenon does on paper. In the second, the camera would take up a few carefully selected vantage points, and the key objects would be linked together by the movements of Mme Maigret. In each case, however, what we would see would be quite different from what Simenon's prose leads us to imagine.

For one thing, the written paragraph—apparently so concretely factual—is filled with half-hidden signs of Mme Maigret's interior life. I have mentioned her pride in the carrot, but she has also put the parsley into the pot in a certain way, and this suggests to us a further fastidiousness as a cook. In her care to "make sure" the gas will not go out, we learn that she has already turned it down, an event that took place before the novel began. She checks that she has not forgotten anything, and is "satisfied." (This in fact is the only time that Simenon reports her feelings directly.) When she closes all the windows "except the one in the bedroom" we are offered a nonevent, something she chooses not to do, a half-formed thought or perhaps a habit—at any rate, a certain logic of mind. In a film, to show these predispositions, emotions, or decisions one would have to dramatize them. Her satisfaction would have to register on her face. Her decision not to close the bedroom window would have to be shown as a momentary indecision or a glance at that window after closing all the others.

It may also seem obvious, but Mme Maigret filmed is very different from Mme Maigret described or, as here, merely named. The Mme Maigret of the film is played by an actor. She is a *certain* woman, with a *certain* face. In a film we would see her face, as we see all faces, not as a series of individual features but as a group, a configuration of features (indeed, "configure"—from *figura*, or shape—comes very close to implying this unified form). Film images would contain additional, parallel configurations. She would not move around the flat against a vaguely suggested background, as she does in the writing, but within a precise context of walls, pictures, and other furnishings. The camera would probably take little note of these—no close-ups, nothing singled out for attention except the stove—and yet, for that very reason, we would see them not as separate details but in their concurrent existence. So, too, with the contents of the pot on the stove, for it is unlikely that the carrot, the onion, and then the parsley would be shown in succession. (In the novel they are, with the suggestion that they were put into the pot in that order.)

What I wish to suggest is that much that is cumulative in writing becomes, in the cinema, composite. We grasp objects and events in their complexes and continuities, and it is the interrelationships of these that are often more important than the components of the images taken separately. This concurrence within the image, which is both concrete and perceptual, is by no means the only important difference between writing and filming, but it is one that has the potential to produce quite different accounts of human beings in their social settings, and indeed will inevitably do so. The cultural complexes revealed in visual media not only involve distinctive sets and arrangements of material objects, but also the relations between objects and actions, and the interplay between actions occurring simultaneously or in close combination, as in the interactive postures and gestures that human beings adopt in conversation.

Without necessarily reducing the level of interpretation to frame-by-frame analysis (although this has its adherents), the composite vision of photographs and films offers a way of exploring connections in the social world often lost in writing, much as writing offers a way of recording conclusions about society unavailable to film. I am thinking here not only of how people and things are culturally organized in their social settings, but also how individuals perceive their surroundings and their fellows in physical and sensory terms, and how this affects how they themselves behave. This is not only a matter of interpersonal relations. We live among cultural practices and culturally mediated environments that exert powerful effects upon us. How we respond to these pressures, and how we in turn modify them, are phenomena that viewing films and photographs (and indeed making them) can help us to understand better.

Speech, Writing, and Image

An understanding of speech, and the differences between speech and writing, may further clarify how films are different from writing and how social research by way of film might differ radically from social research based on words. In his study of orality and literacy, Walter J. Ong makes the point that speech is always located in time and is therefore not only ephemeral but evanescent. "Sound . . . exists only when it is going out of existence. I cannot have all of a word present at once: when I say 'existence', by the time I get to the '-tence', the 'exis-' is gone."[12]

When we watch a film, the individual shots may have a superficial resemblance to words, but they are caught in a continuous flow of time and are mobilized more like the sounds of speech than the sight of words on a page. Speech and writing structure consciousness in different ways, and film structures consciousness in ways different from either of them.

Sooner or later, every film starts with an image, once the titles and opening business have been cleared away. Perhaps it doesn't even matter what we count as an image, whether it is a title, a blank screen with sounds, or a film image in the conventional sense. Once an image has been given, the entire rest of the film is an attempt to explain it—or to explain the other images that have been brought into play to explain it.

The film is a progressive unfolding from that initial, presumptuous image addressed to the audience.

The first image may not be particularly important, but it is a point of departure. From it emerges a conceptual shape akin to a cone or pyramid, a steady expansion outward as further images are added. And it does of course matter very much what the first image is—filmmakers agonize over this—even if it appears inconsequential, such as a landscape or "establishing shot" (in screenwriters' parlance), for everything flows from it. It must have consequences or the film might as well stop at once.

Let us examine this first image. Almost any image will do. Rather than specifying one, it is simpler to take an image from one's imagination, or from a film one has seen, or at random from whatever happens to be nearby. This image is filled with an almost infinite potential, for it could be the start of hundreds of quite different films. It all depends upon what one sees in it and decides to expand upon. Again, of course, this is not how films are actually made. The filmmaker knows very well why that image has been chosen and where it will lead.

And yet again, perhaps not, for very often films are not made with such certainty. The image has its own life, its own content. It has many features, and one or several of these may prove more interesting or fruitful than the idea that the filmmaker started with. In fact, this can happen anywhere along the course of the film, at any point in the filming or editing. Unless the film has been laid out fully in advance in a script that is slavishly followed, the work of the filmmaker is more often that of making the most of the possibilities that arise, while at the same time holding them in check so as not to lose sight of the main idea. If you have ever driven a team of horses or, as is more likely, gone walking with a dog on a leash, you will know what this is like.

To give a clearer sense of it, and of where I am heading, it would be better to choose an image somewhere later in the film. Such an image will have a number of roles. Unlike the first image, it will look backward as well as forward. At this point, let us begin calling it a shot rather than an "image," which is rather too pretentious, like a word in a fine arts catalogue. If we take any shot from within the body of a film, it is part of the unfolding of what we have already seen. Most shots have movement in them, or something happens, or even if they are perfectly static require us to look at them over a certain period of time. They have their own dynamics and create their own expectations and forward movement, unlike a photograph lying on a table. The shot adds one more layer of possible connections and resonances, and it always has the potential to lead us off in a new direction.

Each shot is thus part of the system of understanding and explanation that the filmmaker is trying to erect. But what does a shot actually contain compared to what we see in it? In experiencing a film, we don't ordinarily ask such questions, but film critics do and the filmmaker assuredly does. In most cases, what we look for and see in a shot is what we have been directed to see by the previous shots. This may be a person we have come to recognize, the continuation of an action, or another aspect of the place or set of objects with which the film has been concerned. As it reveals more, the shot also looks backward and amplifies what has gone before it. It may show us in a wider shot something of which we have seen only a part. It may show us who someone is talking to, whom we have not yet seen. It may explain why someone looked startled by showing what startled them. Or conversely, it may start with the startling event and show someone's response to it. There are standard names for such shots—reaction shots, establishing shots, inserts, point-of-view shots, and so on. They are at once the film's syntax and its content.

If we were to reflect more generally on how shots work together, we could describe this process as a progressive form of contextualization, each shot adding contextual matter to what has been shown before and, at the same time, opening up matters that will require further contextualization.[13] This can, in fact, become one of the nightmarish aspects of filmmaking, especially when making nonfiction films. Nothing in nonfiction comes unalloyed. As soon as you clarify one thing you run the risk of introducing new material that requires further clarification. All the same, this process of accretion lies at the very heart of the narrative process, for it is only out of one act that another takes shape. Even if a shot pushes the film off in an entirely new direction, the filmmaker must have laid the necessary groundwork for this departure, whether thematically, emotionally, in the lives of the protagonists, or all three.

Taken out of a film and seen in isolation, a shot becomes more like a still photograph, for it can be made to signify a variety of things, sometimes quite opposite in meaning. Compilation films keep recycling the same stock of archival images to support different arguments. The shot has this potential both because it is disconnected from its former context and because its contents are almost always a mixture of different elements, each of which is capable of being given precedence over the others. It is this multivalency that allows it to be attached to a variety of discourses.[14]

But even within the context of a film, shots do not entirely lose their multivalency. This, perhaps, is the real source of their richness and difference from words. A word carries the potential for both ambiguity and precision through its neutrality, its happy service in many settings. The ambiguity and precision of a shot comes from its specificity. It refers to objects in a unique time and place, but these become ambiguous through their internal complexity and the different levels of potential meaning they make available simultaneously.

When I write and select one or another word, I think about how it fits
or fails to fit the half-articulated sense I have in mind, but when I am
making a film I am constantly confronted by shots that are filled with
both relevant and (to me) extraneous matter at every level. My task is to
direct the viewer toward those aspects of the shot-conglomerate that will
advance their understanding of a particular theme or set of events.
Eisenstein tried to overcome this problem by stripping his shots down to
bare essentials and making them very short, so that no extraneous matter
could creep in. He reached an approximation of this ideal, but even so he
failed. The close-up of a face or a goblet, shot against a dark background,
could not achieve the purity of a word such as "moon" or "heron" that
he so much admired in haiku. A typecast face says far more than "old
peasant woman," for it is a *certain* face, a face perhaps like that of someone we know.

To an even greater extent, those who make nonfiction films are subject
to the actual appearances and unforeseen happenings of the world. Any
shot I begin making will contain multiple events, objects, and qualities
that will either emerge over time or that already coexist in the shot simultaneously. The viewer's attention can take possession of any one of them,
or any combination of them, all at once or progressively as it wanders
among them. Yet far from being a weakness of film (although it does limit
film as a lexical system) this capacity of film for compound expression is
also its greatest asset. As a filmmaker, I cherish the complex structure of
the shot and the possibilities it creates for seeing the interconnections
within it, as well as the interconnections made possible by its resonance
with other shots. I can marshal the complexity of still images in time—
and this, of course, is what, technically, film actually does, 24 or 25 times
a second. The effect, unexpectedly, is to produce not a series of photographs but a single image in which there is apparently movement. Thus I
receive a further gift: the possibility of marshaling the complexities of
moving images in time.

Nevertheless, this richness is potentially uncontrollable. You can see
the problem. You both want and don't want the combinative power that
shots offer, for they constantly drift toward the actual complexity and
indeterminacy of the experienced world. There is no point in making films
if they are mere replicas of what one has witnessed; they must be both
less (selective for a purpose) and more (providing an analysis, expressing
an attitude). In the end, successful films achieve a compromise, sometimes
narrowing the content and meaning of shots (as Eisenstein at first attempted to do), at other times pushing them to the farthest extremes of
their complexity, to the point at which they risk autonomous separation
from the body of the work, even striving for a kind of liberation from it.
Sometimes the filmmaker reserves a special place for something that seems

altogether tangential to the film but intuitively important and thus in a roundabout way reintegrates it. I have in mind certain ploys for saving a scene that has no structural function in a film and may even threaten its coherence but that nevertheless enriches one's experience of it.

Perhaps more frequently encountered is the case in which a shot or sequence of shots has a strong subtext that distracts attention from what one wishes, at that point, to be the dominant focus of the film. How far should one go in limiting or accommodating such material? Often there is little one can do, since one cannot winnow a shot to separate out the part one wants to keep. This is the peculiar nonlinearity of what is in many other respects a linear medium, the characteristic that resists the sort of editing that can be done to a text or a sound recording of speech. When speech is tied to image, as in a film, even this possibility disappears. The only way to move from one part of it to another is by means of an obvious cut or other transition.

Michel Chion has written a series of books insisting that sound in films should be regarded as an integral part of a larger audiovisual construct, not something added, even if the sound (for example, music) was recorded at a different time from the image. Sound and image mutually inflect and transform one another.[15] An image and an appropriate synchronous sound weld themselves together in an effect that Chion calls *synchresis*. The important principle behind Chion's discussion of sound and image, and one that has even broader implications in the understanding of film, is the principle of *co-presentation*. When we see someone speaking and hear his or her voice, we grasp it as a single complex phenomenon. Yet we are affected by it at two sensory levels, and these generate further responses that amplify the effect beyond its simple ingredients of sound and image. A shot of a child's fingers rubbing across the surface of a balloon evokes more than the actions and sounds involved: it suggests the way the balloon must feel, and even an imminent explosion. Sound and image together can generate powerful synesthetic responses, creating a heightened sense of space, volume, and texture. What we see and hear taps into our prior experience of the world and stimulates the imaginative capacity that most of us possess to fill in the gaps left by the cursory acts of perception. Paradoxically, this is true to such an extent that a sound heard off-screen—a distant voice, or the cry of a bird—is often more evocative of a place and its spaces than if we were to see what caused the sound.

In considering how written language differs from speech (and more generally from an oral culture), Ong observes that writing removes speech from the everyday sensory world. It appears to the reader as marks on a page, usually read in silence. "The word in its natural, oral habitat is a part of a real, existential present. . . . Spoken words are always modifications of a total situation which is more than verbal. . . . Yet words are alone in a text."[16] Writing must work all the harder, then, to make up for this loss of its complex interpersonal and multisensory context, as well as the nonverbal forms of communication that accompany speech, and it has devised sophisticated means for doing so. But in the process it has fundamentally altered both readers' and writers' sensibilities and patterns of thought.

Similarly, the sensibilities and thought patterns involved in writing and reading differ markedly from those required for making and viewing films. Film exploits the co-presentation of objects and sensory patterns that writing tends to present in a more selective and linear fashion. In Ong's view, this aspect of writing has in fact given science its analytical edge, permitting it to develop patterns of thought that oral cultures lack. It has fostered lists, charts, subordinated clauses, headings, and other forms of abstraction. It has also changed the perception of time and history. "Persons whose world view has been formed by high literacy need to remind themselves that in functionally oral cultures the past is not felt as an itemized terrain, peppered with verifiable and disputed 'facts' or bits of information."[17]

One could dispute this, pointing to the symbolic systems (such as art and myth) through which nonliterate societies encode abstract relationships and information. However, these systems actually make use of varied and often multiply interreferential sensory stimuli that differ significantly from writing. In other words, they bring into play the co-presentation of elements that writing notably lacks.

Reading Culture

In recent years, a great deal of attention has been directed toward the role of writing in the human sciences. Most of this attention has focused on the assumptions and techniques clustered around writing rather than writing itself. Indeed, the alternatives to writing anthropology or sociology or history have hardly figured in these discussions, although ethnographic filmmakers have from time to time promoted the differences of their own medium. When film is invoked, it is generally to adapt its structures to writing, not to question writing as a method. The primary concerns have been literary ones: how ethnographies are structured, what narrative implies in history, how social research becomes an interpretive process, and so on. There have been experiments in form and style in an effort to expand the writing of these subjects beyond the confines of expository prose—new uses of juxtaposition, the deployment of indigenous texts, and descriptive approaches drawn from fiction. But there has been less attention to writing as a way of encoding knowledge, or the ramifications of reading it.

Part of the dissatisfaction with earlier anthropological writing has stemmed from its assumption of authority and its techniques for making its conclusions appear natural and indisputable, which the new forms are designed to correct. There has also, we are told, been a retreat from grand theory, although interest in evolutionary theory appears to be on an upswing. Despite these shifts, academic writing has retained a deep-seated link with the oral traditions of medieval scholarship, with its emphasis on the reading out of papers at conferences and seminars (even when copies have been precirculated) and the survival of archaic rhetorical structures designed to hammer home each point. Despite their gloss of new technology, most PowerPoint™ presentations also seem founded on these principles. Academic papers tend to leave little to the imagination, generally starting with statements of what they will say, proceeding to saying it in detail, and concluding with a summary of what has just been said. Often an abstract goes over the same ground yet a fourth time. This architecture is purposely clumsy, one feels, as a guarantee of guilelessness, as if the writer were not subject to fashion. The repetition is employed as much to convince as to provide clarity. This may derive, as Ong suggests, from the rhetorical structure of the oral debate, which involves confrontation with an antagonist. In antiquity "rhetorical teaching assumed that the aim of more or less all discourse was to prove or disprove a point, against some opposition" (110).

In other ways, too, writing has contributed to a culture of proof. Without writing, it seems unlikely that philosophy and science would have developed the sort of logic that involves creating a progression of arguments from premises or extracting principles from data. Writing has made it usual—indeed, almost obligatory—to express knowledge in the form of propositional statements. These differ from aphorisms and other kinds of oral wisdom in that they are not taken to be self-evident but the result of a process of inquiry. Social science depends upon writing to perform its three basic tasks: description, explanation, and the codification of more general theories about human society. Anthropological writing is therefore not simply cultural translation, as it is often described, but the creation of a completely new object, an object (on a page) of an entirely different order from its object of study. Ethnography, too, has gradually shifted from more or less pictorial descriptions of human societies in the nineteenth century (usually accompanied by actual pictures in the form of line drawings and engravings) to the greater abstractions of social organization and belief systems in the twentieth. The gap between sensory experience and knowledge has consequently widened.

David Tomas has likened the anthropologist to a photographic emulsion, exposed to another society and then developed at home.[18] He or she is thus seen as an intermediary, registering the contours of the society and reproducing it for the anthropological audience. This implies, too, that the experience of the anthropologist, as a negative, is quite different from that of the reader, who gets a positive. However, the process is more roundabout than this implies, for leaving aside the question of interpretation at the field site, writing involves exposure followed by a process of invention followed by a process of encoding. Unlike a photograph, which has a certain general legibility across cultures, it produces a product for a literate audience that is also culturally specific, for you have to know the language it is written in to read it. The type of encoding is also significant. Writing that uses an alphabetic script, as most languages do, is really a means of recording speech—that is, a series of sounds rather than anything more concrete in the physical world. So a written or printed text can be seen as a quadruple transformation, from initial observations that have a strong sensory component, to a process of thought, to the production of words with their specific sounds, to the rendering of those sounds as letters on a page—a result that is once again sensory, but sensory in a very different way.

Not surprisingly, social scientists often feel uneasy about the huge discrepancies between their own learning experiences, as researchers, and how readers experience their texts.[19] However, they tend to attribute these to the natural limitations of language, rather than to the particular ways in which writing structures the writer's and reader's thinking and imagination. Perhaps the most obvious and yet least often noted effect is the evacuation of human beings from the text. To be sure, human beings are named and their actions described, but they are not in any physical sense *there*, and in academic writing they tend to become examples of general types rather than the individuals the writer has known. This absence haunts anthropology, which has tried to make up for it with photographs, anecdotes, quotations, and museum exhibits. Writing, with its passive, retrospective view of life, entombs the living. In a good novel, characters are said to come alive on the page, but they do so through the expert description of a very few attributes, which if one looks closely are of the most fragmentary and fleeting kind. Yet somehow these activate a waking dream-life in the reader. It is a tribute to good writers that they can evoke the wholeness of a person through such meager evidence. It is also paradoxical that successful reading of this kind requires solitude and separation from the living human beings who normally make up one's social world.

Writing also leads to a deformation of normal social time. Because of the freedom readers feel to read or not to read, and because a book need not be read all at once but can be picked up and put down at will, writers feel a corresponding freedom to pause, make detours, and in effect slow down time as required by their subject. This can lead to an almost infinite expansion of attention to any particular point. Academic writing is prone to various forms of gigantism and disorderings of scale, whole books sometimes appearing to be no more than footnotes to other texts. Novelists, although sometimes more constrained by commercial expectations, have also explored the possibilities of contracted and expanded attention. Olaf Stapledon's synoptic *Last and First Men* (1930) covers 2,000 millennia, Joyce's *Ulysses* recounts the events of a single day, and Proust was able to devote some thirty pages to getting out of bed.

One of the most important features of writing is the way in which it has preserved traces of the speaking voice. This is true not only of the dialogue in novels, but of all writing. All writing, if it uses an alphabet, is based on the transcription of the sounds of speech, and because of this it always refers back to the act of speaking. Whether or not we are aware of hearing their voices, writers are always telling us something, creating a narrative of events or, as in most scholarly writing, of ideas. A great deal of postmodern anxiety in the social sciences has gone into how writers speak to us. To what extent do they beguile us with their personalities or create an impression of omniscient impersonality to convince us of the truth of their statements? How does use of the passive voice contribute to a seeming objectivity? And so on. Expository writing can range from the conversational to the almost impenetrable. Clifford Geertz is one of those anthropologists who writes with such an informal air of speaking to us—with just the right blend of gravitas and humor—that it is as though we were listening to him, not reading words on a page. It's no wonder that he has been particularly adept at unpicking the writing styles of other anthropologists.[20] He has helped make it clear (if more clarity were needed) that qualities of thought are intimately linked to qualities of expression.

Unlike Geertz's writing, a great deal of academic prose seems to be the work of faceless writers. Over the centuries writing has shifted away from speech patterns and assumed an institutional character—the voice of the state, the church, the academy. This shift has allowed it to develop structures that would never be spoken but make possible a high degree of abstraction. Written language tends toward a schematization of knowledge, involving the sophisticated use of categories, oppositions, and mental diagrams. It is no doubt responsible for the excessive reductionism of much theoretical thinking and the propagation of fundamentalist ideologies, but it has also made possible the working out of complex ideas in philosophy and the disciplines that have emerged from it. Writing creates the necessary distance from experience for analysis and theorizing. It also fixes knowledge in an immutable form, which ever after is open to inspection. This encourages care in writing, if the writing is to be published, but it also encourages a certain impunity, since the reader has no immediate way to reply to it except by more writing. Statements put in writing do not disappear just because you refute them and, as Ong observes, this is one reason why books have been burnt.[21]

Along with increasing syntactical complexity, writing has encouraged the growth of a vocabulary of abstraction. Over the past century, social science has created an explosion of abstract terms, the most fought over being "culture," while more recent writing concerns itself with "liminality," "consumption," and "identity." There is a tendency to employ the more obscure meanings of familiar words and other markers of professional membership. With constant use, concepts such as the "Other" become little more than empty gestures. In the military, governmental, and business bureaucracies there is a continuous process of converting verbs into nouns, creating a further level of abstraction, which is quickly canonized in the press. In these and many other ways, written forms seep into general usage and thence into speech. However, this colonization of speech by writing is not entirely a one-way process, nor is it irreversible, as some technological determinists (perhaps including Ong) believe. People are influenced by technologies but they also redefine their uses. Literacy can be used to reinforce oral traditions when indigenous languages are under threat. An innovation like e-mail, while it has given new life to letter writing (against the pressures of the telephone), has also made its written forms far more informal and speechlike.

I have left until last perhaps the most distinctive feature of writing—its linearity. This is not disconnected from the fact that writing is arranged in lines, whether vertical, right to left, or left to right. Its physical ramifications, however, go beyond this. Unlike speech, which it imitates, writing is not evanescent. The whole of a paragraph is left, even when one has reached the last sentence, and it could be said that the whole paragraph lingers in the mind, like a picture. However, writing is a word-by-word process, and reading a description in writing is essentially aggregative, adding one new item at a time, unlike a picture, which is encountered as a composite. To describe the hundreds of details apparent in a picture would require an exhaustive list that could never be taken in as a single entity, much less in its overall form and spatial relationships. It is probably wrong even to speak of a picture as describing, since the very term refers to the process of writing.

There are two arguments against this distinction between writing and images. Speed-readers are said to grasp a paragraph in its entirety, as a unity. Pictures are not in fact viewed all at once but discontinuously, detail by detail, in a series of saccadic movements of the eyes. The impression of seeing the picture as a whole is formed in the brain. Thus reading could be said to be a composite experience and viewing a picture a linear one. I find these arguments only superficially convincing. Like Morin's discovery of cinema in theater (and vice versa), they seem more *ben trovato* than *vero*, for they seem more to describe a secondary level of perception and cognition (speed-reading is a special case of this) than the object itself.

The linearity of writing and reading has had a significant effect on how scholarship and literature have represented the world, and on how (in Ong's terms) this has restructured human consciousness. The aggregative nature of writing encourages the precise ordering of ideas and thus the development of complex chains of reasoning. In the case of descriptions, it has had a similar impact on the selection and ordering of physical details. Since mental images derived from writing are cumulative, there is a limit to how many details can be remembered, and it also becomes important which are introduced earlier and which later. Written description also makes possible the isolation of certain details for emphasis or evocative purposes, just as in filmmaking the camera can pick out a particular object in a close-up. But this resemblance can be misleading. When alluding to a person in writing, it would be impossible (and unnecessary) to include repetitively each time the same information about how the person looked. Pictures are less discriminating in this regard; they are filled with redundancies (such as the appearance of a person) that writing can safely leave out. But by the same token, writing tends to elide the familiar redundancies of the world, with important consequences for how we think about it.

Details in writing are like isolated peaks in a mountain range, leaving huge gaps. They thus have a strongly synecdochic effect, for they leave to the imagination all of the unwritten whole that lies between them. Masters of suggestion, like Graham Greene, know how to choose and place a detail so that it creates the maximum stimulus, at least for a certain community of readers with the necessary prior experience. Take, for example, these glimpses from a train at night: "As he reached his compartment the train was slowing down. The great blast furnaces of Liège rose along the line like ancient castles burning in a border raid. The train lurched and the points clanged. Steel girders rose on either side, and very far below an empty street ran diagonally into the dark, and a lamp shone on a café door."[22] Like this train journey, linearity in writing also tends to project a sense of movement in the direction of completion (of a sentence, of a narrative), which in academic writing assumes the magisterial quality of a movement toward truth. Indeed, the dominant metaphors of scholarship are all about journeys—the path of discovery, covering new ground, arriving at an understanding, and so on.[23] This directionality may arguably produce the emphasis on causality and explanation that seems more characteristic of the narratives of literate than nonliterate societies, in which connections are often mapped as much on places as on time.[24] We might ask to what extent social science is also impelled by writing to produce narratives of cause and effect rather than to expand upon the nature of what it describes.

Simultaneities

I have stressed that "description" is a linear, aggregative process, and that the word itself derives from writing (*scribere*). In the case of films—although they are also in many ways linear—we would be better advised to use the word "depiction." Rather than telling us, in the voice of a writer, a film presents us with a series of scenes. Unless there is a spoken commentary, the narrative of a film is always something unsaid, something implied. Gilberto Perez questions David Bordwell's use of the term "narration" in relation to films, for although the author's hand is often evident in a film, there is rarely a direct authorial voice—which in literature is always potentially there, although not always employed.[25] The "organization of a set of cues for the construction of a story" (as Bordwell puts it) is rather far from a narrative process.[26] In Bordwell's view, the narration is capable of creating a narrator, but it need not, and a narrator, if present, is always a conceit and is never, in any case, the source of the film's narration.

It is possible to extend the principle of *co-presentation* well beyond the simultaneity of sound and image in films. There are many other simultaneities. Physical objects appear together and often jostle for space within a shot, sometimes isolated, sometimes interconnected, and sometimes overlapping one another in foreground and background. Often linked as well from one shot to another, these make up the visible part of the environment projected by the film. We sense not only the co-presence of the objects but their sensory qualities—in form, texture, color, and volume. These qualities figure prominently in Eisenstein's concept of a montage of attractions.[27]

There is co-presentation at several other levels. One could point to the co-presentation of events as well as of objects within the frame. Movements within a shot can be complex and either related to one another or unrelated. Sometimes their relationship is oblique, depending upon a factor not visible in the scene, such as wind blowing upon leaves, each of which has its own separate movement. More obvious are the direct connections between events organized sequentially in time, such as someone reacting to someone else's action within the shot. This may be essentially physical, as in a scene of a tennis match, or at the level of gestures and expressions of emotions. Although in these cases the events follow one other in time and are therefore not literally simultaneous, they nevertheless have a co-presence as linked elements within the shot.

Indeed, it is in the realm of interpersonal relations that the visual complexity of the image has particular relevance for social research, as it does for cinema as an art. The possibility of grasping a complex social event simultaneously through its various dimensions of gesture, facial expression, speech, body movement, and physical surroundings is something that a text can approach only with great difficulty. It can be simulated in the theater, but film allows it to be seen and interpreted as it occurs spontaneously in its original setting. Formal and informal interactions take place over time, but in both cases there is also an element of simultaneity, which reflects the intersubjectivity of the participants. In conversations, teaching and learning situations, arguments, and lovemaking there are patterns of reciprocal behavior that link the participants together and sustain the communication between them, whether this be in the form of looks, physical contact, sounds, or an implicit choreography of movement and posture. In more formal interactions, such as rituals and communal labor, these patterns become more pronounced, to the extent that they often become the defining features of the event (as in military drills and dance performances, for example).

At the more abstract level of social and cultural meanings, film images allow objects to appear in both their guises as symbolically meaningful (to those who know, or care) and not meaningful. Or, to put it another way, they underscore the point that although symbols may be produced by a society, they are not necessarily seen as meaningful by those who observe them or even use them. Film images further suggest that even if objects and forms have symbolic qualities, they have at the same time a simpler brute physical existence, the level at which people most often experience them. This dualism tends to be suppressed in written discussions of symbolism, perhaps because it appears distracting and seemingly contradictory to refer to the countervailing nonsymbolic levels involved. For this reason, anthropologists have taken pains to stress the enunciative and experiential aspects of ritual as coexistent with and often dominant over the symbolic.[28]

Symbols also exist in clusters and complexes, making their copresentation important if one is trying to see how they relate to one another. The "complex" (in the sense of the aggregate) is often more important than its individual elements understood piecemeal, as, for example, in the crossover between painting, dance, poetry, and landscape in the films made by Ian Dunlop and Kim McKenzie about indigenous rituals in Australia. The symbolic aspects of life, as well as sometimes being "dumb," can also be changeable and multivocal. It is important to understand that a single item can simultaneously carry several quite separate meanings in the same context. As an example, I have in mind the sometimes widely varying meanings attached to clothing, colors, and numbers at a boarding school I have studied in northern India.[29]

The principle of co-presentation is not only significant at these various levels of object, event, and symbolic meaning but is also significant in itself for a broader understanding of social experience. People live in a composite world, even though their paths through it have linear qualities. In analyzing and trying to represent that world, it is important not to let the impulse to disentangle its strands displace the effects of its complexity. In providing a different way of addressing such phenomena as multiple sensory stimuli, the interconnections between different *kinds* of complexity, and the unstable nature of symbols, film offers social research and cultural studies a useful alternative to expository prose. It may be objected that film is open-ended, too mimetic, and in a sense too concrete to be analytical. But while it is true that the contents of film images are often in themselves undifferentiated, their further articulations give film its analytical potential, notably the selective use of the camera, the juxtapositions of shots (or, more simply, editing), and the overall organization of shots in time. Like all communicative systems, film is a compromise between order and productive disorder. Writing and film suffer from different kinds of ambiguity and overdetermination. With their shortcomings, they should be thought of as two incomplete but at times complementary systems.

I have mentioned the indiscriminate redundancy of film, its limited ability to filter out what we already know, as writing does, or what the author might wish not to include, such as distractions and potential contradictions. This leads to film projecting an image of the world quite different from what we receive from texts. Photographic depiction differs from description in including massive amounts of detail, sometimes making it difficult to see what the author is driving at. This has led some commentators to equate film with observation itself, lacking an interpretive perspective, as if it were merely reproducing slices of life. And there is indeed a tendency for lazy filmmakers to assume that others will see in their footage what they see in it, and to become indignant when they do not. This is unfortunately one reason why television producers insist on what they call "signposting," to make sure that no one, not even the proverbial little old lady in Nottingham, will miss the point.

That stance, with its implicit fear of film's open-endedness, represents a regressive tendency to return film to the status of text. But what it ignores, or wishes to dismiss, are the very qualities of the "cinematograph" that allow film to perceive life differently. With its constant reiteration of the familiar attributes of things, film presents a differently balanced image of the world, underscoring a range of phenomena that texts ignore as "understood." In films, commonplace appearances regain some of their universality. Connections reemerge that we thought were naïve or misleading. In social research, this becomes a useful brake on the impulse to see every situation as unique, like a doctor inventing a new disease for each patient. It can actually encourage us to look for broader principles amid the admittedly dazzling welter of detail that films also provide. Another perhaps paradoxical benefit of film's composite vision is that it does not pin down meanings too precisely. As in the case of an object that is both utilitarian and potently symbolic, varied meanings can happily coexist within an image. It is the very "dumbness" of the image that permits this. Whatever associations objects may have, they continue to assert their mundane, physical characteristics and remain part of a visual continuum with other objects. In a sense objects gain in symbolic potential and complexity by being left unassigned to a system, for they can then carry forward the varied associations that the film has created around them. This can be as true in nonfiction (take, for example, the red truck in Bob Connolly and Robin Anderson's *Joe Leahy's Neighbours* [1988]) as in the object-laden universe of a Sirk or Hitchcock film.

Like this doubling between object and symbol, one of the distinctive things about film is its routine mixing of different modes of thought and perception. There is a continuous interplay among its varied forms of address—the aural with the visual, the sensory with the verbal, the narrative with the pictorial. There is a semblance of this interplay in literature, as well, but it is actually a construction of the writer's and reader's imaginations, since the actual form of address, words on a page, remains constant. Although films still have a comparatively limited experiential range (one does not smell the flowers in a film, or speak with others, or touch, or feel touched), they do offer the spectator some insight into the integrated and often confusing social reality faced by the protagonists. Writing can provide the jolt of a physical encounter, but films provide a flow of sensory (and other) experiences that requires considerable application to derive from writing.

The material qualities of the objects presented by films are pivotal in this mixing of levels, for these tend to resist abstract meanings, explanations, and conclusions. Also crucial is the fact that each object has its own unique identity, unlike the more casually named objects of writing. An image of a Trobriand yam in one of Malinowski's photographs is forever an image of that one historical yam, now long gone, rather than a member of a class of objects dealt with in his books. It is probably even misleading to call it an example of a yam, as one might do in a text, for even this suggests a somewhat higher level of abstraction. Despite all the commonalities they reveal in human experience, film images suggest a plentitude of cases, not a closed system. By dealing so doggedly with the specific object or moment, films are not very good vehicles for summary statements, but they do nevertheless often imply typicality and encourage viewers to extrapolate from the specific case. The style of the film plays an important part in this. An image taken out of context, overlaid by music and commentary, more easily takes on exemplary power.

One of the ways in which films overcome their potentially indeterminate view of objects and people is through their narrative structures. As Hayden White has pointed out, the closure of narrative implies a moral construction of the world and an ultimate passage from one moral order to another.[30] Along with these judgments, they provide explanations. Paul Roth has examined a number of theories of how narratives explain, including White's.[31] His own builds on White's proposal that narratives explain by replicating a culturally familiar story type that has previously found acceptance as a valid representation of life in a particular society. They thus possess an "explanatory affect."[32] Roth shifts the ground from traditional literary forms to Thomas Kuhn's notion of new scientific paradigms, which provide attractive analogies for confronting unsolved problems in adjacent fields.[33] He sees Geertz's famous essay on the Balinese cockfight as creating such a paradigm, by finding the explanation for an apparently illogical betting system not in familiar rational explanations but in a broader view of Balinese culture.[34] Although this begs some questions, it partly explains explanation as the satisfactory dramatization of a problem and its solution. The explanatory success of Geertz's narrative may thus depend very much on getting us to accept the unexpected paradigm of one logic subordinating another—paradoxical, in view of Geertz's belief in interpretation over explanation.

Another way of thinking about the explanatory power of narrative is to see it as vicarious experience. In an essay like Geertz's, this perhaps lies as much in sharing with Geertz the experience of arriving at a solution as in following the precise logic of how he got there. It involves identification with a first-person narrator. Films, although they occasionally produce narratives of this kind, more often stage them in the third person. The power of explanation in this case may lie more in a process like that described by White—from the recognition of patterns in human life that are recurrent and, according to some anthropologists such as Victor Turner, universal. Narratives based on these "social dramas" explain, it could be argued, because they refer to deep-seated processes by which societies maintain and reproduce themselves. Turner focused on a pattern that, he noted, resembled the phased progression of Aristotelian tragedies, which he formulated as "breach, crisis, redress, reintegration, or schism."[35] Out of such deep patterns are generated the rites of passage and other rituals (and, it could be added, the proto-narratives) that a society creates both to sustain its worldview and explain its own actions to itself.

Because film is time-based, it preserves more concretely than writing does the eventlike quality of experience. If films follow real sequences of events, it could be argued that their power of explanation lies chiefly in making clear the forces working on the protagonists, regardless of the outcome. What is being explained is not necessarily a single problem and its resolution but the accumulated issues and human interactions that occur along the way. Hamlet's indecision is as much an explanation of the contradictory forces around him as is the fate that awaits him at the end of the play. We follow the life of Nanook or Damouré or Charlie Chaplin because we get caught up in making sense of their moment-to-moment experiences. Each film produces a constant stream of low-level explanations. Nichols has pointed out that the plots of Hollywood films are frequently based on problems that are effectively insoluble.[36] It is the film's object simply to demonstrate this in dramatic terms. The ending is more often than not a mechanical release from the situation, lacking in true cathartic effect.

Although films may not construct narratives in the strict sense—that is, as storytelling—they do (*pace* Perez) construct deictic narratives, or narratives of the eye. For films are not simply dramatizations of life; they preserve the traces of a process of seeing and showing. They guide the audience, but they also register (especially in "first-person" nonfiction films) the filmmaker's perceptions and physical presence, much as the speaking voice is physically part of the narrative in an oral tradition. It can be said that the filmmaker's body is inscribed in the camera's vision at the same corporeal level as the bodies of the film subjects themselves. Thus, while in a modernist text we have the transcription of an inner speaking voice, in films we have something ontologically different—direct evidence of the filmmaker's body behind the camera. In viewing a film, we respond in various ways to the bodies of the people we see on the screen, but we also respond to the filmmaker's body as we experience it through the decisions that guide the movements of the camera, how it frames events, and in matters of proximity and positioning in relation to the subjects. The narratives created by the filmmaker's vision carry with them a series of judgments about the world, a moral framework, in much the same way that the narrativization of history does. This becomes quite evident in people's visceral responses to films—their approval or disapproval of the filmmaker's sensibility, of what is seen and how it is seen, and what is left out.

There is another sense in which narratives explain, which in films is accomplished by visual linking. Calvino recounts a legend concerning Charlemagne—that as an old man he successively loved a young girl, her dead body, an archbishop, and Lake Constance—all because the same magic ring had been associated with each of them. "What we have," writes Calvino, "is a series of totally abnormal events linked together."

To hold these together there is the ring, but also "a verbal link, the word 'love' or 'passion,' which establishes a continuity between different forms of attraction."[37] Thus the explanation provided by the narrative is the manner of linking unlike things. Stories such as this are often metaphorical or metaphysical disquisitions disguised as narratives. However, the intentionality of narrative—in Hayden White's terms, its assumed, if unmarked "subject"— implies that connections do exist, even if these are not yet apparent to the reader. In films much of this linking is achieved by visual means, either through the filmmaker's recurrent thematic interests or, more indirectly, through the lives of the film's protagonists. Rouch's characters in the film *Jaguar* create a narrative of travel that ties together diverse strands of social and economic life—from experiencing the exotic and the "primitive" as the protagonists move through the Somba lands in northern Dahomey, to working in the markets and industries of the Gold Coast.

Rouch's film highlights another conspicuous difference between the uses of film and writing. Anthropology (and to a lesser extent sociology) stresses participant-observation and close working relationships with informants. Yet with minor exceptions, the resulting writing stresses distancing from individuals in the interests of more comprehensive statements about society. The individuals are subsumed by the texts in a way that they cannot be in a film.[38] By now it is perhaps a commonplace that synchronous sound contributed to the individualization of the people in ethnographic films.[39] It led to recording speech; speech required translation; translation led to individualization. But the portrayal of people as individuals is also imposed at some level by the very nature of film. It lies in the inherent specificity of film images. In writing one can withhold the identity of an informant and even (if less successfully) a whole village. But one cannot withhold the identity of a face.

The individuality of faces in films also creates an increased potential for identifying psychologically with them. Narratives of individual experience with which viewers or readers can identify have given social scientists such as Rouch and Oscar Lewis (in his transcribed oral histories) a way of conveying the emotional content of social interaction and agency. The impossibility of maintaining anonymity in films may be one reason why a focus on individuals has been more common in ethnographic films than in ethnographic writing. However, it is as much a product of the inherent resistance of film to generality of any kind. Films situate people in a continuum of physical space and material objects that is historically and culturally specific.

The film theorist Béla Balázs wrote in 1923 of the power of film to transform human consciousness. "Its effect on human culture will not be less than that of the printing press," and "it is beginning to be able sometimes to express things which escape the artists of the word."[40] In his analysis, Balázs had two phenomena particularly in mind—the power of film to engulf the spectator in social and geographical space, and the expressiveness of the human face, as experienced in films. The newly emerging syntax of film construction would allow the spectator to experience films as an imaginary participant, "surrounded by the characters of the film."[41] This would play an important part in permitting identification with individuals, but also in delineating human social experience as a feature of both society and environment. In a discussion that presages structuralist interpretations, Balázs writes: "The realities of nature are given their deepest meaning for man if presented as a social experience; even the extra-social nature of the primeval forest or the arctic ice-pack is in the last instance a social experience; the very conception of solitude is a correlative conception and acquires intellectual and emotional content only if we are aware of its opposite, non-solitude."[42]

Perhaps equally important for Balázs, the proximity to the human face, newly provided by the close-up, would make possible a new form of access to human emotions. Balázs believed (with Ong, it seems) that literacy had altered our visual sensibility. "The discovery of printing gradually rendered illegible the faces of men."[43] In film the visible would unveil the invisible—"emotions, moods, intentions and thoughts, things which although our eyes can see them, are not in space."[44] These comments are interesting from the point of view of the concept of co-presentation. Balázs began to develop a theory of what he called the "polyphonic" play of human facial expressions. "By it I mean the appearance on the same face of contradictory expressions. In a sort of physiognomic chord a variety of feelings, passions and thoughts are synthesized."[45] He was also interested in the contrasting ways in which writing and film present the simultaneity of inner feeling and outward expression, concluding (perhaps overoptimistically) that film might collapse the two together: "A novelist can, of course, write a dialogue so as to weave into it what the speakers think to themselves while they are talking. But by so doing he splits up the sometimes comic, sometimes tragic, but always awe-inspiring, unity between spoken word and hidden thought with which this contradiction is rendered manifest in the human face and which the film was the first to show us in all its dazzling variety."[46]

Images and the Senses

In understanding the experiential qualities of visual media, one should not, under the illusion that it is less important, lose sight of the particular kinds of pleasure they produce, for this is indicative of how they function more generally. Written texts may have sensory qualities quite apart from the meanings they evoke. (Roland Barthes, who could find erotic qualities in almost anything, laid the groundwork for an erotics of writing.) Films appeal in an even more direct way to the human sensorium, in part because of the senses they address and the fact that they address them simultaneously. Although films chiefly evoke the tactile qualities of surfaces, Perez notes Ortega y Gasset's observation that the proximate vision of close-ups also emphasizes volume—"corporeality . . . solidity and plenitude."[47] The perception of volume is further influenced by focal length. Long focal length lenses flatten spaces and objects; wide-angle lenses used close to objects tend to heighten one's sense of their roundedness. Sight and sound provoke a further range of secondary sense impressions: of voices, bodies, textures, colors, temperatures, movement, and so on. Without the materiality that this imparts to objects, the power of film to involve the viewer in narratives, and to invite identification with individuals, would be much diminished. This also helps explain why films are revisionist in their descriptions of the world when compared to written texts, through the different emphasis they place on foreground and background, the signified and the ambient, perception and thought.

By expanding vision, films exaggerate differences of scale and the relation of the detail to the whole. Yet this can have a restorative function. Balázs, once again, comments on this. "The camera has uncovered that cell-life of the vital issues in which all great events are ultimately conceived; for the greatest landslide is only the aggregate of the movements of single particles. A multitude of close-ups can show us the very instant in which the general is transformed into the particular."[48] Unlike Walter Benjamin, who saw the camera as a more powerful technology of seeing, revealing things normally inaccessible to vision, and a harbinger of alienation, Balázs saw it as a way of reintegrating the different levels of experience that modern civilization has increasingly uncoupled.

In parallel with this idea, film may also be seen as a method of resensitizing us to the physical presence of objects, which an urbanized culture has attenuated and commodified. The fascination of Epstein, Delluc, and other surrealists with photogénie—the special aura that the cinema imparts to physical objects—was partly a desire to recover the vision of childhood, or (as Balázs and Ong might see it) of preliteracy. The agenda of the surrealists was thus not so far removed from that of those early anthropologists who wished to rediscover the mythological vision of "primitive man"—a vision that could animate the inanimate world.[49] The aim of ethnographic filmmakers may not be so conceived or so ambitious (although Gardner's sensibility is attuned to the inanimate world, and Rouch's to altered states of consciousness), but many nevertheless attempt to redress the imbalance between objects and their written descriptions with a more intensive regard, as in the films of such diverse filmmakers as Rouquier, Preloran, and Ogawa.

Films thus recover a dimension of human experience often lost in texts. This impinges on the viewer in various ways—as hyperawareness, shock, and pleasure. These emotions may in turn help the viewer to understand how and why people behave or interact as they do—how conversations are modulated by looking, gesturing, and touching; why a herder would resist killing an animal; how a craftsperson derives satisfaction from making an object; how power is exercised through material possessions, and so on.

This material property of the image possesses another, more generalized significance. Films, despite their fragmentation, are permeated with the imprint of human environments. Each social landscape is a distinctive sensory complex, constructed not only of material things but also of human activities and the bodies of human beings themselves. For some years scholars have noted the aesthetic features of human environments in terms of art, religion, architecture, urban planning, state ritual, and even bureaucratic organization.[50] This attention has been extended by others to the aesthetics of daily life.[51] This more comprehensive social aesthetics approaches human societies as material creations that structure the experiences of individuals, even as individuals are also constantly modifying them.

Human environments are beginning to be better understood as the culturally constructed settings within which the other dimensions of social life are played out. They reflect historical, economic, and political forces, but also aesthetic judgments that directly affect how people live and the decisions they make. Human life thus has an aesthetic dimension expressed in the environments people create around themselves. In many cases, these settings—whether they be rural, urban, or institutional—provide islands of continuity in what is often a changing and hybrid existence, permeated by other forces.

Viewing human environments as constructions owes something to functionalist anthropology, but it is less prone to seeing societies as hermetically enclosed, ahistorical units. It also resembles the way in which many anthropologists now read certain focal events as texts indicating broader cultural patterns—with the difference, however, that human environments cannot be read so easily as symbolic systems. Their material impact is fully as important as any symbolic meanings that may be encoded in them. Furthermore, these meanings are frequently contradictory in different circumstances and often felt intuitively rather than ever consciously articulated. It is possible (and in fact normal) to go through life participating in social rituals, reproducing aesthetic forms, and obeying rules of behavior chiefly because not to do so invites criticism. At the same time, one is shaped and, in terms of personal pleasure, rewarded by these forces and in subtle (and sometimes more definitive) ways one has the power to transform them.

Our sense of place involves both the perception of a preconfigured space, with its own existential coherence, and our culturally and experientially determined interpretations of it. It is always imbued with our notions of the sort of place it is—jungle, desert, urban, rural, beautiful, ugly, "typical," and so on. (Can one be in Paris without also being in a mythical Paris?) But it is always acting upon us more directly as well, as form and (in human environments) culturally. A place shapes our feelings about it as much as we shape it through our associations with it. This is why Edward Casey argues that places are never neutral spaces upon which we project cultural ideas, but that places exist in our lives and define them from the very beginning, and are thus prior to notions of space in the abstract. Human environments are organized so that they affect us "even—indeed, especially—when a given perception is preconceptual and prediscursive. To be not yet articulated in concept or word is not to be nonculturally constituted, much less free from social constraints."[52]

In many respects we learn the appropriate relations to our social environment without becoming conscious of them. One could even argue that a social "anesthetic" operates to desensitize us and conceal from us the particular conditions of our surroundings—through familiarity, habituation, or lack of a realistic alternative. We are most aware of home when we are away from home. In portraying social environments, films often automatically communicate an entire complex of relations that in writing would emerge only as the result of a firm intention. These complexes are similar to the *chronotopes* that Bakhtin describes in literature and that film theorists see in genres such as the Western and the film noir.[53] (If it were not for its inelegance, *sociotopes* might be a more appropriate term for these social spaces.) To understand them better, the social scientist must explore them as entities in themselves, composed of all the interrelated material objects and activities of community life. This aesthetic dimension of social experience remains a relatively undeveloped area in the human sciences. It is an area particularly open to investigation in the visual media. One can see that many ethnographic filmmakers, while they outwardly pursue conventional anthropological agendas, are already temperamentally and intuitively more attuned to this possibility.

Reconfiguring the Senses

Many anthropologists in recent years have wished to put a new face on ethnography, arguing that social research should give greater weight to embodied experience and the role of the senses in social and cultural life.

Not only has sensory experience been underestimated, they say, but ethnographic description has been dominated by vision and by discursive forms that reduce all knowledge to "information."[54] Among those to act on this are Edward Schieffelin and Steven Feld, who have focused on the centrality of sound among the Kaluli of New Guinea. They and other social scientists have brought to our attention the variations in sensory awareness of human societies.[55] However, Feld is right to insist that renewed attention to the aural-oral, long displaced by an emphasis on the visual, should not become the pretext for a new antivisualism—that there should be a more integrated understanding of the "interplay of tactile, sonic and visual senses" in all societies.[56] The question is how this can be achieved.

One of the unintended consequences of the new focus on the senses is that it risks creating further fragmentation instead of a more integrated approach to sensory experience. In the effort to explore different modes of sensory awareness and different constructions of human consciousness, the ethnographic literature tends to become focused on the dominant modalities of particular societies, such as the role of sound among the Kaluli (Feld), smell and taste among the Songhay (Stoller), bodily movement among the Kuranko (Jackson), and so on. At the same time, other modalities—of place, time, emotion, performance, visual art—become the focus of other ethnographic investigations, giving disproportionate attention to these dimensions of social life.[57] This is perhaps unavoidable in an anthropological practice that has increasingly focused on specific problems and institutions and has preferred ethnographies of the particular to the more doubtful enterprise of holistic description. But it can lead to a kind of extractive modeling of other societies that, despite the authors' best efforts to maintain a balance, may work against an integrated view of social complexity.

A further problem arises from the potential incommensurability of sensory experience and anthropological writing, involving many of the issues of linearity and simultaneity discussed earlier. The continued analysis and description of visual-auditory-tactile experience by verbal means would seem to present anthropological theory with a basic contradiction. It remains to be seen whether innovative forms of anthropological writing can solve this problem. But just as some scholars are searching for parity among the senses, others may have to look for greater parity among modes of expression—at the very least, in the visual, auditory, and textual modes of representation found in film.[58] For their part, filmmakers need to pay closer attention not only to the special properties of film but also to how films can better reflect their own experience of seeing.

Notes

I am indebted to Walter J. Ong's *Orality and Literacy* (1982) for many of the ideas in this chapter. I am grateful to Sara Danius for directing me toward Calvino's writings on literature and for her astute and helpful comments on an earlier draft of this essay. Thanks also to Reinhart Meyer-Kalkus and Steven Feld for introducing me to the writings of Michel Chion.

1. Lienhardt 1961: 1.

2. Ibid., p. 4.

3. Fortes 1945: 1.

4. Ibid., p. 45.

5. Robert Thornton contrasts the language of travel writing and missionary reports, which constituted much of early ethnography, with that of the natural science monograph, arguing that by the end of the nineteenth century, anthropological writing had been "captured" by the latter (Thornton 1983).

6. Calvino 2001: 151–52.

7. See Danius 2002.

8. Eisenstein 1957: 8.

9. Morin 1956: 129.

10. Burton 1993: 16–17.

11. From Simenon's *Madame Maigret's Friend* (1967 [1952]: 5).

12. Ong 1982: 91.

13. Peter Crawford has made the point that narrative is really just another form of contextualization, couched in the language of the arts rather than the sciences. "Visual Anthropology in the Digital Age," presentation at the seminar, Practicing Visual Anthropology—Perspectives on Audiovisual Means for Mediating Scientific Knowledge, Norwegian Institute in Rome, April 2002.

14. Single shots, like still images, are, in Chris Pinney's terms, less bounded than films, which have a narrative structure imposed on them. "Film situates otherwise undecidable images within sequences that produce argument and express intention. They close off plural meanings in the temporal flow of succession and destruction" (Pinney 1992a: 27).

15. Chion 1994: xxvi.

16. Ong 1982: 101.

17. Ibid., p. 98.

18. Cited in Pinney 1992b.

19. For example, Bruner (1986: 7) writes: "Every anthropological fieldworker would readily acknowledge that the accepted genres of anthropological expression—our fieldnotes, diaries, lectures, and professional publications—do not capture the richness or the complexity of our lived experience in the field."

20. Particularly in *Works and Lives: The Anthropologist as Author* (Geertz 1988).

21. Ong 1982: 79.

22. Greene 1932: 15–16.

23. See Lakoff & Johnson 1980: 90; Salmond 1982.

24. Rosaldo 1980.

25. Perez 1998: 60–61.
26. Bordwell 1985: 62.
27. Eisenstein 1988.
28. For example, Lewis 1980, Jackson 1989.
29. See chapters 4 and 5, this volume; also Srivastava 1998.
30. White 1980: 19.
31. Roth 1989.
32. White 1978: 58.
33. See Kuhn 1962.
34. See Geertz 1973.
35. Turner 1986b: 41.
36. Nichols 1981.
37. Calvino 1993: 32.
38. Bourdieu's books (not to criticize them) provide examples of this. However, depersonalization is partially offset in sociological writing by the inclusion of case histories and interview material.
39. For example, MacDougall 1978: 415; 1998: 165–77.
40. Balázs 1952: 40, 42.
41. Ibid., p. 48.
42. Ibid., p. 163.
43. Ibid., p. 39.
44. Ibid., p. 61.
45. Ibid., p. 64.
46. Ibid., pp. 63–64.
47. Cited in Perez 1998: 135.
48. Balázs 1952: 55.
49. Edgar Morin finds numerous references in surrealist film theory to the "soul" of objects, and notes: "Cette âme, il faut l'entendre dans un sens évidemment métaphorique, puisqu'elle concerne l'état d'âme du spectateur. La vie des objets n'est évidemment pas réelle: elle est subjective. Mais une force aliénante tend à prolonger et extérioriser le phénomène d'âme en phénomène animiste" (1956: 74). He adds: "Cette animation des objets nous renvoie, dans un sens, à l'univers de la vision archaïque, comme au regard de l'enfant" (75).
50. See Goffman 1962, Berleant 1992, Coote 1992, Groys 1992, Samier 1997.
51. See chapter 4 in this volume, and also Certeau et al. 1998, von Bonsdorff & Haapala 1999.
52. Casey 1996: 19.
53. Bakhtin 1981: 84–258.
54. See Jackson 1989, Stoller 1989, 1997, Fabian 1990.
55. See, for example, Howes 1991.
56. Feld 1996: 94–96.
57. Turner 1957, Briggs 1970, Fabian 1983, Feld & Basso 1996, Gell 1996.
58. Some writers believe that the future of ethnography lies in hypermedia (see Howard 1988, Biella 1993, Pink 2001, Ruby 2001). In 1988 Alan Howard made a point similar to one I make here, although I believe it is overstated: "Sequential media simply do not lend themselves to apprehending phenomena of great complexity" (1988: 312). Sequential media such as writing can explore many kinds

of complexity, depending upon the strategies employed. The conventions of expository writing in the human sciences have tended to limit these strategies. Film (and video) is both sequential *and* composite. Furthermore, as I have noted elsewhere (MacDougall 1999, 2001a, 2001b), sound films have long been multimedia creations, combining visual, written, oral, temporal, and auditory elements. Hypermedia, while it expands the possibilities of contextualization almost infinitely, also risks dissolving the integrity of an authored work, which normally guides the audience interpretively through a single set of experiences.

PART II

IMAGES OF CHILDHOOD

3

FILMS OF CHILDHOOD

CHILDREN APPEAR in many films, sometimes incidentally, given little more attention than the family dog, sometimes at the center, carrying on their shoulders all the hopes of the adult world. Yet films have a way of reducing children's lives to formulas, replacing their strangeness and individuality with more comfortable notions of what children should be. The emptiness of many fictional children is often a direct index of the filmmaker's own lost childhood. Documentary films, too, often purvey impoverished images of children by looking only for what they expect to find.

If representation is how art and science clarify human experience, then the representation of childhood in films (to say nothing of photographs, paintings, novels, and psychoanalytic theory) would seem to have contributed little but confusion. In the real world, children are by turns kind, cruel, foolish, wise, attractive, unattractive, moral, amoral, innocent, and knowing—but films all too often would have us believe in the essence of the child. Some might ask, what is the point of making representations of childhood when all of us have experienced it (or are experiencing it now), and nearly all of us have observed it as a parent, friend, teacher, sibling, or other relation? Is it simply to correct the myths and commonsense errors about childhood erected by self-protective adults? Perhaps. But such attempts also run the risk of creating new myths or embedding old ones more deeply. If any overriding reason exists for filming children, it is to rediscover their complexity—to give them the respect due to persons living in themselves rather than in our conceptions of them, and to put ourselves in a better position to learn from them.

In the world there are two kinds of people: men and women, we would first say. But in some respects, are there not more profound differences between children and adults? Apart from a few films made by children themselves, most films about children are made by this other group, viewing childhood across the frontiers of age, different generational histories, different generational cultures. Although adults may associate with children constantly, they can never quite recapture what it was like to be a child, with a child's ignorance of adult experience. Films of childhood are therefore often commemorative, even elegiac. Many are imbued with a sense of loss, sometimes when they seem most joyful—for lost sensitivities, lost beauty, lost prospects. What is sometimes called innocence is in fact an amalgam of these losses. Loss and past become intertwined. Some films are quite plainly about the filmmaker's own childhood, such as François Truffaut's *The 400 Blows* (1959) and Vitali Kanevski's *Freeze—Die—Come to Life* (1989). Others are based on literary memoirs or autobiographies, such as Yves Robert's films based on Marcel Pagnol's memories of childhood, *La gloire de mon père* (1990) and *Le château de ma mère* (1990), or Mark Donskoi's *The Childhood of Maxim Gorky* (1938). A few films are more systematic attempts to explore the culture and social life of children, such as Ilkka Ruuhijärvi and Ulla Turunen's documentary series on a group of Finnish schoolchildren. Some may even be attempts to redefine culture itself, as in Truffaut's *The Wild Child* (1969) and Gregory Bateson and Margaret Mead's films on Balinese childhood development, made in the 1930s. Childhood seems to pose a mystery, or a puzzle to be solved. In making films about children, adults often seem to be searching for keys to their own destiny.

Films about children, while important for understanding them, are also a valuable index of how children are perceived in adult society. Most of the films in which children appear—either as protagonists or, more peripherally, as family members, onlookers, victims, witnesses—seem content to fit children into preexistent molds. Even Jean Vigo's *Zero for Conduct* (1933), justly celebrated for its radical depiction of childhood and schooling, nevertheless plays extensively upon the familiar trope of childhood pranks (figure 3.1). Chaplin's films celebrate the cleverness and freedom of children, perhaps in memory of his own difficult childhood. As for Yves Robert's films based on Pagnol's memoirs, never were children more sunny, more scrubbed, more beautiful, more polite than here. Films such as these may appear to undercut the mythology of childhood but, more disingenuously, they promote it. They express a false consciousness, of a childhood paradise regained. Like a certain genre of English children's books, epitomized by those of Enid Blyton, they impose upon children the notion that childhood is an unequivocally happy time, and if they are unhappy it is probably their own fault.

There may be more profound reasons for mythologizing childhood than mere nostalgia. Adults are afflicted with an amnesia about their own childhood that may derive from some deep-seated evolutionary mechanism. Perhaps too vivid a memory of childhood would be unbearable or would challenge the autonomy of the adult personality. Childhood seems to vanish in large swathes from our consciousness, remembered often as if it belonged to other children than ourselves. Sometimes it seems as if we never had a childhood of our own, only fragmentary memories and

3.1. From *Zéro de conduite* (1933). Copyright Centre
National de la Cinématographie.

emotions, filtered through fictions and contaminated by our conceptions
of other children's lives.

Each adult has in fact led two lives, first as a child, then as an adult, with
a screen of forgetfulness erected somewhere between them. The point of
division can be traced roughly to early adolescence, when the child gains
a new consciousness of him- or herself and begins to be reborn as an
individual. Children are often thought to reach a certain state of perfection at eleven or twelve, when the processes begin that will generate massive biological and psychic changes, out of which adults will emerge as
new creatures, like a butterfly from a chrysalis. The period of adolescence
is thus a liminal zone, analogous in some ways to transculturation or
hybridity. The adolescent may even have a quasi-magical status, as if combining in one person the child and the adult and their two spheres of
knowledge.

Our first life, as children, mimics the human lifespan; therefore, in this
sense, too, it can be said that we have already lived another life. Children
pass through an early, middle, and old age, each with its own distinctive
character and appropriate activities. Children at the end of childhood
have an accumulated wisdom that encompasses formal knowledge, piv-

otal experiences, and the learning of social skills. Although guided and restrained by adults, they are perhaps no less limited by this than adults are by their own social and governmental institutions. Adults think of children as unfinished, undergoing a process of socialization, but children do not feel unsocialized. Adults often forget that as children they functioned effectively as social beings. This may account for the condescension many adults display toward the children who succeed them, sometimes tinged with cruelty in recompense for the powerlessness they suffered in their own childhood. The wave-like effects of power are thus felt down the generations, just as they are at the descending levels of hierarchical institutions.

A primary reason for studying childhood is to understand the potential of human society more fully, not because childhood is adult society in miniature (it isn't), but because children are often more experimental than adults in drawing upon the choices open to them. Although deeply conservative in some respects (in relation to their peers), children can be adept at solving problems and resolving conflicts in ways that adults would immediately rule out for ideological reasons. If films are to contribute to the understanding of children and childhood, filmmakers must be willing to observe such social processes closely to reveal their logic. Some filmmakers have done this effectively—for example, Vittorio de Seta in *Diario di un maestro* (1973), Louis Malle in some of his films about children, such as *Murmur of the Heart* (1971) and *Au revoir les enfants* (1987)— while others with fixed ideas about childhood, or who simply use children to advance an argument, as in the allegorical *Lord of the Flies* (1963), show little regard for how children actually think and behave. In this respect, documentary filmmakers may have advantages over fiction filmmakers, for they can show children behaving in concrete situations instead of having to reinvent these through scripts and performances, which in all but the most capable hands leads to oversimplification.

It is often not so much the task of films to show how children think as to show that they think at all. Children have been routinely employed in films as silent witnesses to adult dramas. In this role they are called upon to do little more than watch, out of eyes that show (or are contrived to show) various expressions of incomprehension, sorrow, and connivance. Vittorio de Sica's *The Children Are Watching Us* (1943) is the prototype of this genre, closely followed by his *Bicycle Thieves* (1948), with an exception in between for *Shoeshine* (1946), in which children rather than adults are the main characters. A long list of other films of this kind could be given, in which children act as surrogates for the adult viewer and receptacles for their feelings.[1] These children are opaque and practically mute. They are there to be acted *upon*, not to act. It is their silence that allows us to imagine the impressions and emotions that pass through them, as well as their moral sadness at the sight of human folly. If they act, their motivations must be inferred more from their circumstances than from their own expressiveness. Thus the nearly wooden boy character of Roberto Rossellini's *Germany, Year Zero* (1947) commits suicide for reasons that can never be known but can be variously construed as despair at the state of the world, the madness of warfare, the pettiness of adults, the attentions of a child molester, and so on. The many films that treat childhood in this way, even including, to an extent, Ingmar Bergman's heartfelt *Fanny and Alexander* (1982), place children almost outside the category of humanity, much as ethnographic and travel films for years treated the natives of empire as anonymous types—interchangeable and alien, blanketed in silence. Among nineteenth-century social Darwinists, non-Europeans were often seen as childlike—adult bodies with children's minds. Sometimes even their bodies were found childish. A paper on Chinese ideographs presented at the Anthropological Institute of Great Britain in 1892 contains this observation: "[The Chinese] are, if I may use the expression, an immature people, and just as their eyes are infants' eyes, so far as the absence of the caruncula lachrymalis and the heavy fold of the upper lid are concerned, and their cheeks, the smooth cheeks of young boys, so their written characters represent an arrested stage in the mental development of the people."[2] In fact, the charge of inadequacy once used to discredit foreign adults still remains to discredit children. There are perhaps more gestures now toward acknowledging the child's autonomy, but children in films remain largely instruments and vehicles of adult concerns. This is seen in the many films about single or gay men saddled with babies or children, children as the victims and reconcilers of marital strife, children as accomplices of men on the run, children as go-betweens, children as redeemers, children as comic troublemakers, children as the moral conscience of adults, and so on.

It is probable that many of these formulaic uses of children are the result of the difficulties filmmakers face in imagining child characters and dealing with child actors. Exploring the intellectual and emotional life of a child character requires special knowledge and directing skills. Preoccupied with adult lives, most screenwriters and directors prefer to use children as counters and catalysts. But from time to time a few have taken children more seriously. Among fiction filmmakers, Jean Vigo and Yasujiro Ozu were among the first of these, followed by such directors as Julien Duvivier, François Truffaut, Satyajit Ray, Maurice Pialat, Louis Malle, and Ken Loach, some of whom focused on children in several films. Li Jixian's *A High Sky Summer* (2001) presents an unusual case of a filmmaker directly confronting the question of children's representation in films. The boy protagonist, Wang Schouxian, is cast as the main character in a fiction film, but he refuses to play the part that the adults have written for him because he believes it is false to his own experience.

In making documentary films the need has not been so much for imagination as for sympathy and persistence. Documentary filmmakers must care about children and be willing to take the time to observe them closely and gain their trust. This means not dictating to them as an adult or directing them but allowing them to be expressive in their own ways. One of the first documentary filmmakers to show this combination of interest and restraint was Lindsay Anderson in *Thursday's Children* (1953), a film he made about deaf children with Guy Brenton. Here the camera does indeed watch very young children seriously and records their smallest achievements as triumphs. Anderson was far less successful when he moved into fiction with *If . . .* (1968), where spontaneity is replaced by an actorish self-consciousness. Filmmakers such as Maurice Pialat and Ken Loach, who have encouraged improvisation, or who have managed to import the observational techniques of documentary into fiction, have achieved far more convincing "performances" from children.

Documentaries may also require a measure of collusion, often implicit, between filmmaker and child. Children are usually aware of the filmmaker's presence, but it is always difficult to know to what extent this actually affects their behavior. Perhaps they perform, but this need not diminish a film's truthfulness, for children are constantly performing anyway, if not for the filmmaker, then for each other. An example of a somewhat different approach to collaboration is David Hancock and Herb di Gioia's *Naim and Jabar* (1974). The making of the film set off events that soon became far more important for the protagonists than the film itself. One of the two boys has the rare prospect of entering a secondary school. The film then reports their reactions. But collaborations with children can quickly become one-sided. Some films that are classified as documentaries, such as Robert Flaherty's *Louisiana Story* (1948), are far closer to directed fiction. They reflect the filmmakers' sensibilities more than those of the child-subjects.

Conveying the subjective experience of children has always posed a problem for short story writers and novelists. For filmmakers, who must convey interiority primarily through exterior actions, the problem is even greater. Children tend to go quiet around inquisitive adults, and the clichés of childhood are so powerful and pervasive that they are constantly redeployed in the absence of more detailed and accurate observations. The first-person voices of children devised by such novelists as E. L. Doctorow and Roddy Doyle are special confections that work admirably on the page but would do less well if translated into actual speech.[3] Directors such as Truffaut and de Seta, who have been able to incorporate spontaneous conversation into their films, have generally been more effective than those who rely on screenwriters.

Speech may be the most immediate source of knowledge about children's thoughts, but it is not the only source, nor is it necessarily the best way of understanding their emotional lives. Children often communicate most eloquently through their bodies, especially when they are young, but later, too, often in violence if their words go unheeded. Susumu Hani, who made the semidocumentary fiction film *Bad Boys* (1961) about a juvenile prison, also made a nonfiction film entitled *Children Who Draw* (1956), following the emotional development of a group of schoolchildren by filming their behavior in the classroom and the paintings they made each day. Children not only express themselves with their bodies but also learn through them. Indeed, they generally learn more by imitation and sensory investigation than by more cognitive means. The meticulous observation of children's social interactions and learning processes, as in Helen Levitt's classic *In the Street* (1952)[4] and Ruuhijärvi and Turunen's films, is often more revealing than interviews with children and may even contradict what they would say about themselves. In Abbas Kiarostami's *Homework* (1990), children are subjected to a relentless interrogation about their school and home life. Although they tell us much, both directly and inadvertently, in words, it is how they react physically to the questioning and what they are reluctant to talk about that tells us even more. In his choice of interrogation as a method, Kiarostami underlines the fear of authority and the violence experienced by children in Iranian society in the 1980s.

As this suggests, when adults make films about children, the films are often more about the frontier between adults and children than about the children themselves. Far from being merely incidental, these encounters are of major importance in their implications, for they embody the larger assumptions about childhood prevalent in a society. Every film about children, unless it is made by other children, is the record of a particular kind of adult-child relationship. Kiarostami's relationship to the children in *Homework* was the result of his concern about his own child's schooling. But by the time the film was made, this had expanded into a realization that children are primary indicators of a society's ills. The apparent cruelty of the film is in fact an expression of Kiarostami's horror and compassion.

In Ruuhijärvi and Turunen's films, the relationship between child subjects and adult filmmakers is considerably cooler, although it is difficult to know whether this extended to their relationships outside the film. In Gregory Bateson and Margaret Mead's films in Bali the relationship is scientific. In Danny Lyon's *Los niños abandonados* (1975), a study of street children in Colombia, it is emotional, even passionate. (Lyon says he fell in love with these children.) In Truffaut's *Les mistons* (1958) it is affectionate and nostalgic. It becomes a relationship of complicity in *Bu Doi: Life Like Dust* (1994), *Seventeen* (1982), and *Pride of Place* (1976), a film about an English girls' school that led to the sacking of the school's headmistress.

These films reflect individual approaches, but they also reveal larger societal attitudes toward children. Sometimes the children are seen as happy, sometimes as pitiable. In one subgenre, children are typically seen as victims and are sought out for their victim status. The desires that this satisfies are complex, combining feelings of indignation, parentlike devotion, physical identification, rescue fantasies, morbid curiosity, and sentimentality. Among the recent rash of films about street children are several, like Andrea Varga's *Children of the Street* (1999), that seem to derive a perverse pleasure from plumbing the depths of the children's violation and unhappiness. Others on the same topic, like Alex McCall's *Children of the Sewers* (1998) and Lin Li's *Three-Five People* (2001) appeal to more conventional sentiments, such as the loss of childhood innocence and a desire to save endangered children.

Adults do not always regard children with either sympathy or pity, however. Children in groups can be seen as aggressive and dangerous, as the systematic murder of street children by Brazilian police has made clear. In most countries, in fact, children are treated violently by some authorities. There has long been an American subgenre of fiction films about juvenile delinquency and teenage alienation that reflects these adult fears (e.g., *Rebel Without a Cause* [1955], *Blackboard Jungle* [1955], *Boyz N the Hood* [1991]). The fears emerge more covertly in horror films featuring children (discussed below) and in a steady stream of documentary and semidocumentary fiction films that—while they show children as victims of society—also tend to see them as lost and irredeemably damaged (e.g., *Gosses de Rio* [1990], *We, the Children of the Twentieth Century* [1993], *Pixote* [1981], *Salaam Bombay!* [1988], *Kids* [1995], *Schpaaa* [1998]). Here the hopelessness sometimes seems like an inverted sentimentality, or sentimentality frustrated.

Sentimentality

Sentimentality about children is regarded as a benign weakness in society and also a sign of bad art. It is most easily disposed of by film reviewers (if they approve of a film) with the catchphrase "avoids sentimentality." But this stamp of approval is very frequently too facile and hides a hundred evasions. What kind of sentimentality? There is a sentimentality that conceals itself in toughness and social advocacy. In fact, absolving a film from the sin of sentimentality glosses over the emotional complexity of most of our culturally and biologically determined responses to children. Audience attitudes toward children in films are generated in a force field of suspended possibilities, influenced in part by parental instincts, but also by memory, ideology, identification, aesthetics, and longing. The sentimentality of Mark Twain, Dickens, Kipling, James Barrie, Lewis Carroll, and other Victorians toward children was never as simple, or perverse, or unreflective as a later age made it appear. It varied both in its content and forms of expression, and it contained some important insights about social relations. Kipling's Kim, for example, as an adolescent in the polyglot culture of empire, is able to express sympathies that cross cultural boundaries in a manner impossible for adults,[5] as is Huck Finn in the racist South and Pip in class-conscious England. The literary critic James Kincaid has linked child sentimentality to the rise of romanticism, within which, in his view, the child was mistakenly seen as both "other" to adults and superior to them.[6] But in fact neither of these suppositions can be brushed aside quite so simply. The cultures of childhood and the worlds that children inhabit are beginning to be understood as distinct from adult worlds and not just childish versions of them. Children are indeed "other" to the extent that they are physically and psychologically in a different developmental state. And although the behavior of children often mimics that of adults, the rules of childhood interaction are both more crude (and cruel) in some circumstances and more subtle and caring in others. Nor should the idea be discounted that children are superior to adults in some respects for children have a capacity for invention, for detecting insincerity, for learning, for spontaneity, and for affection that adults often lack. It is perhaps one of the responsibilities of filmmakers to explore this otherness and superiority against the grain of a more insidious sentimentality.

True sentimentality tends to limit the representation of children to traits that filmmakers find attractive or worthy of sympathy. Thus the overarching sentimentality of Italian neorealist films celebrates the toughness and essential incorruptibility of children, whereas the sentimentality of French films dwells on their physical beauty and sensitivity. (Noteworthy exceptions are Rossellini's films in Italy and Bresson's Mouchette [1966] in France.) Iranian films highlight the sanity of children in an indifferent and less-than-sane world. (But Iranian cinema is also perhaps the only national cinema that credits children with playing a central role in society.) British and American sentimentality toward children sometimes seems to have an erotic dimension, with children and adults thrown together in situations of unusual isolation and intimacy. (See, for example, The Kid [1921], The Rocking-Horse Winner [1949], The Browning Version [1951], Tiger Bay [1959], Paper Moon [1973].) James Kincaid has written an entire book discussing what he sees as the pedophilic undercurrent of American films and popular culture. Shirley Temple's film roles quite clearly present an example in American cinema of child sentimentality mérging into sexuality, although the precedents for this were already well established in American advertising and literature. There are certainly other examples, as well, of American films about children with erotic overtones. But Kincaid seems altogether too eager to equate feelings of attraction to children with sexual predation (and the sexualization of children) and yet at the same time, too unwilling to accept that these feelings toward children may have an erotic component, expressed differently in different cultures. Because European cinema is sometimes more open about this, it may in some respects be healthier than its Hollywood counterpart.

What sentimentality most notably ignores in children—with the exception of a certain quick-wittedness—is their thinking. Antoine Doinel's admiration for Balzac in *The 400 Blows* has poignancy and humor, but the personal experiences that led to it are left unexplored. The intellectual life of children and their capacity for abstract thought and moral judgment are almost always implied rather than demonstrated, if they are even acknowledged. Why this should be so is unclear. Perhaps adults feel that to reveal this side of children is to render them unchildlike and less worthy of sympathy. Predictably, adults in films rarely regard children as if they were capable of intellectual reflection. This may indicate how adults frequently treat children, but it nevertheless portrays children's abilities very narrowly. On the other hand, it is perhaps consistent with the fact that few adults in mainstream cinema reveal much of an intellectual life either.

It is not so difficult to avoid the pitfall of sentimentality if, as a filmmaker, one is willing to enter into the reality of children's lives. Sentimentality is misplaced emotion, cultivated at the expense of the subject. It projects upon children a sensibility that is not theirs. In many cases it filters the darker side of humanity out of their lives. But seen at close hand, the capacity of children for self-interest and cruelty soon banishes this, just as their capacity for unexpected kindness adds to one's sense of their complexity. Children are not unsentimental themselves, but they reserve their sentimentality for others. The most perceptive films about childhood reflect the ambivalence that children feel toward the adult world, regarding it with a child's mixture of curiosity and mistrust. These films enter into the spiritual core of childhood, where life is both immense and full of dangers (to use the title of Denis Gheerbrand's film about hospitalized children). They show us how time stops for children and how their sensibilities swing rapidly between boredom and elation. In the best films about children, their inner world is expressed through their own inventions, rituals, and interpersonal relations.

Perhaps related to sentimentality is the almost universal representation of children as sexually innocent. To be sure, many coming-of-age films hint at sexual activity, but few accurately treat the almost obsessive interest in sex that haunts young adolescents and even preadolescents, or their trading of information and sexual experimentation with their peers. Part of this avoidance is due to a reluctance to show the same-sex activities that are part of early sexual awakening. Part is more conventional sexual hypocrisy, of the kind shown toward adult sexuality as well. There is an overriding coyness about this period that is most evident in films that project themselves as being frank and realistic about it. Thus the film *The Year My Voice Broke* (1987) deals, despite its title, almost exclusively with the social embarrassments of puberty rather than the subjective, physical experience of it. An adolescent is preternaturally aware of his or her own body, but in films it remains a mystery. Not all children would support this taboo on sexual content or want imposed on them adult ideas of sexual propriety, even when this is justified as being in their own interests.

The underlying cause of much adult anxiety about these matters is a sentimental attitude to childhood that shies away from the fact that children experience the physical onset of sexuality. This is no doubt related to adults' sense of loss about the end of childhood, but also perhaps to an uneasiness that adults feel about their own relationships with children who are becoming sexual beings. With the institutional prolongation of childhood in modern societies, it may seem to many adults like a contradiction in nature for children to have the desires of adults or engage in clandestine sexual activities.

The representation of children's sexuality may be noteworthy chiefly for its absence in films, yet it is far more important to an understanding of children's lives than many other aspects of childhood that films report upon incessantly. To ignore it is to leave a significant gap in the portrayal of childhood experience. Truffaut's films, although sensitive to many aspects of children's lives, fail in this regard. Roger Shattuck notes, for example, that for the historical Dr. Itard, upon whose case study *The Wild Child* was based, "the boy's immodesty and the onset of puberty posed insuperable problems that no one had adequately foreseen. Truffaut passes over the whole question. Sex does not exist in the film."[7] Nor does it, except by inference, in Truffaut's other films about childhood. There may be good reasons for restraint in documentary films, where the privacy of individuals must be protected, but fiction films provide a context in which nearly all human experiences may be legitimately examined. A number of films have demonstrated that it is possible to portray childhood sexual experiences honestly and without embarrassment.[8] Avoiding such aspects of children's lives reinforces the impression that these are shameful and abnormal experiences—the opposite of what truthful films of childhood should be doing. It may well be important for films to explore why society represses such knowledge, but not to participate in the process.

Such matters form only part of what is exclusive to the life-worlds of children. There are many other experiences that belong only to children, and much of the knowledge that children possess is passed from child to child without ever involving the mediation of adults. Although children's worlds intersect with those of adults, they are not identical to them. Children domesticate the spaces around them with their own landmarks and create mental maps quite different from those of adults. Children's games and verses, studied many years ago by Iona and Peter Opie, are but one example of the distinctive cultures of childhood. Anthropologists are increasingly recognizing that children are not simply socialized passively by adults to become members of the adults' society but are socialized by other children, often into practices not shared with adults. Jean Vigo was one of the first filmmakers to declare the existence of these two cultures in *Zero for Conduct*, giving a surreal edge to the differences and carrying them to the point of intergenerational warfare.

The School Film

Vigo's setting was a school, and films about schools and other juvenile institutions account for a sizable number of films about children. There is, in fact, a distinct school film genre, with a full complement of standard themes, plots, set pieces, and stock characters. Schools have been central to postindustrial childhood. At one level they are childhood writ large, and yet they are in many ways the antithesis of childhood, for they are the most formalized means by which adults control children and seek to shape them into adults. Social control is one of the primary functions of schools, along with child-minding. When it fails, it gives rise to a variety of other institutions such as juvenile prisons and homes for emotionally disturbed children, shown in such films as Hani's *Bad Boys*, *The Quiet One* (1948), *Warrendale* (1966), and *Experiment of the Cross* (1996). Truffaut's *The 400 Blows* provides a bridge between schools and reform schools, based on his own childhood experiences of bad schooling and parental neglect. As in that film, teachers rarely come off well in school films. If they are not monstrous, as in *Zero for Conduct* and *The Blue Angel* (1930), they are irritable and ineffective, constantly defeated by the guile and the war of attrition waged by their charges.

Most films are on the side of the children, who regard their teachers with contempt. This is partly a calculated move on the part of filmmakers to win sympathy for their child characters, but it also builds on the assumption that audiences have shared with them hours of boredom and frustration at school. There is a further perception, apparently prevalent in many countries, that teachers are a socially inferior class, badly paid and in many cases emotionally isolated, as though being confined to years of contact with children marked them out as not quite adequate adults. The most sympathetic view of this is developed in Anthony Asquith's *The Browning Version* (1951), based on the Terence Rattigan play, in which the underlying humanity of a cold and pedantic teacher is recognized by at least one child. The teacher is seen to be suffering from a kind of emotional starvation, resulting in part from the crushing artificiality of schools as institutions. By contrast, a figure like Mr. Chips (in *Goodbye, Mr. Chips* [1939]), or the enterprising teachers of *Diario di un maestro* and *Être et avoir* (2002), are a real rarity in the school film. And occasionally there is a redemptive scene like the one in Satyajit Ray's *Aparajito* (1956), in which the insensitivities of state education are, for once, vanquished by poetry. A school inspector arrives at a village school in a flurry of officialdom and is shown the school's prize pupil, Apu, who gives such a skilled and touching reading of a poem by Satyen Dutta that the inspector's eyes light up in wonder.

The conflict between children and their teachers is the almost universal theme of films about schools, at least in Euro-American cinema. The authoritarian role forced upon teachers is simply an extension of the larger function of the school, which (apart from education) is to control and contain, if not to discipline and punish. The school invariably embodies a set of societal values that run up against the anarchic spontaneity of the children and their quick perception of hypocrisy and injustice. There is the official culture of the school, teaching obedience and devotion to higher values, and then there is the unofficial culture of the schoolyard, which organizes power in its own ways and has different criteria for awarding respect. Schools try to overcome this problem by emphasizing sport, which they see as more in tune with children's values, and to some extent they succeed, but often at the cost of carrying children's competitiveness and taste for heroes to an absurd extreme. Such distortions of childhood emotions are characteristic of schools in any case. Schools can be seen as grotesque enlargements of the individual child, creating new corporate groups such as the team or class or "house." The needs and functions of the child are multiplied a hundredfold, creating massed desks, huge dining halls, ranked urinals, vast playgrounds, and (in boarding schools) dormitories. In the school film the dormitory is the very symbol of institutionalized sleep.

These settings become the canvas of the school film. In many of them the classroom predominates and, indeed, stands emblematically for the school as a whole. But in films about boarding schools, such as *Zero for Conduct*, Lindsay Anderson's *If . . .* (1968), and *Mädchen in Uniform* (1931), an entire physical and social universe is created, more or less functional or dysfunctional as the case may be. This organism is both inanimate and human, the human side imparting a curious aura to the physical setting around it. Thus schools seem to live and breathe even when the children are not present, as though waiting for them to return. They are filled with ghosts. The ecclesiastical architecture of *Mädchen in Uniform* possesses the hushed tension of pent-up emotions, the hallways and lockers of Frederick Wiseman's *High School* (1968), the peculiar ugliness of American cement playgrounds, chewing gum, and textbooks. In *Zero for Conduct*, physical materials—beds, curtains, pillow feathers—take on some of the bodily and spiritual qualities of the children themselves. As in *Mädchen in Uniform*, *If . . .* , and Jean Delannoy's *Les amitiés particulaires* (1964), they also evoke the atmosphere of boarding schools as sensually charged places and sexual incubators.

In many a school film, children are starved and physically abused, their despair mirrored in the bleakness of the institutional setting. There is often little to distinguish the worst private and church-run schools from state-run orphanages and juvenile prisons. In Henri-Georges Clouzot's *Les diaboliques* (1954), a seedy, provincial boarding school with bad food and impecunious teachers serves as an appropriate backdrop for a psychological horror story.

Many of these films underscore the ambiguities surrounding the social function of schools in the modern world. If schools evolved in part to permit the consolidation of the family, as Philippe Ariès argues,[9] and to free children from the apprenticeship system, which often involved children living apart from their families, they also robbed children of much of their independence. Schools, particularly boarding schools, gradually extended the period between puberty and an adult's life of work and marriage. This exposed a fundamental contradiction. Schools were meant to train children for adulthood and yet simultaneously to withhold it from them for increasingly lengthy periods. Films such as *If . . .* and Volker Schlöndorff's *Young Törless* (1966) reveal the resulting tensions—of older children, physically almost adults, kept in a state of suspension, acting as petty tyrants over younger children. At the heart of many films about schools and schooling is the paradox of the young adult who is still treated by the institution as a child and the child who is constantly told to grow up.

The *Bildungsfilm*

If the theme of the school film is conflict, the other great theme of films of childhood is education, in the broadest sense—the child's growth, emotional development, and discovery of adulthood. In the sentimental education of the adolescent we are in the familiar territory of the *Bildungsro-*

man. Growth is seen in some films as a continuous process, but in many more as a moment of emergence or sudden revelation. The dramatic structures of films are typically built around such turning points. In many, such as *Murmur of the Heart*, it is sexual initiation; in *The Fallen Idol* (1948) and *The Go-Between* (1971) it is disillusionment; in *Warrendale* it is a death. As Ian McEwan (or one of his characters) points out: "Turning points are the inventions of story-tellers and dramatists, a necessary mechanism when a life is reduced to, traduced by, a plot, when a morality must be distilled from a sequence of actions, when an audience must be sent home with something unforgettable to mark a character's growth."[10] But like all such conceits, the conceit of the turning point is grounded in a measure of truth, and perhaps especially so in children's lives. There are childhood experiences such as a death in the family, or a new friendship, or a moment of shame that are indeed turning points that impart a new significance to life. In childhood, growth also takes more sudden leaps than in adulthood. In early adolescence these are both physical and psychological—the first menstruation, the first emission, the voice breaking—but also the discovery of music or poetry, a new ability in oneself, a sense of pity for the misfortunes of others, a sudden flood of feeling for another person. The turning point is quintessentially the attainment of a new moral perspective, presaging the gravity and responsibility of the adult.

The turning point is often called "coming of age," but what does this mean? The expression is in fact so laden with meaning that no one attempts to define it. Is it something gained or something lost? It is probably both. It suggests at once tasting the fruit of knowledge and the loss of innocence, the discovery of evil as well as good. Perhaps for adults this moment has special poignancy because it signals the beginning of the discovery of human limitations and ultimately disillusionment. The child is poised at a moment of opportunity that all adults once had but have now lost, and in this respect the child represents humanity in general in its desire to create a better world. Adults know all too well how often such hopes have been dashed.

To study childhood is to revisit our own history, our origins as adults. Some films look back upon childhood through the lens of subsequent knowledge. Sometimes we hear the voice of the grown-up child, as in the nostalgic *Stand By Me* (1986), Yves Robert's Pagnol films, or Stein Leikanger's more sprightly *When I Got Jesus . . . with the Slingshot!* (2000). Other films present childhood as freshly experienced, with its hopes and fears intact and the future uncharted. Still others achieve an ironic mixture of the two perspectives. René Clément's *Jeux interdits* (1952) created a *frisson* upon its release for coolly showing how war had distorted the lives of children without them realizing it (figure 3.2). One step further removed, the image of the world-weary child has a special fascination, as though premature aging somehow endowed a child with a wisdom that adults lack. By the end of Elim Klimov's *Come and See* (1985) the hair of the boy character has turned gray, as well it might after he has witnessed his family slaughtered, people burnt alive, and countless other horrors. Near the beginning of Tarkovsky's *Ivan's Childhood* (1962), the exhausted boy-spy is seen upbraiding a young soldier, then falling asleep once he has completed his dispatch to the soldier's superior officer (figure 3.3). This reversal of roles—boy-for-man, man-for-boy—is reversed once again when the soldier picks up the sleeping boy and puts him to bed. Like Klimov—and the directors of the boy-gangsters in *Billy Bathgate* (1991) and *The Road to Perdition* (2002) (in which the boy always drives the getaway car)—Tarkovsky employs such reversals to evoke the changed state of human relations in a world turned upside down by war and crime.

The premature wisdom and adult skills of certain children have always been a cinematic mainstay, in any case. There is the cleverness of the child prankster upsetting the stodgy adult world, beginning with early silent comedies (it even features in Louis Lumière's first "fiction" film, *L'arroseur arrosé* [1895]), the possessed or demonic child of horror films (e.g., *The Bad Seed* [1956], *Village of the Damned* [1960], *The Exorcist* [1973]), and the children who see through their parents' pretensions and hypocrisy, like the two boys who go on a hunger strike in Ozu's *I Was Born, But . . .* (1932). Certainly part of the interest adults take in childhood owes something to the knowledge that the child's perspective, with its insights as well as its ignorance, is now closed to them. Childhood is a place, another world. As the narrator of *When I Got Jesus . . . with the Slingshot!* says at the end of the film, "I can't return to the world of my childhood, either as an explorer or a tourist, even if I wanted to. . . . The world of my childhood died the moment my childhood ended." For the Romantics, childhood was fascinating for being closer to a feral existence—that of Natural Man. The experiences of actual feral children, like Dr. Itard's Wild Boy, were doubly fascinating for being closer still. "The Wild Boy had escaped from humanity into animality," writes Roger Shattuck, "yet it seemed possible that he could be brought back to inform us about the gap in nature he had crossed."[11] In the chronicles of extreme childhood survival, the child who is wise before his or her time joins the experience of childhood with that of the adult, and this double consciousness has a special power that adults treat with respect. Yet there seems no logical destination for many of these knowing children (nor do films generally show it to us)—except perhaps to become more like the rest of the world, to become as childish as their elders.

3.2. From *Jeux interdits* (1952). Copyright StudioCanal.

3.3. From *Ivan's Childhood* (1962). Courtesy of ScreenSound Australia
National Screen and Sound Archive. Copyright Mosfilm.

To many filmmakers, "coming of age" becomes an exercise in exploring
the child's newfound sensitivity. It is an end in itself, a demonstration that
the child is human. It finishes with the child emerging perhaps even less
well prepared than before to face a harsh world—like Antoine Doinel in
The 400 Blows, although he at least has the courage to turn away from
the sea and face inland. There are innumerable coming-of-age films in
which the protagonist simply becomes older and wiser without other obvious benefit. Some, like *The Getting of Wisdom* (1977) and *Freeze–Die–
Come to Life* (1989), announce the extremes of optimism and pessimism
in their titles. Coming of age is often a period of liminality and transgres-
sion, in which the child slips into a feral world of war or sex where the
rules of both childhood and adulthood are suspended. In Louis Malle's
Murmur of the Heart, Laurent, the fifteen-year-old boy-hero, emerges
from an unconventional sexual initiation (incest with his mother) to take
up normal relations with girls of his own age. As this film suggests, the
period of intellectual and sexual enlightenment is sometimes characterized by attachments deemed inappropriate by polite society—attachments
to adults, to other children, to a cause. There are passionate homoerotic
attachments to teachers, as in *The Prime of Miss Jean Brodie* (1969) and
Mädchen in Uniform, and among children and adolescents in *If . . .* , *The*

Devil's Playground (1976), and *Les amitiés particulières*. At a less fervent level, *Dead Poets Society* (1989) shows the combined effect of discovering an intellectual passion and a charismatic teacher at an impressionable age. These adolescent attachments were anticipated in films that dealt more simply with childish hero-worship, such as Carol Reed's *The Fallen Idol* and Philip Leacock's *The Spanish Gardener* (1956), although even these were not without illicit overtones.

The Visual Anthropology of Childhood

There are many thousands of hours of film and videotape devoted to children, but if one were to break this down into categories, a very large proportion of it would be found locked away in teachers' colleges, university education and psychology departments, psychiatric institutes, family therapy centers, and other institutions that have had good practical reasons for observing and recording children's behavior. Most of the rest would be found in television stations and studio vaults in the form of children's programs (such as *Sesame Street*) and situation comedies (such as *Malcolm in the Middle*). A much smaller proportion has been produced for fiction and documentary films, and of that only a tiny fraction has originated in the social sciences. Children make an appearance in sociological and anthropological films, but almost always incidentally or in subsidiary roles. This is not surprising, since social scientists, with the exception of those studying children and youth cultures, have in the past paid very little attention to children except as adults-in-waiting. The situation is changing—there is now a subdiscipline of child-focused anthropological research[12]—but to many anthropologists this remains very much a specialist area, as if children were a separate and unusual form of humanity. For their part, anthropologists who actually study children believe such studies have important implications for the whole of anthropology. The anthropological study of children may even have the potential to reorient the discipline in ways comparable to the emergence of feminist anthropology in the 1970s.[13]

In the popular imagination and in much social science, children occupy the lower rungs of the human ladder in more ways than one, for they are not only considered to be novices in their own culture, and relatively powerless, but also most frequently the recipients of culture rather than full participants in it. As Marc Henri Piault has pointed out, many scientists have clung to a nineteenth century evolutionary model when it comes to children.[14] Since the development of cultural relativism and the abandonment of racial theories of progress, children have in a sense taken over the position of "primitives" in anthropology. And yet children under fifteen constitute almost a third of the world's population, exert tremendous influence on how adults live, and contribute a significant amount of labor to keep the world running.

None of these reasons is really the important one for taking children more seriously. The most important reason is that studying children's lives, more than the study of any other social group, can give us further insight into what it is to be human. Children are the first and most voracious students of culture. Moreover, they move within society as witnesses and agents, constantly re-imagining and modifying it. They are concerned, in their own way, with the most important questions of human fulfillment and survival. Their conceptions of the world may be largely for themselves, but over the generations these inevitably affect the thinking of adults.

When filmmakers and anthropologists have paid closer attention to children, their interest has generally focused on play and suffering. Play defines childhood, and suffering is the price children pay for not having been born as adults. The earliest films of children show them at play—Lumière's prankster, squirting a gardener with water, and Rudolf Pöch's early ethnological films of children playing on a beach in New Guinea. By the time Robert Flaherty showed an Inuit child playing with a toy bow and arrow in *Nanook of the North* (1922), there were already child movie stars like Mary Pickford and Jackie Coogan active in Hollywood. Many of the subsequent anthropological films featuring children focused on initiation—rituals involving circumcision, subincision, cliterodectomy, tooth avulsion, scarification, stinging with nettles, sleep deprivation, dancing to exhaustion, and, of course, instruction in the knowledge of their elders. In these films, children were viewed as raw material to be shaped and made human by growing up. Perhaps in this, anthropologists were a little too willing to accept the formulations of the societies they studied. Whatever the reasons, they embraced the notion of socialization as the reproduction of culture by direct transmission from adult to child.

But films of initiation rituals said little or nothing about what the child was seeing or thinking. Although ostensibly child-centered, they were really adult-centered, the adult anthropologists in collusion with their adult hosts. When Gregory Bateson and Margaret Mead began their mammoth photographic and filming project in Bali in 1936, the perspective was still much the same, although now reframed by psychoanalytic theory. The filming had simply been redirected to show how child-rearing practices, rather than rituals, shaped the future adult.[15]

If films and television programs have ignored many aspects of childhood, they have generally done so in ways consistent with the ideology and economics of their own countries. How children are portrayed may therefore be taken as an indicator of more pervasive social attitudes toward order, authority, consumption, and individual agency. For their part, academic studies have been more systematic in demonstrating the diverse ways that children have been perceived, both historically and cross-culturally. Although childhood is almost universally recognized as a stage of life, the transitions from infancy to childhood and childhood to adulthood are placed at different points and are more sharply defined in some cultures than others. Behavior considered appropriate to children and adults may also vary depending on the context. Thus child marriage is acceptable in some societies but may be unthinkable in those where marriage is a primary marker of adulthood or is closely linked to sexual activity. Elsewhere, the category of childhood may be extended well beyond adolescence if it is in the interests of the powerful to keep a certain group (such as students or women) in a disempowered state.

Ideas of childhood have also changed over time, but these changes have occurred unevenly according to sex and social class. In one of the first studies of its kind, Philippe Ariès showed how clothing can provide a valuable insight into conceptions of the child.[16] Until the seventeenth century, children in Europe wore the same kinds of clothes as adults, suggesting that before this the category of the child was less clearly defined. Boys were the first to be treated differently, as if given primacy over girls, who remained more nebulously part of family life. However, there was a concurrent tendency to feminize the dress of boys, who had previously been clothed as miniature men. These shifts occurred first in the upper classes. Even as late as the nineteenth century, and into the twentieth, working-class boys wore essentially the same clothing as working-class men, while their middle and upper-class contemporaries were dressed in sailor suits and short trousers. There was also a curious time lag in the style of dress gradually adopted for children: it showed a certain archaism, tending to reflect features of the adult dress of the previous century. Was this yet another way of prolonging the perceived social backwardness of the child?

It is perhaps a human constant that societies maintain a certain level of ignorance about their children, together with a set of supporting myths about them. Children's behavior is explained by these means, but there is a tendency to be dismissive. "Oh, that's the way children are." It is said that mothers know, but how many things did we do and think that our mothers knew nothing about? Child individuality and autonomy are often undervalued, as children of a particular age are categorized as being as yet unformed and much the same. One of the most useful, if sometimes most subversive things that films can do is see through these myths and help to develop a more accurate description of children's lives, uncolored by nostalgia or wishful thinking. For example, how do children spend their time? Little is known about this. It is probably better documented in fiction films than in documentaries, since fiction filmmakers draw upon their own experiences whereas documentary filmmakers are more likely to present a few scenes of children's behavior in the hope that these are representative. There are exceptions, of course. Ilkka Ruuhijärvi and Ulla Turunen have spent years filming what children actually do in groups, and in a more limited way in *Récréations* (1992) Claire Simon has recorded the various small dramas of life in a school playground. Granada Television's *Seven Up* series began with the revolutionary (but really quite obvious) idea of asking children what they thought about jobs, education, and their future. It was only revolutionary because hardly anyone in television had thought of doing it before or thought it would be interesting.

As the first film of that series showed, children are often more frank about their perceptions than adults, because they have not yet learned to be defensive or circumspect. This has earned them a reputation for wisdom when it is nothing more than describing what they see, rather like child prodigies such as the famous Nadia who, perhaps because of her limitations, was able to draw the outlines of a horse as she had seen it rather than the concept of a horse.[17] Children apply ideas to the physical and social world quite indiscriminately in order to see what will happen, whereas adults have generally disciplined themselves to discuss only what is known and sanctioned. The capacity of children for abstract thought has thus very possibly been underestimated because much of the logic of their thinking has been misconstrued as playfulness. Gareth B. Matthews argued some years ago that Piaget's research into the stages of childhood conceptualization was too conservative, discounting the significance of much that departed from the norm as "romancing."[18] But from a philosopher's viewpoint, it is these departures that are most interesting. To Matthews, they demonstrated an early capacity for making conceptual connections. Somewhat as Piault believes anthropologists have cast children against adults as "primitives," Matthews believes that Piaget assumed the early stages of children's thought were more primitive than the later ones and were therefore deficient. By subscribing to a theory of progress in intellectual development, he undervalued children's thought processes, which often open up possibilities that later stages of life actually close off.

Employing a very simple idea, one filmmaker equipped his five-year-old son with a radio microphone and filmed him from a distance talking to adults sitting on park benches. The child was completely uncompromising in exploring the most serious questions of money, death, loneliness, pain, and human happiness. The adults responded, but it took them some time to shed the inhibitions they had put on like layers of clothing since they themselves were children.

Assumptions similar to Piaget's idea of progress in conceptual thinking may have limited the anthropological study of children in other domains, some of them physical. It is well known that nineteenth-century scientists were interested in body movement, with figures such as Muybridge, Marey, and Regnault making photographic studies of animals and human beings in motion. Regnault, in particular, was looking for cultural differences in body movement. Although it was well documented then that horses and people have a variety of gaits, it is still unclear why children use a greater variety of gaits than adults, including skipping, hopping, running, and leaping, or why adults should have limited themselves to so few. This is but one instance of the way in which the study of childhood can have broader implications for the understanding of culture and society. Are gaits like phonemes, from which each language makes its own selection? And if so, does this signal more or less versatility before the selection has become fixed? Are there other aspects of children's lives that are both more fertile and more transcultural than those of adults? If children's lives have distinctive cultural traits, it behooves adults to understand what these are and how they are transmitted. For some reason, fiction filmmakers have so far taken such questions more to heart than visual anthropologists.

Perhaps most ignored in the past, and even today, is the wider agency of children in society.[19] Classed as spectators rather than participants, children normally attract attention only when they are the objects of specific adult interests, as in child-rearing and initiation. That children act upon other children is considered less important, and that they influence society at large is hardly acknowledged. Piault gives an example of a filmmaker, Guy Le Moal, who came upon a moment of symbolic significance for understanding children's agency.[20] Filming a masked procession in Burkina Faso, he almost accidentally followed some children who were playing games under the watchful eyes of a group of elders, who appeared to study the children with great seriousness, as if they were prophets. Piault's point is that children here were regarded as closer to the gods than adults and were looked to for omens. They were crucial to the decisions of the community.

Such encounters with children may be the occasions when we can learn most about their social impact. Indeed, it is in their relations with the adult world that both their lives and those of adults can most clearly be seen mirrored in one another. Adults and children interact most intensively in early childhood, in schooling, in family labor, and (less obviously) when children are using resources by eating, dressing, and buying things, for these are also the occasions when children divert adults from other activities, influence the social infrastructure, produce goods and services, and also consume them. One gets a glimpse here of children's interactive role in society and how much society revolves around them (and increasingly so, as consumers in a globalizing world). Here one may also begin to gauge how children deal with the conceptions adults have of them—to what extent they accept them, pretend to accept them for strategic reasons, or resist them, as we have seen in the school film. Nor in the treatment they receive are children an undifferentiated mass. They are divided by age, gender, temperament, physique, social and economic background, race, and other factors. They quickly grasp these categories and adapt to them in different ways—as when they oppose or conform to the prescribed roles and social aesthetics of boyhood and girlhood. These are no doubt areas that visual anthropology should focus on to correct the notion of children as passive bystanders. But there is a less public domain that deserves equal attention—the interaction of children among themselves, their special uses of language, their social and cultural creativity, and, in short, their creation of other children. Socialization was once thought to be a vertical, or top-down, process. We now have evidence that it is as much a horizontal one. The future is often said to rest with children, but if so it is there to be discovered in their present lives.

Children are very good at giving adults what they want. They are quite willing to impersonate "children" if that is what earns praise and other rewards. The child actors of Hollywood have been aware of this since the early days of cinema. But filming children accurately means granting them complete lives—according them the importance one would accord adults and respecting the validity of their view of the world.

A Personal Note

Although children had appeared in some of the films I had made earlier, I only began to film them seriously in 1997 when I embarked upon a project to film at a school in northern India. In previous films I had tried to give children their due, but they were always in the end minor players in a world dominated by adults. In the new project it was the adults who moved into the background. I found that filming children meant entering a parallel society, one that resembled that of adults but had its own distinctive codes and culture. The children I filmed were not always civil to one another, but neither were they uncivilized. They pondered serious questions and organized their world in intelligent ways. Despite all I had heard about the socialization of children by adults, many of their social instincts seemed inborn. They had a fiercer sense of justice than adults, who so easily learn to adapt to conditions of inequality. They were more willing to express feelings of affection, anger, and desire—or perhaps they had less need to hide them. They constantly taught one another and seemed to learn more from each other than from adults. Moreover, their lives seemed lived on a knife's edge, their actions and emotions on a larger scale. I learned that to film them I had to become a keener observer, quicker at anticipating events. I had to be ready for sudden shifts of mood and unexpected arrivals and departures.

Socialization, I began to think, is both progressive and regressive. Children acquire the skills and wisdom of adults, but adults often lose the skills and wisdom they had as children. Children, who have an almost infinite capacity for body movement and vocalization, soon learn that only certain postures and movements are appropriate, and only certain sounds are required by their language. Adults, who as children demanded frankness and equality, often become ever more "childish" in their social relations, squabbling over precedence and prestige. Filming children raised fundamental questions for me. What qualities of being human do children possess that they must unlearn to become adults? And as we strive to be more humane adults, what qualities must we painfully relearn? Can films about children give us clues to the extent of human possibility?

I think my knowledge has been enlarged by children more as a filmmaker than as a parent or teacher. Filmmaking provides a strange and intensive mode of access to the world, both more immersed and more detached. Initially, the children I filmed were curious about my camera, but they gradually accepted it as part of me, and it continued to justify my presence. The camera symbolized my work and absorbed most of my attention, leaving them with greater freedom to pursue their own interests. Unlike their teachers, I was not required to judge them, nor to make institutional demands upon them. I never asked them to perform for me, with the result that they were not distracted from their usual activities or performances for each other. At the same time, they collaborated with me implicitly in many ways, trying to show me what was important in their lives. Unlike many adults, they rarely questioned the justice of their own existence. The longer I stayed with them, and the more I filmed them, the more confidence they seemed to have that I saw them as comprehensively as they saw themselves. Although this was far from true, it made them willing, and sometimes eager, for me to film them in situations that would otherwise embarrass them. If they sometimes puzzled over why I should take so much trouble, they were pragmatic about my presence. It was an easy sort of relationship for them to have with an adult, unlike most of their other relationships that entailed more complex obligations.

Children are often regarded as unformed versions of adults, and their activities as mere rehearsals for the society in which they will live. Their world is also often seen as a vision of the world to come. This is partly because they are fascinated by their own discoveries, which become fixated on the fashions and preoccupations of children a little older than themselves. But children are also a vision of the past, for they summon up the prehistory of all adults. In children, adults see the beginnings of a future that they have already largely spent and often squandered. I sometimes wondered if the children I was filming would become mere replicas of their parents, whose lives often struck me as emptier and more compromised than theirs. Yet even if this were true, I felt it could never quite negate the intrinsic value of childhood, for each childhood is unique, a discovery of what it means to be alive and human, as if at the dawn of creation.

Notes

This chapter includes revised portions of a brief article published in *Bambini/Children/Pizzinnos*, the catalogue of the Xth Rassegna Internazionale di Documentari Etnografici held in Nuoro, Sardinia, in 2000, which focused on films about children.

1. This seems to be a particular characteristic of British films, such as Carol Reed's *The Fallen Idol* (1948), John Boorman's *Hope and Glory* (1987), and Joseph Losey's *The Go-Between* (1970), but see also *The Devil's Playground* (1976), *Salaam Bombay!* (1988), *The Road to Perdition* (2002), and a number of Iranian films featuring children.

2. R. K. Douglas 1893: 159.

3. The best-known early example is probably Mark Twain's *Adventures of Huckleberry Finn* (1885). The examples referred to are Doctorow's *Billy Bathgate* (1989) and Roddy Doyle's *Paddy Clarke, Ha Ha Ha* (1993).

4. See also Helen Levitt's remarkable book of photographs about urban children, *A Way of Seeing* (1989), with an essay by James Agee, her collaborator on *In the Street*.

5. Randall 2000.

6. Kincaid 1998.

7. Shattuck 1980: 212.

8. These would include *Puberty Blues* (1981), from an adolescent girl's perspective; Bernardo Bertolucci's *1900* (1976), which treats, briefly but explicitly, the sexual curiosity of two preadolescent boys; *The Ice Palace* (1987), approaching the same theme with two girls; and the Swedish film *Children's Island* (1981), about a boy's sexual growing pains.

9. Ariès 1962.

10. McEwan 1992: 50.

11. Shattuck 1980: 181.

12. Institutions and organizations with an interest in the anthropology of childhood include the Child Focused Research Centre at Brunel University in Great Britain; the Norwegian Centre for Child Research at Trondheim University; the Centre for the Study of Childhood and Youth at the University of Sheffield; the Child Culture Research program at the University of Southern Denmark; the Center for Children and Childhood Studies at Rutgers University; the IUAES Commission on the Anthropology of Children, Youth and Childhood, based at Sambalpur University, India; the International Labour Organization, Geneva; and UNICEF.

13. Benthall 1992: 1.

14. Piault 2000b: 26–27.

15. But to give Margaret Mead her due, it should also be pointed out that in her research in Samoa and New Guinea she made a point of studying how the worldview of children differed from that of adults.

16. See Ariès 1962: 50–59. Ariès's conclusion that a clear idea of childhood did not exist in medieval society has been disputed (and effectively disproven) in recent years, but his work remains a landmark in historical ethnography and one of the first extended studies of childhood. Besides, Ariès was not asserting that childhood was not recognized but that the separation between adults' and children's worlds was far less marked than it was later to become.

17. See Selfe 1977.

18. Matthews 1980.

19. Not ignored by consumer research, however. Apart from attempts to create fashions among children, a great deal of corporate time and money has gone into spotting trends in childhood culture in order to exploit them for greater profit.

20. Piault 2000b.

4

SOCIAL AESTHETICS AND THE DOON SCHOOL

Social Landscapes

T HERE ARE moments when the social world seems more evident in an object or a gesture than in the whole concatenation of our beliefs and institutions. Through our senses we measure the qualities of our surroundings—the tempo of life, the dominant patterns of color, texture, movement, and behavior—and these coalesce to make the world familiar or strange. In the 1920s Ruth Benedict suggested that the aesthetic sensibility was an important component in the cultural "configuration" of societies, although her schema of cultural types soon seemed overly reductive to most scholars.[1] Recently, social scientists have increasingly drawn attention to the senses and to how responses to sensory experience may be culturally constructed and specific.[2] Attention has also been given to indigenous aesthetic systems, including, but also extending beyond, artistic activities.[3] Some writers have analyzed the forms and "poetics" of social performance, both public and private.[4] Others have described how the emotions and social interactions of individuals may be closely associated with a society's aesthetic principles and concepts of bodily harmony.[5]

The emergence of these studies points to a desire to remedy certain apparent omissions in anthropological description, often concerning subjects such as art, ritual, and religion about which a good deal has already been written. It also suggests that new methods may be needed to explore these interests, or at least new applications of existing methods. This has led to considerable experimentation in the writing of ethnographies.[6] If one were to look beyond the written literature, one would also have to include filmmaking in this démarche, most notably the work of Jean Rouch, beginning in the early 1950s.[7] Since then, visual anthropologists have been looking for alternative ways of representing social experience, often (like Rouch) at the risk of upsetting more orthodox approaches.[8] Yet it is through such radical moves that anthropology may eventually succeed in reuniting the sensory with the "cultural" landscape.

Defining this larger landscape is not only, or even principally, a matter of making a cultural inventory of the senses—exploring what Walter J. Ong has called the "ratio or balance between the senses"[9] of different cultural groups, or (as another writer terms it) their characteristic *senso-types*.[10] Nor does it lie only in describing the aesthetic preoccupations and preferences of certain societies (as has been done, for example, of cattle-keeping Nilotes of the southern Sudan),[11] nor even in acknowledging the embodied and performative dimensions of rituals and other community events.[12] These are important aspects of the individual's social and cultural consciousness, but gaining a fuller understanding of the relation of individuals to their societies would seem to require further analysis of the societies themselves as complex sensory and aesthetic environments.

So far this task has largely slipped through the gaps between anthropology, art history, and cultural studies. Anthropology remains largely concerned with aesthetics as it pertains to particular art objects and practices and the discourses surrounding them, especially those associated with ritual or myth; art history with artistic production more generally as an institution; and cultural studies with the aesthetics of popular culture, as seen in advertising, mass media, and consumerism. Aesthetics as it relates to everything else in life apart from art or conscious design has received comparatively little attention.[13] As Howard Morphy notes, "in failing to consider the aesthetics of cultures, anthropologists ignore a body of evidence that allows them a unique access to the sensual aspect of human experience: to how people feel in, and respond to, the world."[14]

"Landscape" has seemed to me an appropriate term to apply to these social environments, for like many actual landscapes they are conjunctions of the cultural and the natural. The experience of most anthropologists is that each community exhibits physical attributes and patterns of behavior that, taken as a composite, are specific to itself and instantly recognizable to its inhabitants. That these social landscapes have no individual authors is of no great moment; like the social forces that make individual authorship of works of art relatively unimportant in broadly historical terms, their "authorship" has been collective over time, employing the full range of available media: stones and earth, fibers and dyes, sounds, time and space, and the many expressive possibilities of the human body. Even in its shifts and internal contradictions, a community acquires a character that provides a distinctive backdrop for everyday life. The result may not be a well-balanced whole, but the object in studying such social environments is not to reinvent a holistic typology of societies, nor to return to a hermetic sort of functionalism, but to understand the importance of these settings of human life as they exist in experiential terms. This problem can be approached variously through writing, museum exhibits, sound recordings, photography, film, and video. It demands, in addition to a capacity for analysis, a sensitivity to the aesthetics of community life—to forms and resonances that are often as complexly interlaced as the rhymes and meanings of a poem. Differences in emphasis must also be taken into account. Although aesthetic considerations appear to play a part in the life of all communities, the social aesthetic field often appears more systematically ordered in some than in others. This is particularly true of small "constructed" communities such as schools.

A Constructed Community

I became interested in the aesthetics of social life while making a video study of a boys' boarding school in northern India. Here was a small, self-consciously created community in which aesthetic design and aesthetic judgments seemed to play a prominent part. From my initial intention to study the school as a site of cross-cultural contact and socialization, I soon began turning my attention to more mundane subjects such as clothing, colors, timetables, eating implements, tones of voice, and characteristic gestures and postures. In one sense, this particularity is the very stuff of ethnography, but in anthropology such physical details tend to become adjuncts to larger questions of belief and social structure. Confronted more directly, they produced in me a desire to disconnect objects from the symbolic meanings with which they are conventionally invested. This led to a further shift. While I recognized that the school existed within (and was interdependent with) a complex national, as well as global, economy and culture, I also began to see it as a world in miniature, with its own distinctive material signature. Students moved in and out of this world, to and from other places and other lives, but the school impressed its own distinctive stamp upon them. Recently a former student wrote to me, "I think it will be very difficult to let go, impossible perhaps. I think I will always carry the school with me, wherever I go."

The Doon School is a residential boys' secondary school in the town of Dehra Dun in the state of Uttaranchal. The town lies in the Valley of the Doon, between the Siwalik Hills and the foothills of the Himalayas. It enjoys a comfortable climate for most of the year and, along with the nearby hill station of Mussoorie, is the location of a large number of schools and national institutions, such as the Survey of India and the Indian Military Academy. Of the schools, Doon School is certainly the most famous, perhaps the most famous in all of India. It owes its fame to a number of factors, but most obviously to the part its graduates have played in the ruling elites of India since Independence, particularly in government and industry. The school counts among its alumni former Prime

Minister Rajiv Gandhi, several cabinet ministers, a long list of members of parliament, and major business leaders. The role of its graduates in the professions, the military, the visual and print media, and the arts has been less pronounced but is still considerable. An Air Chief Marshall, a number of army generals, and the writers Vikram Seth and Amitav Ghosh are all former students of the school. The school's impact on public affairs has been enhanced by a powerful network of "old boys" who display great loyalty to the school.

Doon School is also notable for spreading a particular style of education to other schools: a self-consciously egalitarian, secular approach based upon a commitment to public service and a belief in Western-style scientific rationalism.[15] Within this regime, the school aims to produce "all-rounders" with equal proficiency (if not brilliance) in studies, games, and social skills. There is an official emphasis on setting one's own goals and competing against oneself rather than others. Although Doon School and Mayo College (in Rajasthan) have both been called "the Eton of India," in the case of Doon School this is something of a misnomer. It was always a school for the reasonably well off, but it was never the preserve of the upper classes (this was rather the role of Mayo College), and in fact it attracted the sons of the new technocracy that was developing in Punjab and the United Provinces (now Uttar Pradesh) at about the time the school was founded. Over the years many other schools in India have gradually adopted aspects of Doon School's style of education and have, in effect, been "Doon-ized," partly through appointing teachers and headmasters who taught at the school.

The video study coincides with the publication of a written study of Doon School (and two other North Indian schools) by the anthropologist Sanjay Srivastava.[16] It was Srivastava who first interested me in Doon School, although I already knew something about it and had become acquainted with several other schools in nearby Mussoorie. He suggested that the schools he was studying might be suitable subjects for a film, and over the years we discussed many possibilities. We have remained in close communication about Doon School ever since, and I owe much of my understanding of the school to his observations and insights.

Srivastava's study focuses on how the school has both reflected and shaped concepts of the modern Indian citizen and nation in the twentieth century. My interest has been more in how the school, as a small society, has developed a particular aesthetic design in its informal daily life and its more formal rituals and institutions. I believe this kind of "social aesthetic," while it is sometimes elusive, plays an important part in the life of all societies but is very often overlooked by anthropologists and historians. Perhaps because it is more conspicuous in some societies than others—especially those that could be termed "hyperaesthetic" communities, such as schools, religious orders, the military, and certain ultranationalist states—it may not always receive the attention it deserves.[17] Certainly for me, it was only by living in such a community that I began to consider social aesthetics a subject worthy of study in its own right.

"Aesthetics" in this context has little to do with notions of beauty or art, but rather with a much wider range of culturally patterned sensory experience. (It is closer to what the Greeks originally meant by *aisthesis*, or "sense experience.") It is thus not "beauty-aesthetics" in the Kantian sense.[18] Nor does it here imply the *valuation* of sensory experience (as in European aesthetics), except as this bears upon the ability of people to determine what is familiar or unfamiliar. It also includes much that derives from nature rather than culture, such as the geographical setting of a community, and even much in the life of its members that is onerous but to which they become habituated. Doon School's social aesthetic is made up of many elements and consists not so much in a list of ingredients as a complex, whose interrelations as a totality (as in gastronomy) are as important as their individual effects. These elements include such things as the design of buildings and grounds, the use of clothing and colors, the rules of dormitory life, the organization of students' time, particular styles of speech and gesture, and the many rituals of everyday life that accompany such activities as eating, school gatherings, and sport (itself already a highly ritualized activity).

What is interesting sociologically is the extent to which these aesthetic patterns may influence events and decisions in a community, along with the other more commonly recognized social forces of history, economics, politics, and ideology. All these forces are, of course, interconnected, but it often seems that the aesthetic features of a society are too easily assimilated into other categories, to such an extent that they become invisible or are ignored. Alternatively, aesthetic features may simply be seen as the symbolic expression of more profound forces (such as history and ideology) rather than influential in their own right. Although aesthetics may not be independent of other social forces, neither is it merely the residue of them. My working premise has been that the aesthetic dimension of human experience is an important social fact, to be taken seriously alongside such other facts as economic survival, political power, and religious belief. It is important because it often matters to people and influences their actions as much as anything else in their lives. But because aesthetic decisions often appear to be made autonomously, in the face of economic or political logic, we have a strong tendency not to recognize their importance.

The social aesthetic field, composed of objects and actions, is in some respects the physical manifestation of the largely internalized and invisible "embodied history" that Bourdieu calls *habitus*.[19] Bourdieu comes closest to identifying habitus in physical terms when he speaks metaphorically of the "physiognomy" of a "social environment."[20] But this physiognomy is more than metaphorical, more than "a system of structured, structuring dispositions."[21] It is not only an attribute of the self (of whatever class, whatever society) but also exists all around us concretely, in the disposition of time, space, material objects, and social activities. It includes the very areas of practice that Bourdieu himself, in his research among the Kabyle of North Africa, felt previous writers had systematically ignored, "such as the structure and orientation of time (divisions of the year, the day, human life), the structure and orientation of space (especially inside the house), children's games and movements of the body, the rituals of infancy and the parts of the body, values (*nif* and *h'urma*) and the sexual division of labour, colours and the traditional interpretation of dreams, etc."[22]

Some communities ("hyperaesthetic" communities being at the extreme) appear to place greater stress on the aesthetics of social life than others. In the popular imagination, Japanese and Balinese society are particularly noted for their aesthetic preoccupations. However, this should not be seen as unusual but rather as a more conspicuous expression of a concern of all societies, and one that can take quite varied forms. Some societies specifically emphasize artistic expression, others codes of interpersonal behavior, others special regimes of physical activity or public display, and still others particular forms of religious or spiritual experience. In this regard, Vladislav Todorov has observed that industrial production played a largely aesthetic and symbolic role under Stalinism. "Communism created ultimately effective aesthetic structures and ultimately defective economic ones. . . . Factories are not built to produce commodities. . . . They result in a deficit of goods, but an overproduction of symbolic meanings. Their essence is aesthetic, not economic." He concludes: "Society is a poetic work, which reproduces metaphors, not capital."[23]

Whatever its particular local form, each variant serves to define a familiar social space and the individual's sense of belonging, like a lock and its key. Local aesthetic sensibilities may often be attuned to very humdrum activities, such as agricultural or office work, or be defined by painful experiences, such as physical stress, grief for the dead, or (in some religious sects) the infliction of wounds. Appeals to the aesthetic sensibility may also be a means of social control, as in totalitarian states that create a powerful repertoire of public rhetoric and ritual. It does not follow that these states are particularly interested in the arts; indeed, rather than encouraging artistic experimentation, their attitude is more likely to be conservative and prescriptive. Although it is unclear why some societies stress the aesthetics of social life more than others, those that have developed in isolation, or that draw their membership from varied backgrounds, or that need to contain serious internal divisions, may find in the sharing of a strong aesthetic experience a unifying principle.

The School and Its Origins

Compared to many boarding schools in India, such as La Martiniere in Calcutta (founded in 1836) and Lawrence School in Sanawar (founded in 1847), Doon School is a comparative newcomer. It was opened in 1935 on the grounds of the former Forest Research Institute and was the creation of a group of moderate Indian nationalists led by a Calcutta lawyer, Satish Ranjan Das, who, although he died before the school actually opened, had lobbied for it assiduously during the 1920s. Das envisaged an Indian school patterned on the British "public school," which he felt had effectively trained young men to become responsible and resourceful administrators throughout the British Empire. But in contrast to British schools, he wanted an Indian school to be nonsectarian and responsive to Indian aspirations. He and the school's other founders saw Doon as the training ground for a new generation of Indian leaders who would take over the reins of administration and government following Independence. By copying the model of the British public school, the founders were attempting to show that Indians could compete with the British on their own terms without relinquishing their national or cultural identity. This reflected the views of many Indian leaders and intellectuals of the time, but certainly not all. Characteristically, Nehru welcomed the creation of the school, but Gandhi would have nothing to do with it (figure 4.1).

The colonial discourses of imperial Britain celebrated the ideal of strong physical manliness in contrast to the stereotyped image of the ineffectual, even feminized male subject. One of the objectives of Doon School was apparently to counter this colonial view (even as it interiorized it), which in the Indian context had taken on an exaggerated form in the image of the effete Bengali man.[24] The image of the new, masculine Indian was to be built upon a regime of bodily practices borrowed from British schools, not only on the playing field but in the dormitory, classroom, assembly hall, and dining hall. Early morning physical exercises became a permanent fixture of Doon School's daily timetable. In 1937 Sir Jagdish Prasad, a member of the school's board of governors, told the assembled boys:

> The aim of this school might well be to give you the physique of the savage and the cultivated brain of the civilized man. My advice to you is to take pride in the development of your body no whit less than in the improvement of your intellect. Let this school be noted for the fine physique of its students. We in this country have not paid sufficient attention to the proper care of our bodies and have paid the penalty of premature decline in energy and mental vigour.[25]

4.1. Prime Minister Jawaharlal Nehru visiting the Doon School in 1957.
Courtesy of the Doon School.

In some respects the physical regime at Doon proved less spartan and authoritarian than in many British schools, partly due to the fact that the British masters and headmasters who first came to Doon saw it as an opportunity to establish a more benign version of the schools they had left behind. The focus, moreover, was to be upon self-regulation rather than external discipline. The school took the radical step at the time of forbidding corporal punishment. The official doctrines of the school, enunciated by the first headmaster, Arthur Edward Foot, stressed self-control and self-monitoring, exemplifying Foucault's contention that institutions tend to turn their inmates into their own surveillants. "Boys who have apparently been well brought up at home," wrote Foot, "behave well in order to please their parents, or in order to please their school-masters. This is not a sound foundation for conduct. They must behave well and work well to satisfy their own self-respect and sense of personal responsibility."[26]

Vision was to play an important part in this process, through its confirmation of the boys' physical development and their patterns of gesture,
posture, and visible social behavior. Boys were taught to speak and act
boldly and to return the gaze of others steadily and fearlessly, even if that
gaze came from the highest in the land.[27] Their disciplined character was
to be seen in their dress, their orderly formations at assembly, their physical training and games, and the tireless energy with which they followed
the crowded school schedule.

Foot, who could never resist an instructive metaphor, however oblique
or (in this case) sexually allusive, likened the growth of a boy to the root
of a plant observed through a magnifying glass:

> Each tiny shoot on the root is covered with little hair[s] through which it
> takes food and drink from the soil. But the thing I especially noticed was that
> the tip of the shoot was free from the root hair. That is to say the part which
> was leading the way was quite clear from anything which would hinder it.
> This made me think how many of us are handicapped in the things we want
> to do by some little habit of self-indulgence which gets in our way. . . . Don't
> make excuses to yourselves, and don't be handicapped by habits.[28]

The school's emphasis on the body reflects a set of deeper assumptions
about the effects of the physical world on the individual. It also emphasizes individuality itself—the student set apart in body and personality
from the mass of his classmates. "You can think of yourselves," Foot said
at the end of the first year, "as a pack of cards all with the same pattern
of blue and grey on your backs; on the other side is each boy's special
character"[29] (figure 4.2). But each boy's character was also to be reshaped
by his surroundings at the school. What lay outside the boy's body, down
to the very clothes on his back, was to determine the inside. Sharing equal
facilities, for example, such as the minimally furnished dormitories, or
equal responsibilities, such as leading physical exercises or serving at
table, would of itself, and without further intervention, be conducive to
an egalitarian outlook. As Foot himself put it, the individual is not best
shaped by precept but by environment.[30] The school's very buildings, with
their functional, undecorated architecture, and its grounds with their botanical tags on every other tree, would instill a sense of proportion and
orderly thought. Since both were originally designed for the scientific purposes of the Forest Research Institute, the site was seen by the founders
as eminently suitable for this approach to education (figure 4.3). As Srivastava explains, the school's philosophical origins lay in the "Bengal
Renaissance" and the nineteenth-century Brahmo Samaj movement,
which embraced scientific rationalism as a release from the superstition
and archaism of the established religions.[31] The school was eventually
furnished with its own workshops, paper recycling center, "boys' bank,"

4.2. The blue and gray shirt of the Doon School games uniform,
from *Doon School Chronicles* (2000).

store, and hospital. This emphasis on the creation of a setting has the
flavor of missionaries establishing a place of order in a heathen land.

The scientific attitude of the school's founders is perhaps more apparent
today in a kind of brisk efficiency than in appeals to speculative thinking.[32]
In part this takes the form of measurement and labeling. The boys' heights
and weights are recorded twice a year, and at one time the names of the
largest and smallest boys in each house were published in *The Doon
School Weekly* (figure 4.4). Those boys who are overweight are systematically slimmed down by physical exercise and the school diet. Upon joining
the school, each boy is given a number, which he keeps throughout his
school career. At the start of the year, these numbers appear on beds and
desks. They are used on school documents and in announcements at Assembly or after meals when boys are called to meetings or other duties.
They are also essential for the management of school clothing, with a
number tape carefully sewn into each item by the school tailors. The
school day is punctuated by a succession of bells, some rung in the houses,
some at the dining hall, and most importantly on top of the Main Building, signaling the beginning and end of each class. The timing of the Assembly is so precise that this bell usually rings just as the headmaster

4.3. Students near Doon School's Main Building, which dates from the time of the Forest Research Institute. Photograph by David MacDougall.

strides onto the stage in his black gown. This enactment of precision is rehearsed in a hundred smaller ways—in the correct making of beds, arrangement of clothing, and shining of shoes—although it must be said that one of the more attractive aspects of the school is a certain perfunctory attitude toward such matters.

More reminiscent of the Forest Research Institute's interests is the school's own natural history museum, stocked with specimens donated in the early years, ranging from stuffed mammals, birds, and reptiles to a human fetus preserved in a jar of formalin. Scientific apparatus figures prominently at Founder's Day exhibitions, when parents look with bemusement at miniature volcanoes erupting, gas-filled tubes lighting up in different colors, and sparks leaping from one copper ball to another. The school particularly prides itself on the success of its more daring expeditions into the high Himalayas. These occur during the two annual midterm breaks, which are almost sacramental occasions when the entire student body ventures out on trips of varying difficulty into the surrounding countryside. That groups of schoolboys, led by a few teachers, regularly climb to altitudes of more than twenty thousand feet not only proves astonishing to other schools but provides a sentimental link to the past prowess of Empire.

4.4. Measuring a student at Doon School. From *Doon School Chronicles* (2000).

The School-World

When I first went to Doon School it struck me as a kind of theater. There was a performance going on. A bell would ring and everyone would rush onto the stage, dressed in the same costume. Then they would depart. An hour or two later another bell would ring and they would rush on again in a different costume. It was at this point that I began thinking it might be possible to view a small community such as a school much as one would view a play or other creative work. But who in this case were the creators, the players, and the viewers? Clearly the boys themselves were the raw material of this creation, upon whose bodies the aesthetics of the school was imprinted. But at the same time these same boys were also its foremost audience.

By the creation of a social aesthetic, I should stress here that I do not mean a system of signs and meanings encoded in school life, but rather the creation of an aesthetic space or sensory structure. I am not proposing the exegesis of a cultural text, a hermeneutic anthropology.[33] Signs and meanings there clearly are at the school, for a great deal of history and ideology underlies its aesthetic choices, but these qualities both exceed and are experienced differently from any interpretation that might be placed on them. Nor would such meanings necessarily be understood by the boys themselves—either upon first arriving at the school or, indeed, ever. What does speak to them is a particular structure of sense impressions, social relations, and ways of behaving physically. This must be assimilated and acted upon—and therefore be "understood"—in quite a different manner. In a sense, it is a code without a message. As Bourdieu puts it, for them the acts they learn "may have, strictly speaking, neither meaning nor function, other than the function implied in their very existence."[34]

When I came to the school I was not thinking of such distinctions. And as must frequently happen to others, the ideas with which I began were gradually overtaken by ideas that assumed greater importance. My interest in the school as a site of cultural cross-currents gave way to what was for me a new way of thinking about the configuration of forces in community life. Rather than looking at a multiplicity of intersecting histories and cultures (postmodern anthropology's currently ascendant conception of social experience), I found myself much more interested in a cultural phenomenon that could more accurately be viewed as homogeneous, or at least as a temporary coalescence of elements. Through the viewfinder of the camera I found myself drawn into a matrix of life that I felt exerted a powerful influence on all around me. What I began to realize was that the boys in the school lived neither in a homogeneous society nor in a multiply fragmented global one, but in both. Like many of us, they moved between "little worlds" of family and school and a larger world that they encountered in the streets, during their travels, and on television. And like many of us, they learned to accept and adapt to a state of more or less permanent cultural confusion. Perhaps all the more reason, then, for them to bind themselves closely to the islands of relative coherence in their lives.

In certain respects, and more than most other communities, a school aims at a steady state. As older students leave, younger ones come to take their place. Schools can thus be seen—beyond their role in training the young—as institutions for capturing the ephemeral state of childhood and youth. In this they serve a utopian dream: to create a regulated world, insulated from aging and historical change. Adults look across the borders into childhood much as colonial administrators once looked upon "primitive" societies. The ideal school community thus resembles the archetypal community of functionalist anthropology—inward-looking, ahistorical, conservative, and self-perpetuating. Conversely, the functionalist model of anthropology can be seen as permitting an infantilized vision of remote, small-scale societies, investing their inhabitants with some of the same utopian qualities that inspire the makers of schools. The "natives" were characteristically seen as childlike in both their virtues and excesses. The administrator and the schoolmaster habitually regarded their respective communities (albeit often benignly) from similar positions of worldly power and experience.

Schoolmasters, however, must also relate schools to the wider community. At Doon School there have been two views, seemingly opposed, one introspective, the other nationalistic. On the one hand, the school is seen as a microcosm of the larger society. Arthur Foot remarked, "it has been truly said that [the] school should be the replica of the larger and progressive community outside."[35] The more utopian vision is that the school is the microcosm of a nascent society—a society-in-waiting. It is both an exemplar and a kind of hatchery. Its role is to contribute to the making of society, or, as Foot put it, "the production of boys for the service of a free India."[36] This was also the vision of Doon's Indian founders, who wanted the school to produce a new generation of leaders who would guide the nation. The same goal could also be put in more negative terms. Sir Jagdish Prasad, speaking in 1937, said, "this school will indeed have made a notable contribution to Indian advancement if by this intermingling of creeds, castes and race . . . a type is produced free from the communal, racial and regional antipathies that so disfigure our lives."[37]

Conceived as an ideal community, a school at its inception and as it is built up over time has much in common with other creative works. There is a gradual integration of its official doctrines, ceremonies, and physical attributes, so that none stands in need of independent justification. Indeed, where justification is sought it is not so much in particulars as in an appeal to the whole. There is a synthesis of the material and metaphorical. In the botanical garden that forms the school's grounds, the most solemn events are enacted in the Rose Bowl—a setting that joins together botany and the neoclassical order of a Greek amphitheater. Foot's comparison of a boy to a root cannot be seen as entirely coincidental. A year earlier he had compared a boy to a growing flower,[38] and a month before to a path that required annual weeding.[39]

To those who desire change within the school, the call is often to draw closer to the ideals of the original design or to restore what has been lost. There is a tendency to deplore the erosions of present-day life and hark back to the school's Golden Age, placed somewhere between 1936 and 1945. To those who support the school through the Doon School Old Boys Society, the school has acquired a retrospective perfection that absorbs even the things they hated most, such as early morning P.T. (physical training). This creates a resistance to change that extends, irrationally, to even the most trivial matters, which are heatedly opposed, such as the proposed removal of some quite inappropriate statues from the Rose Bowl. One reformist master confided to me that the most dire word for him at the school was "Dosco"—the universal term for a Doon student or Old Boy—because it was used as the ultimate defense against change. "Doscos don't do that" or "That's not for Doscos" eerily recalls Bourdieu's formulation of class conservatism: "That's not for us."

Filming Social Aesthetics

In any field the pursuit of an unforeseen object presents a problem of representation: how to begin defining it in a language that was not intended for it and for which it is opaque or simply nonexistent. Can methods that were designed for exploring quite different sorts of objects be successfully adapted to the purpose, or must new methods be devised? In the end, both approaches are probably necessary.

At Doon School I began asking myself whether it was possible to film something as implicit and all-pervasive as social aesthetics. Could it in any sense be isolated as a subject? I concluded that it could not, or at least not directly. One might be able to focus upon certain features of life in which aesthetic concerns seemed paramount, but this atomized the subject and caused it to disintegrate. Its reality lay elsewhere, in a wider aggregation of features. Unlike cattle among Nilotic pastoralists, there was no single, dominating locus of aesthetic interest.

Something as visible as the patterns and colors of clothing might be singled out for attention, but this was to risk giving these features an excessive symbolic importance, divorced from the actual contexts in which such meanings were submerged or overwritten by other, more immediate, forms of experience. In the case of school uniforms, these contexts included the obvious ones, such as the practical requirements of different activities, the division of the school into manageable groups, and the student hierarchy, but also less obvious ones such as academic achievement and methods of punishment.[40] It was important to see how these links produced new and complex associations, often naturalizing or justifying apparent incongruities, much as chemical compounds exhibit properties quite different from their constituent elements.

I concluded that social aesthetics, as both the backdrop and product of everyday life, could only be approached obliquely, through the events and material objects in which it played a variety of roles. The events might be small and incidental, or ordinary, or large and extraordinary. In the end they included everything from simple hand gestures to the school's annual Founder's Day extravaganza, the torchlight tattoo.

The aesthetics of a society might very well be regarded as an aesthetics of management: an ordering of the elements of life for the balancing of physical needs, comfort, time, space, power relations, and sexuality. The aesthetic sense would then be seen as a regulatory feature of our consciousness, telling us when to be pleased and content or, on the contrary, anxious, disgusted, distressed, or fearful. It would be accepted as one among the many regulatory systems of society, although considerably less specific than, for example, kinship or customary law.

Despite this generally more diffused role, there is one particular manifestation of social aesthetics of which one becomes very conscious at a school like Doon: the aesthetics of power. However, the exercise of power can rarely be distinguished from its aesthetic expression, even when one or the other is clearly marked. There is nothing very edifying about a senior boy bullying a junior one, but there is nevertheless a pattern and protocol to it. In the many instances of explicit aesthetic display that I witnessed at the school (such as the lining up and grouping of boys at assembly, the ritualized cheering at sports events, morning physical exercises, and special events such as the annual Physical Training Competition) a lesson was being inscribed in the bodies of the participants, much as a repertoire of movements is gradually inscribed in the body of a classical dancer. These were not, in fact, symbolic expressions of power relations but their result. When boys cheered for their side at a house hockey match, the sense of power over their rivals—the power of their house—was part of a larger regime of power in which older boys of the house felt it their duty to order younger boys to cheer.

The aesthetics of power is thus as much an enactment of power as a representation of it and is codeterminate with a wider range of activities and social relationships, each with its own aesthetic manifestations. Power cannot be abstracted from such agencies as self-preservation and desire, which form part of the substratum upon which it rests. It would be difficult to determine which of the designs and rituals of a school such as Doon were created with clear objectives and which are part of a more unconscious adaptive and evolutionary process. Certainly the school has borrowed heavily from other, older schools, which have in turn taken much from religious and military institutions. The combination desk-lockers at which the boys study—called "toyes" at Doon—were an importation from Winchester College but have all the hallmarks of the monastery (figure 4.5). In some cases the school's procedures seem to be clear applications of principles developed elsewhere. The school's use of house captains and prefects mirrors the British colonial policy of "indirect rule," in that senior boys control many matters that in other schools, in other countries, would be directly controlled by teachers. But it is also plausible that indirect rule is itself a product of the British public school system.

Again, the design and management of school clothing, which is highly elaborated at Doon, cannot be ascribed to simple motives, although functional and utilitarian explanations abound. Pure cotton cloth of Indian origin was chosen for summer uniforms by the first headmaster on the

4.5. "Toyes" at Doon School. Photograph by David MacDougall.

grounds of simplicity, hygiene, and support for local industries, but this rougher material also framed the growing bodies of the boys in an appealing way that may have been more pleasing to the masters than to the boys themselves. An item by a master in the school newspaper in 1985 runs as follows: "The boys standing on the lovely green turf, in their blue shorts and singlets; with the leaders in white ducks and singlets presents a refreshing sight."[41] Here the line between aesthetics and erotics is unclear. School uniforms become not only indicative of social relationships but also a way of controlling, concealing, and exhibiting the human body, reflecting correspondingly complex motives in those who institute them. Differences in uniform for juniors and seniors, or ordinary boys and prefects, mark intersections of visual pleasure and power, as well as conceptions of discipline, disorder, childhood, adulthood, innocence, and experience. Another, more ironic school newspaper item reads: "Lo and behold. Not a pair of white shorts in sight. The whole school lined up properly in games clothes! . . . Here was symbolism at its subtlest. The School dressed in the blue and greys of Sin while the angelic prefects flitted around . . . in radiant white."[42]

Perhaps the most curious example of the school's preoccupation with clothing is to be found in its system of punishments. The most commonly given of the school's punishments (and considered among the least severe) is called a "change-in-break." It is given for minor infractions, such as making one's bed badly or having unpolished shoes. Boys can often be seen before Assembly polishing their shoes with leaves or bits of paper to avoid the notice of beady-eyed prefects. If caught, the boy is given a chit and must run back to his house during the mid-morning break and change into his P.T. uniform. He must then run back to the Main Building to have the chit signed, return to the house, change into his school clothes again, and return to have the chit signed a second time. If he lives in a nearby house he may have to change into his games clothes as well, and run two more times, with two more signings. Another punishment, more common in the past than now, was to have to put on all of one's uniforms, one on top of the other, and then report to the prefect or house captain. If one was lucky that was the end of it, but sometimes a boy was made to do exercises or run "rounds" of the playing field dressed in these many layers of clothing.

The change-in-break seems designed to make one aware of one's clothing in the most acute and immediate way. Its various gradations and sensory qualities are intensified and become ever more keenly experienced as they are impressed upon one's consciousness. Here, as in everything else around one at the school, the social aesthetic field is never neutral or random: its patterning creates forces and polarities with strong emotional effects. Ordinary objects with which one comes in daily contact take on a particular aura, and this aura is augmented by repetition and multiplication. Both occur in the case of the stainless steel tableware used at the school. Every piece—the hundreds of plates, cups, porridge bowls, serving dishes, pitchers, knives, forks, and spoons—is made of the same bright, hard steel, which produces its own distinctive gonglike tones and clashing sounds. Its surfaces are unyielding and reflect back the bluish colors of the boys' uniforms and the overhead fluorescent lights, meal after meal. The strength and obduracy of this material cannot but be communicated as a direct physical sensation to the boys and to inform the whole process of eating with an unrelenting, utilitarian urgency. Stainless steel tableware is of course common in India, most notably in the South Indian *thali*.[43] Here it is elevated to a fetish of modernity (figure 4.6).

A Pattern of Study

During the first months of my stay at the school I observed these complexities and began to consider my approach to them. I gradually adopted a three-pronged filming strategy. I first identified a set of themes that seemed to provide conceptual keys to the school's aesthetic structures and their

4.6. Stainless steel tableware at Doon School. Photograph by David MacDougall.

importance in the lives of the students. These included abstract concepts such as hierarchy and threats to personal identity, but also more immediate topics of school life such as clothing, eating, informal games, and organized sports. I found another conceptual key in the phenomenon of homesickness, which was succeeded among older students by what they themselves called "schoolsickness." I next focused on certain classes of objects that seemed to be focal points in the aesthetics of everyday life. These included uniforms, the stainless steel utensils already mentioned, trophies and prizes of various kinds, beds and bedcovers, and semi-illicit dormitory foods (or "tuck"). Lastly, I decided to follow the activities of first-year students in an attempt to "discover" the school through their own discovery of it. In one instance, I spent three months filming a group of these students from their first day at the school. Here I concentrated on certain individuals, trying to see how they learned the rules and became sensitized to the school as a complex environment.

Over a period of two years I spent nine months at the school, recording some eighty-five hours of material. This might be thought to constitute a kind of visual ethnography of school life, but because I was pursuing particular interests rather than attempting to be encyclopedic, it falls short of that in many respects. There is little about the teachers, and the footage is disproportionately about younger and middle students rather than older ones. Within the youngest group, a few individuals receive a great deal of attention. In selecting them I was more concerned that they were expressive of their condition than representative in any statistical sense. As we know, anthropologists often select their informants from those who stand out in a crowd, but this is perhaps even more the case in visual anthropology, where one looks for people who are particularly eloquent in their relations with others, either in speech or manner.

At the beginning I identified certain boys who were expressive or distinctive in some way. This eventually led me to a group of four fourteen-year-olds who shared a room together. I had noticed at least three of them already, so to find them sharing a room was a welcome discovery. In a similar way, I was led to two others who were to figure prominently in the first film. The older of these, a sixteen-year-old, was already an important figure around the school, noted for his self-assurance and skill as an actor in school plays. In the film he became the exception who tended to prove the rules about peer pressure and conformity. He had successfully made a name for himself by being different from others and going his own way as a forceful but sensitive person. He was never good at sports, the safest avenue to success and power at the school. But his view differed from that of Vikram Seth, the writer, who had been unhappy at the school in the 1960s and who felt it was not a good place for a sensitive person.[44]

> I found myself thinking: Is this true that if you don't play a sport you can't survive? So very early on I took the attitude that, "I'm not going to play a sport, but I'm definitely going to survive." And—you can. It's all about being at rhythm with yourself, being at peace with yourself, not really caring if you're popular amongst 90% of your classmates or not. I mean, it's very important to have your friends, and your soul mates, and the people you can really talk to, which you sometimes desperately need in school. But no, I don't think it's a hard and fast rule that if you're sensitive you can't survive in school.[45]

A younger boy whom I noticed at an early stage also became a prominent figure in one of the films. I began filming him on my first brief visit, perhaps because he seemed to regard everything around him with the same mixture of trepidation and curiosity that I felt toward the school, but also with an eagerness to adapt himself to it. He radiated a sort of nervous courage. In the film he was to become a different type of survivor: one who accepts the school at face value but who delights in it, who tries everything and takes as much from the school as the school has to offer.

Among my tactics during my early days was to seek advice about possible subjects for filming from the teachers, particularly some of the younger ones who had formed close ties with the boys under their care. The following notes may give some idea of the variety of comments I received from one such teacher. They are given here almost as they appear in my note-book, minus of course the names. At the time I knew none of these boys.

Boy A: Tough, open, expressive, a little scatter-brained, good at drama & sports.

Boy B: Good-looking, willing, competent, good all-rounder, a leader.

Boy C: Mature, articulate, clear ideas, excellent boy.

Boy D: Outgoing, mature, excellent academically, computer expert.

Boy E: Quiet, introverted, but strong boxer, good at soccer; English weak, on scholarship.

Boy F: Very academic, good singer, from rich family but unassuming.

Boy G: Precocious, bright, self-conscious, friendly, sweet.

Boy H: Shy, a recent arrival.

Boy I: Tense, rather stressed, insecure, subject to teasing.

Boy J: Has adapted well.

Boy K: From the hills, good sportsman, leader, photographer.

Boy L: Small, silent, mature, won't be pushed around.

Boy M: Pleasant, academic inclinations.

Boy N: Mischievous, lively, nice, weak academically.

Boy O: Seeks bad company, troublesome, anti-academic.

Boy P: Very decent, dignified boy, nonathletic.

Boy Q: Mature, strong ideas, clear thinker, a leader.

Boy R: Easygoing, comic.

Boy S: Boisterous, popular, lively, funny.

Boy T: Academic, not an extrovert, good talker, gets on well.

I was fortunate to have the trust of the new headmaster, who gave me the run of the school. I was allowed to live there, take my meals with the students, and film where and what I wanted. There was never an attempt to direct or censor my work. The teachers were somewhat more guarded, but perhaps because I rarely filmed them, I was able to establish good relations with most of them and friendships with several. It was under-stood that I was engaged in a long-term research project, but the headmas-ter also saw my presence as an opportunity to create a greater awareness of visual media at the school. As one way of contributing to this I trained a small group of students to produce their own video journal.

I came to know two successive groups of first-year students better than any other students at the school, although for one period I made a point of focusing on the group of four older students (fourteen-year-olds in B form) who shared a room together. Here I was attempting to achieve greater breadth, both because they were older and because, as a group, they varied greatly from one another in personality, background, and ma-turity. These boys always maintained a certain reserve toward me. The

4.7. A group of first-year boys in Foot House. Photograph by David MacDougall.

younger boys were more unconcerned and came to regard the filming as a routine part of dormitory life. Perhaps because I was never a teacher at the school and only rarely exercised a teacher's authority, I was accepted more readily as a harmless observer, and very occasionally as an honorary schoolboy (figure 4.7).

From this material would come five "public" films and additional compilations of footage for specialist interests, such as studies of children's games and pastimes. I have made other compilations in order to return the material to the boys themselves and to their parents. From the parents' point of view this is a precious resource. Most of them long to see what has been happening to their children, growing up rapidly in a world that remains largely closed to them. From the boys' point of view, the films are both a memory bank and a confirmation of what I have told them of my aims. One boy wrote to me: "I am going to treasure [the film] for my life. After all nobody is so lucky to have a film of his school days."

Although I soon focused my study on something other than cross-cultural topics at the school, the project remains cross-cultural in several respects. First, and most obviously, it registers my encounter as an outsider with one small microcosm (among many) of contemporary Indian life. It also explores the intersection of India's colonial past with its present national identity and, at another level, the school's intersection, as a cultural enclave, with the wider Indian community. Most importantly, perhaps, it is cross-cultural because it involves childhood and what is increasingly seen by anthropologists as a significant separation between the cultural worlds of children and adults. In the case of a boarding school, this separation is made all the more acute by the added distance between family and institutional life.

The Doon School project, like many similar studies, can be seen as part of a larger effort internationally to apply visual media to fields such as anthropology, sociology, and history that have traditionally developed as disciplines of words. They are intended partly to explore alternative approaches to these disciplines, both as a method of research and as a means of professional publication. But to a greater degree, their purpose is to find out whether the use of visual media will in fact transform these disciplines, leading to forms of knowledge that were not envisaged before. The present project provides one more test of these possibilities. I can say at least that it was through the use of the video camera that I discovered new interests and was directed away from more naïvely preconceived ones.

If the study of social aesthetics sometimes seems quixotic, this is not, I believe, because it is an obscure or illusory part of human experience but because, on the contrary, it is both very obvious and yet highly dispersed through a wide range of cultural phenomena, many of which have already been closely studied in other contexts such as the anthropology of art and cultural history. Perhaps for that very reason, the broader aesthetic aspects of social life, and aesthetic experience itself, appear to many scholars to have been adequately accounted for as aspects of something else. To a certain extent this is the logical consequence of the fragmentation of academic fields, but it also has to do with the constraints of expression. Most description in the human sciences is beholden to the writing skills of scholars. To describe the social role of aesthetics properly (its phenomenological reality) we may need a "language" closer to the multidimensionality of the subject itself—that is, a language operating in visual, aural, verbal, temporal, and even (through synesthetic association) tactile domains. To me, this suggests a new line of approach to what has long been inadequately called "visual" anthropology. It is an approach that has the potential to restore to anthropology the material world within which culture takes its forms.

Notes

My thanks to the following people for reading and commenting on earlier versions of this paper: Kalissa Alexeyeff, Roger Benjamin, Dipesh Chakrabarty, Mary Eagle, Chris Gregory, Judith MacDougall, Howard Morphy, J. David Sapir, John Shannon, Sanjay Srivastava, Lucien Taylor, and Salim Yusufji.

1. See Benedict 1928, 1934. In *Naven*, Gregory Bateson acknowledged his debt to Benedict while proposing several hypotheses for the "standardizing" of the psychology of individuals in a society. See Bateson 1936: 112–14.

2. See Feld 1982, Stoller 1989, 1997, Howes 1991.

3. See, for example, Scoditti 1982, Forrest 1988, O'Hanlon 1989, Coote & Shelton 1992.

4. See Turner 1981, Kapferer 1983, Herzfeld 1985, Hardin 1993, K. Stewart 1996. Earlier, Erving Goffman (1959, 1967) convincingly analyzed social interactions in terms of performance. (For related work, see Brown & Levinson 1987.)

5. See Desjarlais 1992, Alter 1992. Desjarlais's approach intersects with mine, but somewhat obliquely, since his focus is more upon the physical and psychic state of the individual than upon the physical and social environment.

6. See Marcus & Cushman 1982; Marcus & Fischer 1986. The more radical approaches include experiments in intertextuality and juxtaposition such as Michael Taussig's *Shamanism, Colonialism, and the Wild Man* (1987) and Oscar Lewis's oral autobiographical transcriptions (see O. Lewis 1961, 1964, 1967).

7. In particular, such films as *Les maîtres fous* (1955), *Moi, un noir* (1957), *La goumbé des jeunes noceurs* (1965), and the cycle of *Sigui* films (1966–73).

8. A film that provoked anthropological outrage (as well as praise) was Robert Gardner's *Forest of Bliss* (1985). In documentary films there is a long history of interest in exploring the aesthetics of everyday life, dating back at least to the "city symphonies" of Vertov, Ruttman, and Cavalcanti, and continuing in such postwar films as Rouquier's *Farrebique* (1947). Ethnographic filmmakers have tended to approach the subject more indirectly through material culture, ritual, and art, perhaps considering it insufficiently recognized as a topic of social analysis. But interest in this aspect of social experience is certainly evident in the films of Robert Flaherty, if not earlier, and is explicit in Basil Wright's *Song of Ceylon* (1934). It was also a concern of Gregory Bateson in his studies with Margaret Mead of Balinese society in the 1930s. Although Jorge Preloran's *Imaginero* (1970) is ostensibly about a craftsman and artist, the film explores his larger aesthetic world comprehensively, as do other Preloran films, such as *Zerda's Children* (1978), about an impoverished family of woodcutters. One problem for filmmakers has been how to distinguish their own aesthetic responses from those of their subjects. Another has been how to separate the broader aspects of cultural style from a society's officially consecrated aesthetic practices. Still another is how to define aesthetic experience in contrast to "nonaesthetic" experience. This is a very large subject that I plan to treat at length elsewhere.

9. Ong 1991: 29.

10. A concept proposed by Mallory Wober. See Wober 1966, 1991.

11. See Coote 1992. E. E. Evans-Pritchard (1940: 16–50) and Neville Dyson-Hudson (1966: 96–103) had already devoted some attention to the aesthetic role of cattle among the Nuer and Karimojong, respectively.

12. See Bloch 1974, G. Lewis 1980, Jackson 1989.

13. It is of course possible to argue that these other aspects of life often function as works of art, as Gell (1995) argues in his response to Coote (1992) on the aesthetic role of cattle in African pastoralist societies, but in the end this is perhaps a category dispute. For another view, see Kupfer 1983.

14. Morphy 1996: 255.

15. This is succinctly expressed in the 1948 Founder's Day speech at Doon School by the Governor General of the United Provinces, Shri Rajagopalachari: "It is wrong to think that science teaches only science. Science brings about a change in the whole attitude of boys. It brings about correct judgment, alertness and obedience to laws" (*The Doon School Weekly*, 30 October 1948).

16. Srivastava, 1998. I began the video project in 1997. *Doon School Chronicles*, the first part, was completed in 1999 and released in 2000.

17. Among those who have discussed the aesthetics of ultranationalist states are Umberto Eco (1977), Klaus Theweleit (1987), Boris Groys (1992), Vladislav Todorov (1995), Susan Buck-Morss (1994), and Alla Efimova (1997).

18. See Gell 1995: 21–22.

19. Bourdieu 1990a: 56.

20. Ibid., p. 60.

21. Ibid., p. 52.

22. Ibid., p. 9.

23. Todorov 1995: 10–11.

24. See Rosselli 1980; Sinha 1995.

25. *The Doon School Weekly*, 13 November 1937: 3.

26. *The Doon School Book*, 1949, reprinted in Chopra 1996: 40.

27. Foot wrote: "By 14 he should have learnt all the ordinary principles of social behaviour. He should know how to stand up and speak to a variety of different types of people—to his own mother, to someone else's mother, to his father, to his schoolmasters, to servants, to Mahatma Gandhi or to the Viceroy, and to do this without any self-consciousness." From "Fourteen," *Doon School Magazine*, 1938.

28. *The Doon School Weekly*, 13 March 1937: 1.

29. *The Doon School Weekly*, 20 June 1936: 1.

30. "We believe that character-training is more a matter of organisation than instruction. . . . The purpose is achieved not by precept or instruction, but by creating an environment in which a boy is led to do things for himself." *The Doon School Book*, 1949, reprinted in Chopra 1996: 40.

31. Srivastava 1998: 60.

32. Srivastava devotes considerable attention to this topic. See especially chapters 3 and 5.

33. For Clifford Geertz, the task of anthropology is "scratching surfaces" by examining the representations people make about their lives, and it is a piece of bad faith to try to go further (Geertz 1986: 373). My view is that it is important to try to go further if we are to go beyond the play of textual understandings to a more physically grounded understanding. One reservation about hermeneutic anthropology is its selective focus upon what are considered to be exemplary cultural performances (or "performed texts"). This approach is seen as a way of exposing indigenous symbolic systems and as a guarantee that the objects of study are "socially constructed units of meaning" rather than ethnocentric projections of the investigator (Bruner 1986: 7). However, the underpinning of this selectivity (usually of highly ritualized and emotionally heightened events) presupposes an equivalence between the meanings of such events and the conduct of everyday

life. The problem is not that interpretive studies produce sterile exegeses, or that the events themselves are unilluminating about the assumptions and modes of self-representation of a society, but that they may convey to us rather little about actually living in it. The fear of the hermeneuticists is that too close an experience-near focus leaves the anthropologist "awash in immediacies" (Geertz 1983: 57), but it is in fact very much the task of the visual anthropologist to deal in such immediacies and to fashion out of them a work of analysis.

34. Bourdieu 1990a: 18. Bourdieu also refers to this form of understanding, which need never rise to the level of consciousness, as "learned ignorance" (ibid., p. 19). Anthony Forge (1970: 289) makes a related observation in the case of Abelam iconography, which he believes is meant to produce an effect upon its viewers "directly" rather than through its symbolic meanings—a view quite opposed to the "cryptological paradigm" of cultural description, to use Chris Pinney's phrase (1995: 94).

35. *The Doon School Weekly*, 23 May 1936: 1.

36. *The Doon School Weekly Supplement*, 27 May 1944.

37. *The Doon School Weekly*, 13 November 1937: 3.

38. *The Doon School Weekly*, 7 March 1936: 2.

39. *The Doon School Weekly*, 27 February 1937: 1.

40. In 1969 the school began awarding students a black blazer for high academic achievement as a counterbalance to the blue blazer, awarded since 1940 for achievement in sports. Clothing is also a feature of school punishments, such as the "change-in-break" described at the end of this section.

41. A. N. Dar, "The Ethos of Sport in Doon School," *The Doon School Weekly*, 1 November 1985: 5.

42. "The Moving Finger Writes, and Having Writ, Moves On," *The Doon School Weekly*, 6 April 1985: 2.

43. A *thali* is a meal served on a large, circular stainless steel tray made with indentations to hold the portions of the various foods.

44. Vikram Seth, Founder's Day Speech, Doon School, 1992.

45. Personal communication, 14 November 1997.

5

DOON SCHOOL RECONSIDERED

I N THE PREVIOUS chapter I described the sequence of films that I
began to make at The Doon School in northern India in 1997. When
I wrote it the project was far from complete. I had done most of the
filming, but I had edited only one film. I was launched on a second, and
eventually there would be five. In this chapter I shall try to give an account
of how the project developed in its later stages and how it appears in
retrospect with the completion of the fifth film, *The Age of Reason*.

There are several aspects of the Doon School project that I feel, perhaps
unreasonably, I should have understood better at an earlier stage. Although I was aware of a shift in my perceptions of the school soon after
I started, I was unaware for some time of a more gradual shift that was
taking place in how I was filming it. The actual experience of filming was
in fact changing a number of my ideas about the characteristics of social
spaces. Secondly, I failed to see the connection between this project and
my filming projects in Africa some thirty years earlier, although the link
now seems obvious. Trying to reconstruct the Doon School project has
become part of the project itself, which I hope will guide me in the future.
Perhaps for others it will illustrate how ventures of this kind are affected
by changes in one's persepctive and in what one finds important.

Filming at Doon School

The anthropologist Sanjay Srivastava first suggested the idea of filming at
Doon School, the most famous boarding school for boys in India.[1] He had
spent some months there in 1991–93 doing the research for his doctoral
dissertation on three prominent boarding schools in northern India—
schools which, despite their different origins, had in many ways con-
verged in their educational philosophy. His interest was in how these
schools had reflected and helped define notions of the modern Indian citizen and had served as a staging ground for India's postcolonial elite. He
saw the schools, and Doon in particular, as places where differences that
threatened to split the Indian intelligentsia, and indeed the nation, were

domesticated in the interests of maintaining that group's dominance. This was consistent with the school's origins, as a copy of the English public school on Indian soil, created by an Indian professional class that had largely benefited from British rule.

My interests developed along different lines, but at the start I had in mind the not unrelated idea of finding out how students of different backgrounds got on together within the dominant culture of the school. Was it possible for friendships to be created across social and cultural boundaries? The school seemed full of contradictions—an institution that sought to promote egalitarian principles within a hierarchy, Indian culture within a British model, and old-fashioned liberal values against the pressures of a rapidly globalizing youth culture.

The idea of filming at a school appealed to me for other reasons as well. I had been to a boarding school myself. Although it was very different from Doon, it seemed to me that boarding school students had certain fundamental experiences in common, not least of which was the experience of having to adapt themselves to a communal life.[3] How to represent children's lives also interested me as a problem, for I had never before taken a group of children as my primary subject. My impression was that fiction filmmakers had done a better job of depicting childhood than documentary filmmakers. Whether or not one agreed with that, films about children generally seemed to me more patronizing than those about adults, as if children were more predictable or of lesser consequence, both to society and in themselves. Children were often indulged in films, as well as sentimentalized, but they were rarely developed fully as individuals. I felt that if I paid close attention, I might be able to show some aspects of childhood that had not been adequately filmed before, or at least show children behaving in less clichéd ways than I had seen in other films.

At first I looked for television funding to make such a film. I found some support for this at the Australian Broadcasting Corporation and the BBC. Both gave me verbal commitments to co-finance the film, but I soon discovered that they were less interested in the film I would make than in the overall topic of the school itself, and even this held limited interest for them. When the BBC commissioning editor who had first encouraged me was replaced, I followed up the idea with his successor, only to have it dismissed in a brief fax message, saying, "there have been films about British equivalents, and they never really seem to work —I just don't feel the subject is energising enough."[4] I realized that although hundreds of different films could be made about a school, it was probably pointless to argue that how I made the film, or what it was about, mattered. Television doesn't work that way.

The rebuff proved to be a liberation. I had originally planned to make the film in 16mm, but by 1996 we were at the beginning of the digital video revolution. I realized that I did not have to use film, that I did not even have to make a "film" as it was understood in any conventional sense. Instead, I began to think about a long-term study of the school using a video camera as my means of inquiry. What would emerge from this I did not know, and therein lay one of its attractions. I was not tied to a script or a deadline or a commissioning editor looking over my shoulder. I could do this work within a modest university research budget, at a tiny fraction of the cost of my previous film, which had been a BBC co-production.[5]

When one hears of a film or television series, or even a series of books, one tends to think of an ordered progression. The separate parts may be built around a single character, or they may follow a set of characters chronologically, as in soap operas and drama series. Successful films lead to sequels and even prequels. Documentary series usually present a succession of historical or cultural figures, or else they develop a historical theme or argument over a number of episodes.[6]

The Doon School project resulted in a series of five films, but they were never organized in such a linear way. [7] In fact, they are tied together according to several different kinds of logic. When I began the project I did not know how many films I would make, nor their probable lengths, nor even how they would relate to one another. This emerged over time through a more organic, even fortuitous process. I had considered a chronological approach, but I was also aware that it was possible to create a cluster rather than a string of works, as Lawrence Durrell had shown in his Alexandria Quartet. In a series such as this, the parts comment on one another more obliquely and expand laterally rather than longitudinally. One can see or read them in any order, and the order one chooses produces different perceptions and paths of discovery. I had had one previous experience of structuring films in this way when making the Turkana Conversations trilogy in northern Kenya. This consisted of a narrative film, a portrait film, and a film constructed as an essay.[8] Although the trilogy was not a direct model for the Doon project, it no doubt influenced it.

At Doon School I decided against any overarching plan, believing that it might impose a false structure on what I found, or at the very least blind me to the alternatives. I felt that the filming should be an inquiry leading to a structure, not a structure demonstrating the ideas I had started with. I wanted to find out what it was possible to learn about the school by filming it. When students asked me what I was doing, I told them I was studying the life of the school, but instead of writing a book about it I was going to try to write it with my camera. Was this sophistry? It was the best explanation I could find, and it seemed to make sense to them.

As a filmmaker, I was aware of the difficulties of working within both an academic and a personal paradigm. However, I wanted to hold in equilibrium the elements of my intellectual and emotional life, so that each could guide rather than dominate the other. I believed that scholarship should be an expression of one's sensibilities as well as one's mind. Perhaps this was always an unattainable ideal; there would always be a process of alternating excess and correction between these impulses. As I look back on the project, I see that this was indeed the case, that the way I conducted the project, and even my reflections on it, occupy two different areas of understanding, perhaps never to be reconciled. I see faces, and I am lost in them. I must drag myself back to find any "reason" in them.

Two Contrasting Films: *Doon School Chronicles* and *With Morning Hearts*

I have described in the last chapter how my interest in the school soon shifted from thinking of it as a cultural crossroads to seeing it, despite all its ambiguities, as a homogeneous community exhibiting the strong aesthetic patterns and concerns that are characteristic of what Goffman called "total institutions"—mental hospitals, prisons, religious orders, ships at sea, military organizations, and, not least, boarding schools. Although such institutions are connected to the rest of society, I had come to the conclusion that aesthetic considerations were a significant force in their sense of identity and governance, and that the principles that applied to them might apply to human societies more widely.

This interest in social aesthetics was foremost in my mind as I filmed *Doon School Chronicles*, which by this time was taking shape as a study of the school's social and physical environment, ideology, and student hierarchy. I found that part of what interested me could be shown by observing the school's rituals and quoting from historical documents that I found in the school archives, using these as epigraphs for each of the film's ten "chapters." For the rest, I needed to follow individual students in order to understand their experience of the school at a sensory, emotional, and intellectual level. When one does this, it is not so much that one sees through their eyes or feels their feelings but that one is present with them, sharing a consciousness of their surroundings and the social forces bearing on them (figure 5.1).

I wanted to listen to them, as well. I found two boys who expressed their ideas about the school clearly and could present their own critiques of school life. One was a thirteen-year-old, Rohan, who turned out to be an amateur sociologist. When I asked him if the composition of the school's student body had changed over the years, he told me he had made a study of this. In earlier days, he said, most boys came from professional families in the big cities, or from the rural landowning class. Increasingly they were coming from smaller towns, the sons of newly successful busi-

5.1. A Doon School dormitory. From *Doon School Chronicles* (2000).

nessmen. At home they were more likely to speak Hindi or another Indian language than English. I asked him if this meant the school had become more Indian. "Not more Indian," he said, "but less cosmopolitan."

Another student, Veer, age sixteen, was a nonconformist who had nevertheless made a success of the school on his own terms. He was an actor, writer, and theater director. He even staged his own video production, which in my film becomes a sort of film-within-the-film. In contrast to him, I found a younger boy, Arjun, who was making a success of the school through the very things that Veer repudiated, such as sports. Then there was another boy whom I could never understand, who seemed to me to pose a mystery. Although at times funny and sociable, Rishabh appeared to live in his own inner world. I kept him in the film for the very reason that I found him opaque, a sign of the limits of this kind of inquiry or my ability to go beyond them. Later I saw that I had cast as my protagonists an intellectual, an artist, a sportsman, and a dreamer. When I came to edit the material, I was faced with the problem of how to maintain a sense of forward movement in the film and at the same time develop this diverse cast of characters. I eventually solved this by introducing them in gradual stages and then progressively drawing them together toward the end of the film. Thus Arjun makes his appearance only in chapter 6, and the development of Veer is held off until chapter 8, although he appears once in an earlier scene.

It is clear to me now that *Doon School Chronicles* is very much a hybrid, tending in one direction toward analysis and abstraction and in another toward a more experiential grasp of students' lives. It also serves as a web in which the other films are suspended. Its experiential aspect reflects the shift that I was already beginning to make in the second Doon film. The scenes in this mode are typically filmed more casually and intimately, whereas the abstract scenes tend toward more formally constructed studies of the material and ritualized aspects of school life. One of these latter scenes, focusing on the school's preoccupation with bodily prowess, is the most impressionistic of all.[9] Here, as elsewhere in the film, I began including still images, to produce in the viewer the sense of time being suddenly suspended. I hoped that the shock of these images would give greater physical immediacy to people and objects and make more evident how the vitality of the present is at every moment slipping into an irrecoverable past. I hoped also that they would force one to inspect the contents of the images in a fresh way.

I took the title of the next film, *With Morning Hearts*, from one of the prayers regularly read out at school assemblies. As it implies, the emphasis of the film is on the emotional life of boys who are just beginning their careers at the school. The prayer reads in part:

> Go with each of us to rest;
> If any awake, temper to them
> The dark hours of watching;
> And when the day returns,
> Return to us our sun and comforter,
> And call us up with morning faces
> And with morning hearts,
> Eager to labour, eager to be happy
> If happiness shall be our portion,
> And if the day be marked for sorrow,
> Strong to endure it.[10]

The boys I filmed were a group of thirty twelve-year-olds staying in Foot House, one of the two "holding houses" where new boys are put for their first year. There was a dark side to the prayer. It adjures the boys to suffer bravely the fears and loneliness that beset them at night and even into the day. I began making this film almost simultaneously with *Doon School Chronicles*, and it indicates the direction that the rest of the project was to take. However, it grew quite naturally out of the first film, for I had wandered into Foot House one day to get out of the rain. I found there a community that seemed more self-contained and coherent than any I had so far seen at the school, partly because the boys were all about the same age. They accepted me quite readily and I soon began filming regularly in the house. As time went on they gave me access to increasingly diverse and intimate aspects of their lives.

The house itself was an old colonial bungalow with three long rooms that served as dormitories. It had cement floors, twenty-foot ceilings, and civet cats living in the roof. A fourth long room was filled with the boys' desks, which at Doon School are called "toyes." There was a separate bath house at the back and an unkempt field where the boys played improvised games of cricket and "pittoo." I lived just beside this, in a building that contained flats for guests and a few teachers. It was almost like living in the house itself.

There is very little crossover between the first two films. In fact, one catches only the briefest glimpse of the Foot House boys in *Doon School Chronicles*. I was somehow able to keep the two films entirely separate in my planning and thinking. It was like living in two worlds, one the enclosed and intimate space of a first-year dormitory, with all its small-scale details and dramas, the other the larger world of the school as a whole. And yet in many ways the dormitory was for me the larger world, richer in individual lives and more deeply experienced. Paradoxically, Karam, the boy who soon emerged as the main protagonist in the film, was someone I hardly knew at the time, nor in fact ever knew very well. All the same, I found in him an expression of many of the feelings that the others were keeping to themselves. He was the smallest of the group and seemingly the most vulnerable. I could tell he was often unhappy, but I was touched by his courage in living with his unhappiness. As he told me, he managed his life in such a way as to keep himself busy and not to disappoint his family, who had placed great hopes in him.

It was at this time that I began to understand what children could teach me about the strengths and skills they develop early in life. It was also a lesson in what children have to give up, or unlearn, in the process of becoming adults. I realized that what I most admired in children was their surprising versatility compared to adults, their "experimental" side, their way of working out a view of the world as they live it, as they speak about it. I sometimes felt that to show this it would have been sufficient just to film some of these boys talking, although my training as a filmmaker insisted this was not enough. As much as I pushed it aside, as much as I resisted its limitations, this image continued to invade my filmmaking at the school. At first, in place of the students talking to me, I preferred to film them talking to each other, but in the later films I arrived at a more equitable acceptance of both.

With Morning Hearts marks a shift away from an abstract interest in social aesthetics to a more direct practical interest in how it is manifested in the experience of self, place, and sociality. For the boys I was filming, the process of making Foot House their own meant exploring all of these things. Filming them was a way of allowing the viewer to discover the school as they were discovering it, but it was also a way of examining the smaller worlds within the school: the world of the dormitory and the world that surrounds each boy. It is perhaps emblematic of this that Karam constructs a "room" out of the area around his bed, and indeed within the carapace of his own personality. Foot House, in the severity of its interiors, in its limited colors and textures, expressed for me even more strongly than the school at large the influence of a physical environment on the consciousness of individuals. For their part, the boys seemed inexhaustible in the variety of their responses to their setting and to one another. More interesting to me than how they adapted to the school was how, thrown together from their separate families, they struggled to reinvent themselves as a community in an alien place. No doubt my interest in this derived in part from my own years of boarding school life, for even today when I dream, I almost never dream about living in a family. I am part of a group, often among strangers—a collection of people trying to make a life together.

Perhaps because it is so obvious, it is easy to forget that people not only inhabit social spaces but also create them. Our sensory worlds are to a large extent defined by the presence of others. Each group of people has its own specific gravity—whether this be a crowd in a subway, a group of university students, or children in a playground. Even one or two people in a room change it as an environment. Our awareness of others varies according to how close they are, their appearance and actions, their actual relationship to us, and how we feel toward them. We may distinguish them as individuals or simply sense their presence as an undifferentiated mass. We may feel aversion or attraction to them. Among them, we are always both participants and observers.

One of the difficulties with the "total institution" model of a school, and indeed with other models of institutions based on their structure or symbolism, is that it risks leaving out of its imagining the actual physical presence of human beings, as though institutions were mainly defined by their administration and architecture. But the weight of an institution exists as much in the massed bodies of its members as in the rituals they perform, the traditions they observe, or the material setting they inhabit. A school without its students is a ghost of itself. Moreover, human beings are not merely a physical ballast (although this is important) but a social and psychological presence, the sum of their different backgrounds and personalities. It became apparent to me that to try to describe the character of Foot House as an institutional space was absurd without taking into account the boys who filled its rooms and hallways. The house was saturated with their presence, an amalgam of their faces, bodies, movements, gestures, and voices, further concentrated by the fact that they were all of about the same age. Within the range of different masculinities represented in the school, the house radiated its own distinctive sort, poised somewhere between childhood and adolescence. I felt it was important to try to capture the character of this particular strain of Indian boyhood, whose basic pattern was worked out with variations in each one of them.

In their first year, Doon School students are still partly isolated from the rest of the school. Although they mix with older students throughout the day, they do not yet live with them. One of the teachers told me: "These boys are in a transitional period. They are still under the influence of their home lives. As soon as they shift to the main house they will be completely changed, completely transformed by the school culture." This was a frequent refrain: the boys would change. But it was often unclear which changes were due to adolescence and which to the influence of the school. What was clear was that when they moved into one of the school's five main houses they would be exposed to the full force of the school's institutional culture.

This culture was as much a creation of the students as of the school's founders, teachers, and headmasters. It was a culture that had grown, adapted, and in many ways sustained itself as a separate organism within the school's official culture, and it required the constant induction of new members. It would therefore be a mistake to see the Doon students as merely acted upon by the institution. Almost from the beginning they were complicit in their relation to it. As the new students learned the school's ways, they were already becoming its agents and preparing themselves to pass on what they had learned to the next set of newcomers. (This was formalized in the assignment of "guardians" from the second year to boys in the first year, immediately upon their arrival.) Much of this acceptance was due to the fame of the school and the sense of superiority it bred in its students and would-be students. Being a Dosco promised success and advantages in one's future career. Most students were willing to suffer the indignities and loss of personal identity this sometimes imposed on them in exchange for the rewards to come later. There were also immediate rewards, beyond the prestige one gained outside the school from being a Doon student. In negotiating their way through the school's countless competitions, prizes, and petty sanctions (largely administered by other students), each boy became the manager of his own program of transformation. In doing so he reaffirmed and reinforced the entire system.

The school culture was by no means static. It was in a continual state of being reinvented by the students as they adapted it to trends in the wider world and the youth culture they had brought with them. But the changes were incremental. They were seen as small modifications of a tradition, as were the changes introduced by the headmaster or other school authorities. Thus, for each student entering the school, its customs and rules seemed timeless. Much of the attraction of these customs lay in their exclusivity—the codes, however pointless in themselves, that marked one as a Dosco. Over the years the students had evolved their own argot, which each new boy was quick to learn. There were senior boys who were scoping ("scopats," angling for authority) and lendy boys ("lends," happy to do "favors" for seniors, a little too eager to please). "Jamming" meant skipping an event (cutting class or Assembly), but "jamming up" was making a mess of things. To cog and to crib and to bunk all had meanings that differed from usage outside the school.

Language was but one of these codes. Along with other aspects of the school's regime and aesthetics—such as the color and cut of uniforms, the use of numbers for boys and acronyms for teachers, the rituals of deference and punishment—it was part of a wider system of exclusivity, so that even practices that were irritating to the boys assumed (especially in the nostalgic minds of Old Boys) a certain distinction. New boys assimilated these patterns gradually, so that what at first were fleeting experiences gained increasing significance and power in their lives through steady repetition. The insistent messages of these codes were subliminal and often quite different from their avowed purposes. The boys were hardly aware of their effects.

I soon realized that my task was not simply to depict school life, in the hope of somehow conveying it transparently from observed behavior to film. Rather, it was to produce a distillation more intense and more selective than observation, as I (and the students) experienced it and as I tried to make sense of it through the camera. By doing this, I believe nonfiction films can move beyond the simulacra of documents to a more analytical and, at the same time, more personally engaged understanding. The Doon School films focus on certain themes and objects: faces, bodies, clothing, colors, food, beds, and so on. These elements, as in any institution, form a physical environment open to the senses. But a school is also an environment of the emotions. There were certain pivotal moments in dormitory life: waking, dressing, studying, bathing, resting, and intense physical activity. These formed a routine within which it was possible to film how the boys organized the spaces around them, cared for their few belongings, and expressed their physical and social awareness of one another. These were also occasions for filming characteristic expressions of playfulness, joy, aggression, anger, tenderness, loneliness, and mutual support.

5.2. Karam during his last lunch as a Foot House boy.
From *With Morning Hearts* (2001).

Although one can capture specific emotional states on film, it is perhaps only through narrative, both extended and small-scale, that one can grasp emotion as a more integral part of social life. When I was editing *With Morning Hearts* I showed it to a historian friend. I told him that I thought the film was fundamentally about attachment to a place. The boys leave their families, form an attachment to Foot House, and are then forced to leave it a year later when they are moved into the school's main houses. He suggested I was wrong—that the film was really about their attachment to one another. I realized then that the house, while it unconsciously colored almost every aspect of their lives, became important to them in quite a different manner in retrospect, as an embodiment of the social relationships that had developed within it. Foot House, when they were about to leave it, was already being transformed from the Foot House that they inhabited to a memory (figure 5.2).

A crucial person in the making of *With Morning Hearts* and several of the later films was the director of the school's outreach Teachers' Centre and a tutor at Foot House, Minakshi Basu. With her I endlessly discussed the boys' personalities and backgrounds, and how they were adapting to the school. Although she was formally attached to the house and was responsible for overseeing the progress of about half its students, her own house was always open to all of them. In her, many of the boys found a wise and understanding counselor. She was responsive to the qualities of each of them, and unlike so many adults at the school, she never talked down to them or treated them summarily or with disrespect. It was her matter-of-fact acceptance of them as they were that inspired their trust. At first I looked to her for information and guidance, but I soon began to see a role for her in the films. In *With Morning Hearts* and two of the other films she comments on the boys' lives—an astute and knowledgeable observer. Because of our shared concerns, her voice at times seems almost to merge with my voice.

The other adults in the house were Ashad and Abia Qezilbash, its house master and house mistress (or "dame," in school parlance). Like Minakshi Basu, Ashad comments on the boys' lives in the films, but somewhat more generally. His importance to *With Morning Hearts* and *The New Boys* lies more in his direct interactions with the boys, whom he encourages to solve their own problems and treats with kindness and consideration even in moments of frustration. He resisted the "barking" style of addressing boys that was favored by many of the teachers and housemasters at the school.

Three Comparative Films: *With Morning Hearts,*
Karam in Jaipur, and *The New Boys*

With the making of *With Morning Hearts* I was committed to a new direction in the project; or perhaps in the making of it I had been captured by my subject. The idea of focusing on first-year students had initially been a strategy for gaining a newcomer's view of the school. Now it was raising questions for me about human development and human capabilities, for this period of preadolescence seemed to mark a high point of proficiency and self-confidence, and yet also to herald the first stirrings of adult compromise and self-limitation. I felt it offered more than enough scope for exploring these countervailing forces in the school and in individual students.

Karam in Jaipur reflected these interests. It is a sequel to *With Morning Hearts*, the only film in the series to be a direct continuation of another. I wanted to follow Karam into the next phase of his school life, when he leaves the "holding house" and joins Jaipur House, one of the school's five main houses. I had at first intended to make this material part of *With Morning Hearts*, as it would have preserved the unity of Karam's story, but I soon saw that the film was not fundamentally about Karam, even though he was prominent in it. It was important that *With Morning*

Hearts end with the entire group vacating Foot House. I made *Karam in Jaipur* in order to look more closely at the next stages of self-discovery and self-discipline. I also made it for Karam. I wanted to give him a film to take home that showed him succeeding at something. In one sense the film is a footnote to the previous film, but taken on its own it perhaps gives a more rounded picture of the life of a Doon schoolboy than any of the other films. It also allows one to compare life in one of the main houses with the "holding house" that Karam has just left. In the main house Karam learns new rules, plays hockey, studies, sings, contends with older students, and looks for some way of making his mark. He finds it in gymnastics, for which he has a particular aptitude.

After Karam's group left Foot House a new group of twenty-eight students was due to arrive to take their place. Outwardly the situation had changed little, with the same housemaster and house mistress in residence. I assumed that the backgrounds of the new boys would be much the same as the earlier group. I decided to make the next film about this new group, to provide a direct comparison with the one shown in *With Morning Hearts*. I wanted to see if the two groups differed, and if so how. And unlike my filming of Karam's group, I planned to be present from the moment they arrived. I imagined these two films forming a pair.

In filming *The New Boys* I was surprised to find that the social dynamics of the new group were quite different from those of the previous group. The boys seemed more divided, argumentative, and class-conscious. There was much less of the former group's solidarity or kindness toward one another. Certain boys were subject to teasing; others remained isolated and quietly unhappy. My filming this time focused more on themes of homesickness and conflict. And yet I felt an affection for many of these boys, for they were as spirited and inventive as the former group. It seemed as if they were more unsure of themselves and lacked the guidance of a few calm and fair-minded leaders. However, an important difference was that I was seeing them at an earlier stage in their school life, when they were first grappling with the strangeness of their surroundings.

Although the film was meant to provide a basis of comparison to *With Morning Hearts*, I was closer to the students this time and able to interact with them more freely. This affected the tenor of my filming. I was more involved in day-to-day events. Boys would speak to me more spontaneously while I was filming, for the camera had been part of the life of the house from the beginning. As before, I avoided the authoritarian role of a teacher, but there were times when I had to intervene in a dispute or look after the house when the housemaster was away. I was also searching for ways to make the film more multidimensional than *With Morning Hearts*. For one thing, I decided it would have no major protagonist like Karam. Instead, several boys would gradually emerge from the group as subjects.

As it turned out, some of these were involved in fights, another was being bullied, others simply became more prominent through the force of their personalities. Still another boy, Angad, was suffering from a severe case of homesickness. He remained a rather distant figure, but I developed a section of the film around him during which his parents appear and both his housemaster and his fellow students address his problem.

Even more than in the earlier films, I wanted to look closely at conversations as an insight into the boys' concerns and patterns of thought. Sometimes these conversations erupted unexpectedly. One evening several boys began talking about ghosts—whether anyone had seen one, how to call them, and if they appeared, how to speak to them. It was at once a joking conversation and a compendium of schoolboy folklore. It eventually moved on to other topics, including vegetarianism, cannibalism, and kung fu. What I found curious was that although I said little, the conversation revolved quite naturally around me and the camera, as if my presence acted as a focus or stimulus for it. However, the forms of interaction fluctuated: sometimes the boys addressed me and sometimes talked among themselves.

There were also opportunities during the evening study period when small groups of boys were allowed to talk in the dormitory. I filmed a number of these discussions, which covered such topics as food, money, and unhappiness. One was about the causes of conflict. Several boys took the position that competitions, such as the school's interhouse sporting rivalries, actually resembled communal violence and might even prepare one psychologically for the tensions and periodic warfare between nations such as India and Pakistan. So important is competition at the school, and so great is the approval for it, that I doubt whether many students would have been willing to express this idea later in their school careers. In this film and throughout the project, the words, thoughts, and perceptions of children about the adult world were always at the back of my mind.

Films in Dialogue: *The New Boys* and *The Age of Reason*

By now the project had moved from the wider focus of *Doon School Chronicles* to the narrower focus of Foot House. In the fifth and last film, it reached its narrowest focus in a portrait of one student. Once again, this film grew out of another; however, it parallels it exactly in time. Although the two films are self-sustaining, each can be seen as a companion to the other. *The New Boys* and *The Age of Reason* form a pair based on their common origin and how they intersect with one another.

I began making *The New Boys* a few days before the boys appeared, when the house was being cleaned and prepared for them. I was present as they arrived, struggling with their trunks and suitcases, looking for their beds in the dormitory, and having their clothing checked off on a list. As a filmmaker, I kept an eye out for those boys who might become important in the film. Nonfiction films are "cast" no less carefully than fiction films, but the casting takes a more evolutionary and subterranean course. I filmed parents talking with one another and boys regarding each other cautiously, wondering who might be friendly. I watched two boys forming an instant bond, one of them following the other wherever he went. It made me aware how quickly attachments can be formed, apparently on such slender threads as chance, manner, or social class. I saw and filmed a boy who arrived from Nepal with his parents. As he looked at his new surroundings his expression conveyed both awe and determination, a quality that intrigued me, for I detected an unusual spark of intelligence and knowingness in him. He kept his distance from the others and yet was cheerful when spoken to. Later I learned he was one of the few boys who had spent his earlier years at a boarding school, starting at the age of six.

This boy, Abhishek, began accompanying me and talking to me as I was filming. I must have encouraged him, for I enjoyed his company. He played a game with me, looking into the camera lens and directing it toward different objects, all the time giving a spoken inventory of what he imagined the camera was seeing. As time went on he told me about books he had read, films he had seen, the school he had been to in Kathmandu, and his ideas about education and learning. I was trying to be impartial in my attention to the boys, but in Abhishek's case this proved difficult. I had never heard a twelve-year-old (and he was barely that) speak so assuredly or so wisely. If he had been merely precocious, he might have been a bore, but he had a speculative way of moving from thought to thought as if considering each thought for the first time. He also had a luminous, open disposition and a funny side to him. He struck me as an outsider, not only because he came from Nepal but also in temperament. He was often the silent observer, preferring his own company to that of the other boys, but he was not unsociable with them, nor did anyone seem to dislike him. I wondered how he would get on at a school like Doon (figure 5.3).

Along with several other boys, Abhishek was becoming a contender for prominence in the film. He had qualities of intellect and character that made one question the supposed superiority of adults in such things. I had begun filming our conversations, or rather, his outpourings of talk. We never discussed this at the time, but it was clear he knew what I was doing. And yet the more he talked to me, the more I wondered what to do with this material. There was no way I could put his extended reflections into the film without overburdening it, and to use only brief frag-

5.3. Abhishek, from *The Age of Reason* (2004).

ments would, I thought, do him an injustice. It gradually seemed to me that I should make one further film, an offshoot of *The New Boys*. This eventually became *The Age of Reason*. At the time I envisaged it as a series of scenes of Abhishek talking, interspersed with glimpses of his daily life. Meanwhile, I got on with the business of making *The New Boys*.[11]

The two films proceeded together, and at some point it occurred to me that certain scenes should appear in both films, edited differently for each. There would thus be points of crossover, and the films would, in a sense, speak to each other. Abhishek might be the focus of one film, but in the other he would be just one of the large group of boys. He would be seen from time to time but the film would not single him out for attention; yet if you had seen *The Age of Reason*, you would have a special regard for him. In any case, whichever film you saw first, you could never see the other innocently. I felt this would create an additional level of interplay between the two films, possibly more interesting than the parallels between the earlier films. Instead of simply permitting general comparisons, the films would be in constant dialogue. I was beginning to think of the series of films as a three-dimensional structure: if you looked through the gaps between them, you could see the others. Each provided a different perspective on the school, but it also provided a different perspective on each of the other films. Taken together, the five films might even be considered a single film eight hours long.

My filming of Abhishek expanded from the first few encounters to include scenes revealing different aspects of his character. It also followed his progress from his arrival at the school to attending his first classes, his treatment for viral fever in the school hospital, his return to the house, and receiving his marks at the end of the term—a period of only about eight weeks but one in which he seemed to grow both physically and emotionally. I worried whether his friendship with me was preventing him from fully integrating himself into the house, and whether I should try to create a greater distance between us. But I also saw that he was methodically working out his place in the school, and I was a part of this process. As far as his housemates were concerned, he was only one of about five boys I had been filming regularly, and they seemed to accept that I would devote more time to these than to others. Toward the end of the term, Abhishek became less talkative and his thoughts more inward. He was beginning to outgrow his need for me. This is covered in the final "Postscript" of the film.

I made *The New Boys* as an observer and occasional participant in the boys' lives. That approach is apparent in the way I shot the film, the boys' relation to me, and my occasional interactions with them. *The Age of Reason* was a more personal and fundamentally interactive film. My voice was already on the soundtrack when I spoke to Abhishek. I added a further spoken commentary, linking events, commenting on Abhishek's progress, and reflecting on my relationship with him. I realized that for some audiences, Abhishek's English might be hard to understand, and there were times when my own off-camera remarks were hard to make out. I decided to try a selective subtitling, here and there highlighting an opening sentence or a difficult passage. As the film progressed, the necessity for this diminished, as Abhishek's way of speaking became more familiar and events became clearer from their context.

During the time that I filmed Abhishek I sometimes wished that I could present him whole to the viewer. It was not that he was necessarily more remarkable than other boys, but with him I constantly felt a sense of discovery and pride. If one child could encompass so much, should we not be revising the way we portrayed all children in films, giving them the sort of respect we accord adults? Children are not just the appendages of adult society, nor the raw materials for it; they are strong and independent personalities. I felt that they merited our fuller attention, and that our attention should start from a different position. It seemed to me that the line between childhood and adulthood was too artificial and was taken too much for granted, based on a possibly faulty developmental premise and a whole string of stereotypes. Sometimes, as an adult in the presence of Abhishek, I felt like an impostor.

The New Boys is structured around the evolving cohesion of the group and the problems they encounter along the way: disorientation, homesickness, and conflict. *The Age of Reason* is structured around a deepening understanding of Abhishek and the question of how well he will fit into the school. In the two films it is possible to see him sometimes in isolation and sometimes as part of a social unit, but his presence also produces an altered perspective on the school, that of someone who comes from another country and a different educational background. I felt he had arrived at an important way-station in his life, but it was hard to know whether this was due to his age or training or his outsider position.

Films and Feelings

Films are often regarded as documents and publications, but they also contain the traces of experience. Making them can induce an intense engagement with the world that sometimes verges on the painful. At times this brings joy, at other times a sense of loss. Filmmakers sometimes feel themselves emptied, for in reaching out to assimilate the experiences of others there is a certain erosion of their sense of themselves. In sharing the worlds of others so intimately, it is possible to lose sight of your own boundaries. It is not uncommon to discover yourself inhabited by your subjects. Long after making a film, you sometimes feel in yourself a gesture or hear in your mind an intonation of voice that is not your own. Filmmakers and film viewers have this in common, that things seen and heard are capable of reaching out and possessing us. The possession is not so much a matter of spirit as of material being. It may come from how someone moves, speaks, stands in a room, or handles an object. We nevertheless experience it in ourselves—how it is to be someone else in the world. Our consciousness comes alive in watching others' actions, which resemble but differ from our own. We respond to the stimulus of familiarity, but also to the stimulus of difference. This is corporeal knowledge, only lightly mediated by thought.

Filmmakers are often compared to hunters, searching out and acquiring the materials for a film, but the actual experience is more often one of being immersed in the details of daily life. In much documentary filmmaking, this is more an act of recovery than acquisition, gathering up what has been overlooked by everyone else. It is in this modest sense, I think, that Agnès Varda casts herself as a gleaner.[12] To make the ordinary events of life reveal themselves involves a process of exchange. A film borrows something from the world and then returns it, adding something in tribute.

This paradoxically is what can give great consequence to what at first seems inconsequential. As I finished each of the Doon School films, I had to consider how it would be seen. It was not the reputation of the school that particularly concerned me, for inevitably there would be grumblings that the school had been misrepresented. I knew, for example, that there were worries that the plumbing in Foot House, which was soon to be upgraded, would seem archaic. Several teachers questioned why I began *Doon School Chronicles* with the *dhobi ghat*, the school's laundry, rather than something more modern or impressive, not grasping the significance of clothing in the film. Beyond such feelings of embarrassment over details, there would be the more usual objections about what the films had left out and what they chose to dwell upon. I was far less concerned about this than how the boys would see themselves, and whether this could in any way harm them. There were always risks, because in the end such consequences are often unknowable, even to the persons themselves. The only sure solution is not to make films, but I had made them. It was natural that there would be feelings of self-consciousness. It was therefore important that the boys accept this and put it in perspective.

I showed each film first to those boys who were most concerned in it, usually in the company of a few friends whom they had selected to see it with them. This last was important, because it is easier to respond to how you appear in a film with someone else present, preferably someone you trust. I also showed it before it was quite finished, in order to take account of the boys' reactions. When particular boys such as Karam were given prominence, I would discuss the film with them afterward to try to gauge their feelings. Then, if they agreed, the film would be shown more widely. As for Abhishek, I assured him that his film would not be shown at the school while he was still a student there. This was my precaution, not his, but he did not object to it.

All the films were completed several years after they were shot. This gave the boys some distance from them and a degree of objectivity. In most cases they saw the films with amusement and nostalgia. After I had shown *With Morning Hearts* to the Foot House group, several of them went immediately to the house to try to find their old beds. One boy in *The New Boys* was embarrassed by his former behavior and said he hoped never to do such things again, but he was adamant that the scenes concerning him should stay in the film. For him, as for most of them, the film was an important documentary record and a reservoir of memories. I gave each of them a copy to take home. Karam took some pride in the attention the two films had given him and was willing for other students to see them, although I withheld *Karam in Jaipur* from screenings for several more years. I found that the most appreciative audience for *The New Boys* was the latest batch of Foot House boys, who found it fascinating to see the school's godlike seniors as they had once been at their own age of twelve.

When I showed *The Age of Reason* to Abhishek, he was seventeen. By then he was reading Marx, Nietzsche, and Dostoevsky. It was strange to watch the film with him. I kept looking back and forth between the two Abhisheks in the room, the one on the screen and the other sitting near me. Perhaps he had similar feelings, for he told me he felt like a different person now. But then, upon reflection, he said he would say the same things today as he had said in the film, only in different words. Later he wrote to me about it, and about how films transform the fluidity of memory into something concrete. After some doubt, he concluded he had come across well in the film and thanked me for making it with care and from a personal viewpoint.

My concept of social aesthetics changed as a result of filming at Foot House, where I was almost always surrounded by boys involved in their own activities. In the house, the aesthetics of the group proved to be even more important than the aesthetics of place or culture. It not only created the collective character of the house but also determined how each boy was categorized, recognized, and, in some respects, treated.[13] Such forces operate in society at large, but they are even more evident in a highly organized and circumscribed community where everyone knows everyone else. I have mentioned the almost palpable sense of life that I felt in Foot House. What was the particular texture of this that made it so recognizable? It was, in fact, the sum of the boys' age and development, the manners of an Indian middle-class upbringing, and the rules imposed by the school itself. This had a density that I tried to convey on film by concentrating on how the boys used their voices, its pitch, their characteristic postures, their faces, how they wore their uniforms, the uniforms themselves, their attention to their appearance, their expressiveness in conversation, what they talked about, and so on. Sounds were very important. One was always aware of the scuffling and running sounds of boys' shoes and of shouted imprecations such as "Are you mad?" echoing through the house. There was the constant tap-tapping of a table tennis ball on the back veranda. One would only have to enter a dormitory at a comparable girls' school to see and hear a quite different aesthetics of gender operating at this age, many features of which extend far beyond the borders of India.

The aesthetics of the person bears upon one quite differently when one is filming an individual rather than a group. Each person then projects a preternatural presence that one feels with an intensity one rarely experiences in daily life. I sometimes had the feeling that I knew Abhishek better than he knew himself—which was possibly true at least of his external appearance. When filming certain people, it is difficult not to sense a unity as profound as any in a song or poem or other creative work. Nuances of expression become more than the external signs of thought and feeling; they sum up the person's being in some much more elemental sense. Characteristic gestures and tones of voice encapsulate the pungency of the entire person. The amplitude of a single human life can thus be overwhelming in its individuality and yet exhibit all the dignity of human life more generally. In *The Age of Reason* Abhishek represents a certain norm of childhood shared with many of his classmates, but the film is also witness to his difference from them, and indeed from all other people.

Abhishek's position as a foreigner and, at times, onlooker at the school symbolized for me the outsider status of many children today. Unlike working children, who are immersed in adult society from an early age, those at school are held apart, where they become increasingly separated from adults in culture and power. They have time to watch and form their own designs on adulthood. They also fill these years by evolving in their own directions. Boarding schools, in particular, create a space for this separate development with their communal dormitories and endless rounds of games and other activities. The transition to adulthood is blunted at schools like Doon, where older students act as a buffer between children and adults. To some extent children preserve and guard their outsider status as a self-protective measure until they reach adulthood. They have a sense that their strength lies in numbers. This is usually expressed in silence and solidarity in the presence of adults, but it may take the form of resistance or even rebellion.

Continuities and Discoveries

Ideas do not develop in an orderly fashion; they begin with a notion that gathers authority until it is altered by experience or some new understanding. This can result from a discussion with others, but it can also occur quite naturally in the thinking of any one of us. As it is in our minds, so it is with our projects. It is rare for a plan to be followed through without modification, and the modification often calls into question the very idea we started with. This is why so many projects seem internally inconsistent, as if they were trying to accommodate the transition from one way of thinking to another. Any project—any work of art or science—is nearly always better viewed as a process than a statement. It marks out a trajectory toward a destination beyond itself, which is perhaps best foreseen at its point of extremity, where it leaves off. Understanding that trajectory may only come later, and by degrees. Often one grasps at it with a sense of discovery, only to realize that one knew it intuitively all along. These moments lie in wait for us, vaguely perceived but pushed aside until we are finally ready to accept them. Their appearance may be triggered by someone's chance remark or by a fragment of writing that bears little relation to the idea. At all events, it seems we cannot rush this process of making connections.

There are threads of continuity in everyone's work, although some are less obvious than others, sometimes especially to the author. One apparent interest may conceal another. Certain themes may appear fleetingly in work after work. In my case, an obvious link between this project and earlier ones was my interest in how to represent human societies. Another was a continuing interest in how communities renew and pass on their culture. However, the Doon School films, which had begun as another "cultural" project, marked a shift toward questioning the very nature of cultural learning. At the school I not only concentrated on children for the first time, but I found myself preoccupied and puzzled by childhood itself. My preconceptions about childhood development had inevitably been shaped by European and American models of progress and improvement. But my filming suggested to me that adulthood was not necessarily a refinement of childhood—rather, that children might actually write the agenda for adults, and that adult society might more properly be regarded as a paring down of children's discoveries. At the very least, childhood could be looked upon as a laboratory for the fundamentals of adulthood.

In public culture, the agency of children still seems to be underestimated. If a significant range of social processes are being forged and tested in childhood, how does this affect the emphasis we place on socialization and culture itself? And yet this is not the popular view, nor one widely supported by psychologists and social scientists, who generally subscribe to "top-down" theories.[14] I have stressed this point not so much to defend it as to suggest how exposure to a field situation throws up all manner of refractory ideas. Films and filmmaking, I think, are valuable not so much for conducting theoretical arguments as for transporting the viewer into unfamiliar circumstances and creating more radical perspectives.

An adult often feels as much of an outsider among children as a visitor in a foreign land. Membership in childhood is limited and nonrenewable. As far as children are concerned, adults have always been adults, and it matters little that they were once children. At best, adults gain a kind of provisional access to children's affairs. My access, based on making films, allowed me to spend months with children who, separated from their families, were engaged in a form of social experimentation that is perhaps too often overlooked by adults. In the midst of childhood's cruelties and anxieties, the skillful ways in which they organized themselves and their moral judgment often took me by surprise. I had the impression of seeing remarkable things and of preserving these moments for others to see. It was something I had experienced only a few times before, most memorably in Africa.

What link could there be between filming herders in a remote part of East Africa in the 1960s and filming at Doon School? I had never thought to ask this question. Doon School was, after all, a place of privilege, well connected to the centers of national and international power. The answer only struck me when a colleague wrote about the attention the African films had paid "to speech, and to the careful representation of ethnographic film subjects as intellectuals."[15] How had I missed this? It described in many respects my recent approach to children, whom I had identified, perhaps unconsciously, as a similarly marginalized group. For, to many adults, the minds of children appear as alien and "primitive" as those of the Jie and Turkana herders I had filmed in Africa. Even at a school like Doon, children are routinely seen as more instinctive than rational, more acted upon than acting, more impressionable than creative, more "natural" than cultural. Africans were once widely viewed by Europeans as childlike. In the colonies grown men were called "boys." Today children are arguably the last group still stigmatized as incomplete human beings, in need of civilizing. Yet I had found them in many ways more civilized than adults. I realized that what had inspired me was nothing new. It was the same sense of discovery, the same fascination and respect for what I had seen. Children had given me a broader perspective on human life. It was a perspective that, through film, I hoped to convey to others.

Like most projects, this one began more abstractly than it finished. From an initial interest in schools as structured institutions, I had begun to look upon them increasingly as social environments. How did the students adapt to a new environment? From this I had tried to film how students experienced their surroundings, and then how they actually created much of their social world. I had regarded the students as the inhabitants of a place, only to find that they were in themselves the greater part of the place that they, and I, experienced. If aesthetics played a part in the life of institutions, then the physical qualities of human beings, both collectively and individually, were an essential part of this. Finally, Abhishek had provided the focus for many of my emerging convictions about the dignity and rationality of childhood.

Others might well have arrived at such ideas simply by living at the school, but for me the act of filming was crucial to arriving at them. I think that if I had not had the opportunities the camera gave me and experienced so much through using it, I should probably have accepted a more prosaic view of the school and its inhabitants. But the camera was constantly propelling me into new situations and changing my view of things. It is perhaps axiomatic that filmmaking, at least of this kind, does this, for before films can express ideas, they are a way of engaging with the world. I wrote at the beginning of this chapter that the Doon School films were not a series in the chronological sense. Yet this is not entirely true, for if they provide an image of the school, they also provide a narrative of my changing relationship to it.

Notes

I am grateful to Salim Yusufji for his comments on this chapter and for the ideas that he generously contributed to it. Thanks also to Anna Grimshaw for her comments and suggestions.

1. I knew of the school, having lived nearby in Landour and Mussoorie in 1988–89 while making the film *Photo Wallahs* (1991) with Judith MacDougall. However, I did not visit the school until September 1996.

2. See Srivastava 1998.

3. Even if we have never attended one, boarding schools can figure in our imaginations through reading fiction and memoirs. This literature is considerable, marked by such key works as Thomas Hughes's *Tom Brown's Schooldays* (1857), Kipling's *Stalky & Co.* (1899), and Graham Greene's collection of accounts of school life, *The Old School* (1934). There is also a large school film genre, discussed earlier in chapter 3. Perhaps the images in films such as *Zero for Conduct*, *Mädchen in Uniform*, and *Au revoir les enfants* impress themselves even more vividly upon our dreamworlds than books do. With the growth of anthropological studies of childhood have come a number of ethnographies focusing on schools and boarding schools. The latter include Srivastava's study, *Constructing Post-Colonial India* (1998), Meenakshi Thapan's *Life at School* (1991), Anthony Simpson's essays on a Catholic boarding school in Zambia (1998, 1999), and Judith Okely's analysis of her own boarding school in *Own or Other Culture* (1996).

4. Fax from Nick Fraser, Documentary Department, BBC, London, 5 August 1996.

5. *Tempus de Baristas* (1993), about three generations of goatherds in Sardinia.

6. For example, Thames Television's *The World at War*, or Ken Burns's *Jazz*, or Bernard-Henri Lévy's *The Spirit of Freedom*, or Kenneth Clark's *Civilization, A Personal View*.

7. The five films of the Doon School quintet are *Doon School Chronicles* (2000), *With Morning Hearts* (2001), *Karam in Jaipur* (2001), *The New Boys* (2003), and *The Age of Reason* (2004).

8. The films in the Turkana Conversations trilogy, codirected with Judith Mac-Dougall, are *The Wedding Camels* (1977), *Lorang's Way* (1979), and *A Wife Among Wives* (1981).

9. It was also filmed in an almost trancelike state. This was perhaps augmented by a fever that I had been running for several days.

10. This prayer is by Robert Louis Stevenson and is one of a number that he wrote during his stay in Samoa, later published as *Prayers Written in Vailima*

(Stevenson 1910). Like other prayers read at Doon School assemblies, it is sufficiently nondenominational in character to be used with students of Hindu, Muslim, Sikh, Jain, Parsi, and Christian backgrounds. Several other prayers by Stevenson are used at the school, along with prayers by Rabindranath Tagore and a prolific prayer writer, J. S. Hoyland.

11. I was also at this time filming *Karam in Jaipur*, so I was very busy.

12. In her film, *Les glaneurs et la glaneuse* (2000).

13. That appearance may affect how students are treated by staff is illustrated by an item in the school newspaper, the *Doon School Weekly*, dating from 1941:

> When a thin boy has not done his homework, he goes with a friend or two to the Dame.
> "Madame, please could I have some ointment for my ankle?" he says . . .
> The boy, assisted by his friends, will tell a long story. "Poor boy," the Dame will say, and hearing this the boy will quietly and most politely ask,
> "Could I be excused P.T. madame, please?"
> "Yes, dear," the Dame will say, "report to the hospital tomorrow." . . .
> But if a fat boy should go once in a blue moon with a real hurt and ask to get off P.T. he would be ticked off for shamming and shirking, and made to do P.T., when he would be called all sorts of names and made to do extra rounds for not doing the exercises properly.
> —R. Janaksinhji, *The Doon School Weekly*, 29 November 1941 (Saturday, no. 59): 2.

14. The main exception is in the anthropology and sociology of childhood. In the past, children were considered to be relatively passive in the socialization process. Despite pioneering studies by Margaret Mead (1930) and O. F. Raum (1940), the emphasis of anthropology was on how children received instruction by adults in their own culture. Today, studies of childhood and youth focus instead on how children participate actively in society and are instrumental in socializing themselves and one another. This varies greatly among different societies, as does the conception of childhood. Scholars such as Christina Toren, Allison James, Olga Nieuwenhuys, Alan Prout, and Paul Willis have been in the forefront of efforts to challenge theories of passive socialization.

15. This observation was made in a reader's report for this book by Faye Ginsburg, New York University.

PART III
THE PHOTOGRAPHIC IMAGINATION

6

PHOTO HIERARCHICUS: SIGNS AND MIRRORS
IN INDIAN PHOTOGRAPHY

That which makes the eye see, but needs no eye to see,
that alone is Spirit.
—Kena Upanishad 1, 7

MIRRORS AND photographs are the most mechanical means by which we see ourselves, and they are usually considered the least mediated forms of representation. But when one looks in a mirror, is it an image of the transient self one sees or the eternal Self that looks back? What if one dresses the worldly image in the apparel of the gods? In photographs of ourselves, do we see our private being or the mere surface of a public, predestined role? What photographic practices support and deny these possibilities?

On the top of Gun Hill in Mussoorie, an Indian hill station in the Himalayan foothills, middle-class Indian tourists look into mirrors and dress themselves as idealized peasants, bandits, Arab sheiks, and pop stars. They are then led to points of scenic beauty to have their photographs taken. It is a good-humored diversion, not unlike a party game, but like many games it also has the formulaic toughness of ritual. The tourists deliver themselves up to the photographers who, like priests, conduct them through their parts. The photographers know exactly where and how to pose them, and they do it with the speed and offhand manner of long experience. If the tourists see such photography as dressing up and "playing" someone else, the photographers often see it otherwise—as a catalyst for the release of the true self from the social self. According to one of them, H. S. Chadha, "all the emotions flow out in photography," and he has described how he discovered by taking photographs that a Chief Minister and an astrologer (who looked like a holy man) were both in fact thieves. The process, he maintains, produces an emotional transformation, one that we might compare to a religious experience. But for Chadha (as for priests) there may be no clear boundary between religion and science. "Photography is a psychological, scientific way of bringing out inner feelings, through the use of costumes and objects," he says. "You can test anyone with it."[1]

Two Photographies

Photographs, like mirrors, double us and create a parallel world, what Susan Sontag has called "a reality in the second degree."[2] They represent us, and they also serve to reidentify us. Edmund Carpenter has concluded that photographs are fundamentally shocking, doing a violence that tears something out of us as social beings.[3] They enjoin us to do something before the event to prepare for the photograph, or afterward, to "save" ourselves from the attack of representation. Most people profess not to like their own photographs. Photographs of ourselves are things other people prize.

Carpenter's notion is that photography confronts us with our own individuality, forever alienating us from collective social experience. But it is for "stealing our souls" that photography has more commonly been indicted in popular clichés derived from ethnography. The capture of the spirit or ghost is indeed the fear of many peoples when first exposed to photography, but this is often put more physiologically. F. J. Gillen, who accompanied Sir Walter Baldwin Spencer to central Australia in 1901, wrote in his diary of "a morose old fellow" who "expressed his opinion that our object in taking photographs was to extract the heart and liver of the blackfellows."[4] Turkana women in northern Kenya told us in 1973 that they feared photography because it "might make us weak" or "make our blood thin."

But there is another side to photography, an alternative to this draining and predatory one. It offers us the chance to add something to ourselves and review our varied appearances. It takes nothing from us; indeed, every image increases us and attests to the possibilities within us. The preparations surrounding such photography are often elaborate. In the early days it was normal for people to dress up for their photographs, often in borrowed clothes. They were also often pictured among their belongings, or they held symbolic props such as books, even if they could not read. The rich and powerful could to some extent control their images (figure 6.1). The middle classes tended to collude with photographers, while peasants and working-class people were more often dominated by them and pictured uncomfortably in the trappings of the bourgeoisie[5] (figure 6.2).

India has long offered instances of both the threatening and the genially additive faces of photography. Photography came to India soon after its invention and was taken up both as an instrument of government policy and as an adjunct to the arts of court life. The official photographic documentation of "ethnic types" began at least as early as 1851, and the eight-volume photographic project, *The People of India,* begun in 1861 and published between 1868 and 1875, is an eloquent document of the imperial

।। भाहाराजासाहृ ब श्री राघोरीसिंहजोो ।।

बुन्दी ४ मईसन्‍ू १९१२ईस्वी

6.1. The Maharao Raja Raghubir Singh of Bundi with some of his
possessions, 1912. Photographer unknown.

6.2. Studio portrait of a working-class man. France, ca. 1910.
Photographer unknown.

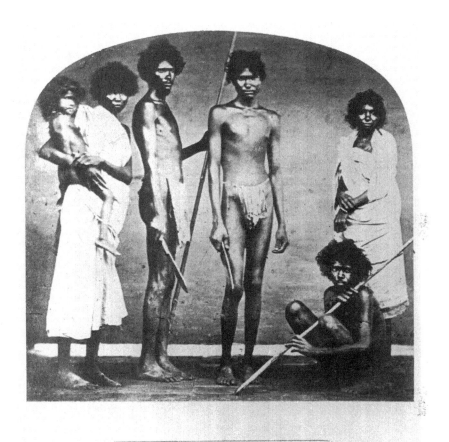

YENADIES.

FOREST TRIBE.

CHINGLEPUT.

441.

6.3. Plate 441 from Watson and Kaye's *The People of India*, 1868–1875.
Courtesy of the State Library of South Australia.

Panopticon taking the dimensions of its subject population.[6] These human beings are objectified as neatly and perhaps as innocently as butterflies impaled on pins (figure 6.3). Although this and similar ethnographic photography obviously required some staging, there is a clear effort to present the subjects as unvarnished scientific specimens. In many of the works that followed *The People of India* they are often shown in "anthropometric" profile and frontal views or accompanied by measuring rulers, even if, as Pinney has noted, these markers are more symbolic than useful.[7] It may not be stretching a point to say that these images are unmistakably European in their intellectual heritage—they could have been produced by no other society on Earth.

If photographic representation as violence is evident here, it is to be found in the manner in which the figures are extracted from their social context and reduced to lonely individuals before the camera. It may be evident, too, in the look of fear on many of the faces, a look perhaps quite unconnected with the personality of the photographer (who may have been kindly) but induced by the photographic situation itself. One has a sense of bereftness, of shells from which the living core has been removed. At the extreme are photographs of famine victims, whose hold on life appears so tenuous that one expects the camera to extinguish it in extracting its few photons of light.

A different photography, opposing this, is abundantly evident in Indian court photographs. Photography was taken up enthusiastically by Indian princes, including some, like the nineteenth-century maharajas of Jaipur, Tripura, and Bikaner, who made a personal hobby of it and imported the latest darkroom equipment from Europe. Among the many subjects photographed by Sawai Ram Singh II, the Maharaja of Jaipur, his favorite seems to have been himself.[8] Perhaps best known in the West are photographs by Lala Deen Dayal (his title "Raja" was but honorary), taken of the family of the Nizam of Hyderabad and his startlingly mustachio'd fellow princes. When in 1891 the Maharaja of Jodhpur (Marwar) ordered a photographic census of "ethnic types" in the colonial tradition, the result—the *Report on the Men of Marwar State*—was, it has been argued, subtly different in mood and content from its British predecessors.[9] Although that claim seems more wished-for than apparent, Indian court photographs of the period are unquestionably statements of local power, and they are ruled by a supreme confidence.

Indian court photographs are noted for their degree of tinting and overpainting, sometimes reaching the extent that only tiny faces peer out from the surrounding layer of color (figure 6.4). In the process the perspective is often flattened so that, as the conventional wisdom has it, in India this kind of photographic art is subordinated to an older tradition of court painting.

Vinod Kumar, the proprietor of a shop in Mussoorie, possesses two works, one of which (probably a portrait of the Maharaja of Alwar) is heavily overpainted with scarlet and gold. The other, another court portrait (probably the Maharaja of Patiala), is much smaller, and of this, because its surface is completely painted, Mr. Kumar can only say, "I don't know whether it is a colored photograph or a miniature painting."

6.4. Painted photograph of a young prince. Bourne & Shepherd, ca. 1890.

Only by means of X-rays, or by taking off the paint, could one know if a photograph lies beneath.

Here, as in much else in Indian life, appearance (photographic emulsion) and ideal (paint) exist in close contact but occupy separate layers of consciousness. This is not so much a separation of sign and referent as a much more comprehensive splitting of the two domains in one setting, just as Indian signs advertising the world of Hindi cinema tower, huge and extravagant, over the life of the streets. Indian religious art can be equally monumental and, in the case of oleographic posters, painted statuary, and television programs (such as Doordarshan's *Ramayana* and *Mahabharata* series), equally extravagant with color. Most popular photographic practices in India explicitly serve the second domain, but there are others that severely test the splitting off of the ideal from the "social" self.

Mirror vs. Self

In Mussoorie the work of one young photographer, Raja Dass, seems to exemplify the tensions between the two. Not long ago he began to make a specialty of matrimonial photography, which is to be distinguished from wedding photography in that it consists of photographs of young men and women to be sent to suitable families for the arrangement of their marriages. These photographs are in many ways visual equivalents of the texts to be found on the matrimonial pages of Indian newspapers, such as the following from the *Hindustan Times*:

> SUITABLE match for Punjabi Khatri, beautiful, slim, fair girl, 22/154, convent educated, employed in International company, drawing four figures, belongs to educated family, early decent marriage, C.A./Doctor/Engineer etc. preferred.

Just as the matrimonial advertisements specify subcaste, complexion, and economic requirements (or assets), so the photographs have the potential to convey considerable information about the appearance and status of their subjects. Skin color is made visible (ideally, "wheatish") and the subjects may wear certain clothes, be shown in certain milieux, and be associated with certain objects that are implicitly coded as caste indicators and dowry objects (or in the case of men, evidence of income). In advertisements like the one above, "decent" is the code word signaling that appropriate dowry will be given (or required). Attributes necessarily expressed by words in the written advertisements, such as "attractive" and "slim," are here replaced by the direct indexical evidence of the image. But equally, such photographs may exaggerate assets and conceal defects through lighting, retouching, and "set dressing." The problem for the photographer is to find a balance between the ideal and the evidential, and in the case of faces, between what Gombrich calls "mask" and "likeness."[10]

To make this point, Dass tells the story of a woman who, upon meeting a man whose photograph she has received, immediately runs from the room. "The picture was saying something else," he says, "but the person was not like that." In the past such photographs were made in the studio and often heavily retouched. The modern trend, according to Dass, is toward more informal photographs taken in the subject's natural surroundings. He showed us a photograph of his sister before her engagement, posed in a field of flowers, and another of her perched on a motorcycle in the street. It was not necessary to read the motorcycle as hers; it was, rather, an emblem of her modernity. But on another occasion Dass posed a young woman beside a television set, with the words, "Now your husband won't have to get one." And later, he lent a subject his watch when she had forgotten her own. Thus today in matrimonial photography, the practical strictures and complexities of Indian society force an accommodation with the idealization that figures prominently in so much popular Indian iconography. A matrimonial photograph, if it is excessively retouched or stage-managed, begins to fail as evidence.

In the Mall Road in Mussoorie there is a shop called the Kala Nikitan. Inside, an artist named Bishmber Dutt paints life-sized, cutout portraits, basing them on photographs that his clients have provided. When finished, the paintings are mounted on stands, and from the street you would think they were living persons—or life-sized photographs. In fact, many represent dead persons, commissioned by their relatives. One of Mr. Dutt's figures has stood in the drawing room of a nearby house for many years. It is a likeness of the former owner of the Savoy Hotel, and, like an ancestral deity, it dominates the room in which his widow sits.

This style of naïve hyperrealism can be found in other parts of India and is reminiscent of certain kinds of photographic advertising. But Mr. Dutt maintains that he does not copy photographs. Often he has only a few blurred snapshots to work from. "Although it seems a photograph, it is not," he says. "It is not a photograph because it is 'processed' as a color painting . . . but from the beginning I painted so that [my work] seemed a photograph. . . . In fact, it is the product of the mind." It seems that Mr. Dutt has found a solution to what may be viewed as a historic Indian ambivalence toward photographic representation, or at least its more intrusive, evidential side. Although his paintings look like photographs, they are not photographs. They mimic the persuasiveness—the indexical "truth"—of photographs without in any way having to be "truthful" or indexical. Mr. Dutt's figures seem like a later permutation of the Indian tradition of overpainting. Where once the paint all but obliterated the photographic image, there is no longer any need for this. Paint has triumphed, disguised as photography.

"In order to have surrealism, there first has to be realism," said Michel Leiris, litérateur-ethnographer, member of the Dakar-Djibouti expedition of 1931–33 and author of the anthropological curiosity, L'Afrique fantôme.[11] Mr. Dutt's portraits are surreal as well as hyperreal, but their realist referent lies in many respects outside Indian art in the photography and painting of the West. In a perverse way they sum up the latent surrealism of all photographic reproduction, in which the sign threatens to defy its referent. This is a transcultural surrealism, a mirror image of the sort that attracted the cubist painters, with their heritage of European realist painting, to African and Melanesian carvings. Resolutely photographic and yet antiphotographic, Mr. Dutt's portraiture provides a kind of baseline for considering the other photographic practices of Mussoorie, and perhaps of India more widely.

From Hill Station to Street

Mussoorie confirms all the clichés about Indian diversity. As a tourist town it attracts some eight thousand visitors a day in the summer "season," from as far away as Madras and Bombay. They come in regional waves according to the progress of the monsoon and local holiday timetables, so that June is the month of Delhi-ites, July of Punjabis, October of Bengalis (celebrating Durga Puja), November of Bombay-ites, and so on. As a hill station within easy reach of Delhi, Mussoorie also has a history of permanent settlement and summer occupation by British colonials and Indian princely families. Its many boarding schools draw better-off students from the whole of the subcontinent. It has also been a destination for Punjabi refugees (many of them Sikhs) following Partition and for Tibetan refugees since 1959. Beneath its cosmopolitan veneer is a population of ordinary Hindu and Muslim traders and workers, and a daytime population of local people from the surrounding Garhwal hills. There are also Nepalis, who provide much of the labor for hotel construction and road building.

This has proven a fertile environment for photographers, of whom there have been many hundreds since the nineteenth century in a town that even today has a permanent population of only about thirty thousand. Photography has found customers among almost all the social groups in Mussoorie, with the result that the profession here, and its history, is stratified to a remarkable degree along social and economic lines. There has been a correspondingly broad range of photographic styles, and over the years a shift in the balance between photographers riding different waves of technology and the fortunes of different clienteles.

One may start with the primitive but highly effective technology of the street photographer. A Mussoorie shopkeeper, Indra Prakash, remembers these photographers in Mussoorie fifty years ago "on the roadside, [with] the big box camera with the big cloth." They would take your picture and "sell it for maybe one rupee in those days." One no longer sees such photographers in Mussoorie (at any rate, I saw none during eight months in 1988–89), but they still exist in Dehra Dun, the large commercial town only 24 kilometers from Mussoorie at the foot of the escarpment (figure 6.5).

It may be significant, or perhaps merely symbolic, that this humblest class of photographers, with no studio but the street, is now found only several thousand feet below Mussoorie in a more rough-and-tumble urban environment. Mr. Dutt's life-sized painted images, one might say, gaze down upon images at the opposite end of the representational scale: tiny, rough prints produced from paper negatives, destined to be pinned to applications, licenses, and examination papers. The likenesses on them have no refinement (they have passed through no one's mind) and have much the same status as fingerprints in the bureaucratic apparatus of social control. They have the same stiff appearance as their subjects, as they pose nervously against a cloth backdrop on the street. Like fingerprints, they are used for identification, and but for a wash of red watercolor on the paper negative to lighten the skin color, they are (in Sontag's phrase)

6.5. Bharat Kumar, street photographer, at work in Dehra Dun, 1989.
Photograph by David MacDougall.

like "something directly stenciled off the real."[12] They are like mug shots
and I.D. photos made anywhere in the world, and they have an eerie
resemblance to the ethnographic photography of the nineteenth century
(figure 6.6).

The clients for these pictures are often the urban poor and farmers from
rural areas. More prosperous or sophisticated people would go to a small
studio in the bazaar, pay a bit more, and sit in comfort. The street photographers are aware of their own low status. They are unlicensed and occupy their streetside locations at the pleasure of the police, whom they
must pay off from time to time in order to keep them. One street photographer whom we wanted to film refused, saying, "I am too ashamed. I
was once a prosperous farmer in the Punjab. Look at me now!"

Yet their work, to bystanders, must seem a kind of miracle. The subjects
sit on a narrow bench against a temple wall, a green cloth hung behind
them. If the sun is too bright an umbrella, hung against the wall, shades

them. The camera has no shutter. There is a lens cap that the photographer removes for two to four seconds to make the exposure. With the other hand (inserted through a lightproof sleeve) he manipulates the paper and a tray of developer inside the camera. Sheets of Agfa printing paper, torn into passport photo–sized rectangles, are kept in a rack or behind a piece of elastic within the camera and are moved into place on the plane of the focusing ground glass. After the exposure, the photographer can watch the paper developing in the tray through a hooded eyepiece, rather like that of an old stereoscope, mounted on top of the camera. The viewing light is daylight, filtered through a window of red glass that at other times is covered by a small door. Once developed, the paper is slipped through a slot in the bottom of the camera into a vertical tray of fixer. When this is slid out, like a small drawer, the print can be removed and dropped into a pail of wash water on the ground. This, of course, is only half the process. It produces a paper negative, which is usually retouched with watercolor and then rephotographed on a small easel at the front of the camera to yield the final positive prints.

I have described this apparatus in some detail because despite its crude appearance, it is extremely practical and ingenious. The process is quick and cheap, which accounts for its survival in a country now awash with plastic disposable cameras and well equipped with sophisticated 35mm models. The technique is identical to that practiced by itinerant photographers at country *melas* and by the street photographers at the end of Chandni Chowk in Old Delhi. In Dehra Dun I heard of a proposal to install automatic photo booths at the premises of one of the larger photographic studios. I suspect this will be a failure, so long as the street photographers can continue to produce, within ten or fifteen minutes, three passport-sized photographs for five rupees (about 20 U.S. cents, or 12 pence).[13]

I have suggested that one can read Mussoorie's social complexity in its photography. This is not only a matter of how people are presented (and present themselves) in photographs but also extends to the physical disposition of the photographers and their clients. Here class status appears to play a more important part than caste, religion, or ethnicity. On one level this may be no more than a truism of economic geography, but it may have more significance in cognitive terms as a factor in how people map their social environment.[14] In certain situations, such as arranging marriages, photography may serve to reinforce traditional corporate groups; in many others, such as business and tourism, its role and people's perceptions of it may be based on quite different factors. In Mussoorie physical and economic geography appear to coincide with photography to create a kind of vertical *photo hierarchicus*.

6.6. Photograph of the author by a street photographer, using the paper negative process. Bharat Kumar, Dehra Dun, 1988.

A Photographic Hierarchy

On the highest crags and forested hills of Mussoorie stand the houses built by former British settlers and Indian princely families. In the past they patronized a few elite studio photographers on the Mall Road. Living lower down were the "old" middle-class residents of Mussoorie, comprising established professionals and merchants, as well as visiting British tourists and the populations of the many boarding schools, all using a second rank of studios located at either end of the Mall Road in the Kulri and Library bazaars (the latter so called because Mussoorie's earliest lending library was there). Artisans and tradespeople tended to go to smaller studios in the bazaars. Poorer people and Garhwali villagers from the surrounding countryside used the street photographers who, as we have seen, are now only to be found still lower down in Dehra Dun. The recent phenomenon of the costume photographers on Gun Hill, catering to the "new" middle class of Indian tourists, is poised somewhere in the air between the bazaars and the highest hills, its clientele moving uncertainly upward and downward in a cable car.

In the Mall Road, once the promenade of "children, nurses, dogs and sickly ladies and gentlemen," as an early visitor described it,[15] is one of the older photographic establishments, Doon Studios. The proprietors, J. P. Sharma and his son M. M. Sharma, are the latest of four generations of photographers who began their business in Saharanpur in the nineteenth century. At one time there were more studios like this in Mussoorie and Dehra Dun—Kinsey Brothers, Vernon Studio, and Thomas A. Rust (and later, Julian Rust) among them. They catered to the upper classes, producing principally two kinds of photographs. The first was large formal portraits, carefully retouched and often tinted. J. P. Sharma, who was trained by Kinsey Brothers, still has his father's wood and brass plate camera, as well as tinting materials, and can demonstrate the tinting techniques. These photographs were sometimes very large indeed. One at the former Vernon Studio (now a television shop), portraying the Maharaja of Gwalior, is fully a meter by a meter and a half and hangs in a heavy gilt frame.[16] Photographs of this kind can still be found in some of the older houses in Mussoorie.

A member of one of the princely families, who still maintains a summer cottage in Mussoorie, has many examples of the second genre. Although part of the clientele of the larger studios was British, perhaps an even greater part was Indian or Anglo-Indian. In addition to single and group photographs, these photographers produced what might best be called "art snapshots." These documented the daily, sometimes informal events of court life in well-composed photographs of technical excellence and often great beauty. The princess whose albums we saw had full-plate photographs from the 1890s with hand-printed captions such as "His Highness Out Shooting on Elephant" or more personal notes: "Grandpa in his younger days!" and "The four brothers all bejeweled . . . " These pictures represent an unusual coupling of the intimate and the formal (figure 6.7). The photographs are private in the sense of belonging to the family, and public in their professionalism. Some of them show people in fancy-dress costumes for parties or dressed for state occasions in traditional regalia, which creates a curious resonance with the dressing up of the tourists on Gun Hill. When is dressing up not dressing up? Perhaps only when one is a prince.

Many of the photographs described above were made by Bourne & Shepherd, a firm that despite its English name employed many Indian photographers, as did Kinsey Brothers. In their combination of formality and domesticity, the pictures are not unlike those made for the Nizam of Hyderabad by Lala Deen Dayal. But the clientele that once supported such photography no longer exists. Doon Studios in Mussoorie, which once had wealthy Indian and British clients, now carries on primarily

6.7. Four young princes of Kapurthala. Bourne & Shepherd, 1890s.
Courtesy of Princess Sita of Kapurthala.

through such sidelines as photocopying, passport photography, and acting as agent for color laboratories in Dehra Dun and Delhi. The fourth
and last son is going into politics.

There is a strongly Victorian character to many of these pictures. They
are not overpainted or transformed by Indian artistic conventions in the
manner of photographs from many of the smaller Indian states. Despite
the culturally-distinctive features of much Indian photography, these pictures (with some important exceptions) have more in common with the
photography of Europe. Here, as elsewhere, the expectations of the clientele cannot be discounted. It was cosmopolitan and often equally at home
in the salons of Paris and the palaces of Punjab or Rajasthan.

Doon Studios and its chief competitors were located in the most fashionable part of Mussoorie, along the Mall Road (every hill station had its equivalent, often bearing this same name). The next set of studios, which catered to the middle class, was more widely scattered through the commercial areas of Library and Kulri and up into Landour Bazaar. Some, like Thukral Brothers and Bhanu Art Studio, are comparatively new, founded in the forty years or so since Partition. Many others that flourished earlier, such as Sharma Studio, Bora Brothers, Hari Sharn, and New Light Studio, are now gone. Almost all their work was portraiture, either single or group, and an important part of it was (and still is) for the boarding schools, which required an annual selection of class and team pictures.

A photograph by D. S. Bora, in the Ram Chander food and dry goods shop in Landour Bazaar, is typical of the style. It is one of two such framed portraits of the shop's earlier proprietors, both of which hang in a prominent position, hung with garlands. This is the same position in which religious pictures are normally hung in Indian shops, and one can find many examples in Mussoorie of a founder's portrait hung alongside that of a Hindu god or Guru Nanak. Here the borderline between the holy and the ancestral is blurred, like that between worship and reverence.

The differences in style between the Bora portrait and portraits by Bourne & Shepherd and the Mall Road photographers are largely matters of degree. The studios catering to the middle classes no doubt emulated the styles of the "top" photographers. But there is a subtle shift toward a greater generalizing of the image, evident in more retouching, shading, and removal of background detail. The negative has been masked, or painted before printing, to create the effect of a halo around the subject, enlarging the white area between the photographic image and the frame. This vignetting produces a more remote and ethereal situating of the image and an attenuation of its historicity. As André Bazin has noted, citing Ortega y Gasset, lightness is a significant feature of picture frames, whose purpose is to create a zone of indeterminacy between the world of the image and the viewing world.[17]

In all, the aim here seems to be to capture not so much the person at a particular moment in his career but an eternal image, a statement about his being perhaps more suitable for reverence. In comparison to the anecdotal, "occasional" photographic portraits in the albums of the princely family, this portrait has more of the qualities of a facial mask and seems less "European." (Although, it must be said, many older European photographic portraits, particularly from rural areas, display just such qualities.)

Perhaps connected to the retouching and manipulation of such photographic images is the fact that many Indian photographers, including many in Mussoorie and Dehra Dun (such as B. S. Thukral, S. N. Nautiyal, and the late J. S. Bhumbra), started their careers as painters. Indian photographic studios commonly put on their signs such phrases as "Photographer and Artist" and "Artists in Painting and Photographing." In Hindi the word for "picture" is that normally applied to photographs, and in English the two words are often used interchangeably. Another Mussoorie photographer, Bhanu Chandra Jasani, owner of Bhanu Art Studio in Library Bazaar, who also began work as a painter, once made retouched and "finished" photographs much like D. S. Bora's. His uncle before him had taken 10 x 12 inch glass plates and used his camera as an enlarger, directing the sun's rays into it through mirrors. "When I see some old photographs, I think, 'Beautiful!' " says Jasani. "People's faces are not photogenic. And they want in photography to look nice, you see, not ugly. . . . So this is the photographer's duty." Today most of Jasani's commissions come from the boarding schools. But he is aware that further changes lie ahead and is now thinking of installing a semiautomatic color lab.

A different manifestation of the conjunction of painting and photography can be seen in the work of another Mussoorie photographer, J. S. Bhumbra, who until his death in 1990 had a small shop between the Kulri and Landour bazaars. Bhumbra was perhaps the most skillful of the recent generation of photographers in detailed painting on photographs, although he stopped doing this some years ago. He used not only transparent watercolors for tinting but also opaque oil paint, which gave some of his portraits the look of a Botticelli or Bellini. Unlike most of the local studio photographers, he responded to color photography not as a threat but as an opportunity, and he began to make dramatic portraits with colored lights. These works have a theatrical quality, and Bhumbra consciously treated his subjects like actors on a stage in his small studio. He fussed with them, talked to them, and sometimes played music to them to put them in the right mood. He was after a certain emotional look in the face, which did not necessarily have anything to do with the personality of the sitter.

Bhumbra considered himself first and foremost an artist, striving to express something within him, "the concept of Art, the Art that we all seek," as he put it, and he carried this about as far as his commercial life would permit. I am not in a position to know how his clients may have responded to wedding and matrimonial pictures that looked like publicity stills from *Gone with the Wind*, but judging from his straitened circumstances he was not a commercial success. Until the end he made a very meager living from the sale of greeting cards, which carried his own color photographs of the local landscape.

On Gun Hill

In a sense Bhumbra's dramatic, cinematic portraits are the link back to the costume photography of the self-styled "outdoor photographers" of Gun Hill (where in imperial days a gun was fired daily at noon). Their stalls surround a large rectangular space like a parade ground. These stalls are hung with glittering costumes and at first glance look like booths at a fun fair. (One of H. S. Chadha's is even called "Fun Fair.") At the height of the tourist season in June and July there may be more than fifty photographers here, with another fifty scattered around other tourist sites in Mussoorie. As each cable car load of Indian tourists reaches the top of Gun Hill, the photographers and their touts descend upon them. The tourists are invited, cajoled, and sometimes physically hauled to the photographers' stalls. Although some resist, many others do not seem to mind, for this is one of the things they came for.

At the stalls the photographers and their assistants quickly dress them in brightly colored costumes that sparkle with sequins and gold thread. They are given props, such as metal jars, baskets of plastic flowers, and rifles. They are then taken, sometimes singly, more often in couples or groups, to points overlooking the mountain scenery. Rather than trying to describe the poses, the photographers demonstrate them or simply push their subjects into them. They use 35mm cameras and work expertly, like surgeons in the days before anesthetics, so that the photography is sometimes over before the subjects think it has begun. The photographs are paid for, or a deposit is given, and the clients receive the prints either at their hotels the following day or by post when they return home.

Domestic tourism is relatively new to the Indian middle class, which is now estimated at more than twenty million.[18] Travel in the past, even by poor people, often occurred in connection with pilgrimages or labor migration, but the idea of travel for pleasure is novel and glamorous. For many of those who come to Mussoorie, this is their first such trip, and often their honeymoon. Their objectives are often vague, but one seemingly paramount objective is to bring back photographs of themselves—what Bourdieu has called "monuments to leisure."[19] As few people have their own cameras (although this is rapidly changing), the work of the "outdoor" photographers provides both the photographs and an element of adventure.

The photographs themselves suggest what sort of adventure this may be. The costumes in which people are photographed conform broadly to three ideal types. The first are versions of traditional regional costumes, primarily those worn by women (although there are a few for men, including Punjabi-style turbans). These include a version of local Garhwali village dress and costumes modeled on the regional dress of Kashmir, Rajasthan, Gujarat, and so on. The resemblances are often approximate, and the amount of gold and silver tinsel tends to give the dresses a similar look. Certain modifications are necessary. For example, to simulate the amount of jewelry worn by some village women, imitation jewelry is sewn directly onto the headscarves and dresses. As H. S. Chadha explained, this became necessary because it took too long to put individual pieces of jewelry on the customers, and the jewelry was always getting lost. The usual prop accompanying any of the rural dresses is a water jar, which is to be held in formalized ways in the photographs (figure 6.8). "We give a water jar with the dress," says Chadha, "and this has cultural implications. . . . In the olden days when there were no water taps, the women went out to get water for the household. The water was carried only by women." Here Chadha appears to be linking the appeal of the water jar not only to nostalgia for rural life but perhaps also to its role as a sacred vessel in religious rites and to the association between a sexually ordered, traditional world and women's fertility, which is consistent with other Indian poetic imagery about water. The link with sexuality is perhaps supported by the second major female photographic prop, the basket of flowers, and the major male prop, the gun.

The second category of costumes, apparently only for men, are those belonging to "outlaws" or powerfully exotic figures, such as dacoits, Pathan tribesmen (figure 6.9), and Arab sheiks. These are accompanied by rifles, bandoliers worn across the chest, pistols, and (for the sheiks) obligatory sunglasses. According to Chadha, "When we asked the customers to dress like Gandhi they refused and said, 'Give us the costumes of bandits.' Bad characters are more powerful than good characters. . . . Truly, people prefer the costumes of a bandit, a thief, or a Shahenshah [lit. 'king of kings'/hero of a recent Hindi film of that name]."

A third category of costume epitomizes urban and especially Western sophistication. Its current most common form, intended rather vaguely for both men and women, is a sequin-covered "cocktail dress," sometimes with a butterfly motif, which in India is closely associated with romantic love. The main prop is a guitar, which is held in the various positions used by rock stars. Other symbols of urban power are at the moment absent on Gun Hill, but there was a period when, because of the Hindi film *Haré Rama Haré Krishna* (1971), a fascination with "hippieism" led to hippie costumes being devised.

It may be difficult to say precisely whether interest in the hippie was as a sophisticate or an exotic "outlaw" figure, but there seems little doubt that one further genre of Gun Hill photography relates to the social liberation promised by urban life, at least as it appears in the cinema. This kind of photograph requires no costumes but does require a certain daring,

6.8. Tourist in costume with water jar. Gun Hill, Mussoorie.
Gopal Ratorie, 1990. Courtesy of Glory Studio.

and in this sense a pose can indeed be regarded as a kind of costume,
equivalent to a disguise. (The standard poses for Gun Hill dacoits, for
example, are as much a part of the character as the turban, bandolier,
and rifle.) If one looks through the more private stock of the "outdoor"
photographers' photographs, one finds many couples embracing or arranging themselves like lovers on the ground. Most of them are newly

6.9. Tourist posing as a Pathan. Gun Hill, Mussoorie, 1989.
Photograph by David MacDougall.

married couples who have come to Mussoorie for their honeymoon. There is nothing more sexually explicit here than a kiss, but in India a lovers' kiss in public is shocking. On the screen, Indian film stars can writhe into extraordinary positions in the process of approaching the consummation of a kiss, but (until recently) the shot was always cut just before this moment was reached.

In the Gun Hill photographs one finds the full range of positions including the kiss, and once again one is reminded, as one is meant to be, of publicity photographs from Hindi films. Here the repression of sexuality is a powerful inducement to fantasy and idealization, as it perhaps is in other aspects of Indian popular culture. And for many young visitors to Mussoorie, tourism itself is closely associated with the cinema. In the periods of relative tranquility before the recent political disturbances in Kashmir, its valleys and mountains were the stock backdrop for holidaying film-star lovers, but these are now being replaced by the scenery of hill stations such as Mussoorie.[20] For the honeymoon couples who come here, tourism is perhaps the ultimate extension of the cinema experience, with themselves, for the only time in their lives, in the leading roles.

It will be apparent that each of these categories represents a major theme in mainstream Indian cinema: the nostalgia for a more benign rural age, the power offered by lawlessness, the wealth and greater social freedom of the city. The formulaic poses go beyond the cinema, however, and can be found in traditional and popular iconography. The pose with the water jar on the shoulder comes out of Mogul paintings. Images of the bandit's rifle held high and the Arab sheik's hands held out in prayer can be found in magazines and advertisements. But the link with Indian cinema is strengthened by the slightly low camera angles used on Gun Hill, so that the subjects appear against the sky in the dramatic manner of "filmi" heroes painted on cinema hoardings. H. S. Chadha is explicit about the link with cinema. The ideas for some costumes were taken directly from films (such as Amitabh Bachchan's character in *Shahenshah* [1987]), and he describes how certain costumes induce customers to speak lines from famous films, such as those of the bandit-hero Gabbar Singh, played by Amjad Khan in *Sholay* (1975), and a line of Raj Kumar's about "people in glass houses."

Dressing up as dangerous characters or as more familiar regional "types" (perhaps vaguely echoing nineteenth-century ethnography) does not require real contact with such people, and Gun Hill photography appears to provide purely vicarious pleasures. Having contact with the real seems a pleasure more sought after by European tourists.[21] In the anthropology of tourism, the Western tourist characteristically "kills the thing he loves" in the pursuit of "authenticity."[22] Indian tourists in Mussoorie appear to find satisfaction in the pursuit of the authentic (at least in the case of regional culture) without going very near it. Although a tourist may dress in a Garhwali costume ("hilly dresses," as they used to be advertised), one would be unlikely to find Indian tourists visiting a Garhwali village, whereas a European might go there to see "real" Indian peasants. At least outside their own countries, many young Westerners seek the *frisson* of a brush with Third World hardship, on the one hand, and the purity of exotic cultures on the other.[23] Chadha says Westerners don't like his costumes; they prefer to be photographed as they are. They go to see but not to be. If Mussoorie's outdoor photography is any guide, Indian tourists go enthusiastically to *be*, without hazarding actually being "in touch." They have little interest in such authenticities, which in any case are a matter of daily avoidance in Indian society.

Gun Hill photography is perhaps a perfect demonstration of the Indian principle of separation in proximity. Assuming another identity for a photograph is no threat to one's own. The costume never really touches one. In this respect constant negotiation of matters of ritual purity and pollution may provide Indians with a certain immunity, or at least confidence. "A millionaire would never wear such a costume," says Chadha, "but after seeing the attraction of it he will put it on, no matter how filthy and stinking it is. . . . He forgets everything because he has a strong feeling to wear the costume and look like a Garhwali man." It will also be remembered that Indian tourists had no hesitation in being photographed as hippies, who were regarded as filthy, drug-crazed, and foreign.

Photography is thus not a medium for contact with the dangerous, in oneself or others, but a consciously mediated form of representation. This allows it a certain freedom and wisdom. It is not caught up in the search for unitary truths; it need not be afraid of paint or of being self-referential. Indian popular photography is full of magical effects and frames within frames.[24] It is not afraid of "dressing up." Only in H. S. Chadha's private testing of his clients can it be called subversive.

Revelation and unmasking are clearly not part of this construction of photography, as they so often are in the West. Photography is not meant to break through class indifference or bridge social divisions. Nor, in domestic use, is it historical, in the sense of catching people unawares as part of a family narrative, a chronicle of change. Its purpose is not so much to define, for people already exist as defined beings, but to acknowledge and enlarge. Thus photography assists in the creation of a reality, not in the discovery (or uncovering) of it.

Missing Persons

What I have described above is a commonly held and culturally consistent view of Indian photography, but it is by no means universally applicable, and there are times when a different, more corrosive use of photography breaks through. If people ever actually looked closely at I.D. photographs they would find it there, in faces reduced to the status of numbers. And every night on Indian television there is a painful display of the invasion of the private domain, rupturing the carefully preserved protective membranes between Indian social groups. For five or ten minutes photographs are shown of missing persons. It is clear that these are often the only photographs that exist of them, for many are almost indecipherably fuzzy images enlarged from group photographs, or pictures of the persons at a much younger age. Some are school, matrimonial, or wedding photographs. Many are of children (figure 6.10). Here, images that are redolent with unfathomable personal meanings are thrust into public view and are transformed into emblems of vulnerability and loss. They reach the public stripped of memory. Part of the poignancy of seeing these photographs is that of perceiving them simultaneously as (privately) known loved ones and mere (public) bodily envelopes. The surface of the face is what matters if the persons are to be found, or their bodies identified. But the piece of paper may be all that remains, a reminder that in the end every photograph is that of a missing person.

6.10. Photograph of a missing boy shown on Indian television, November 1989.

And what are we to make of the work of R. S. Sharma, another Mussoorie photographer? In their stark, "realist" look these photographs stand in sharp contrast to almost all the other kinds of photography practiced in Mussoorie. Sharma is the proprietor of a small studio in Landour Bazaar called Glamour Studio, which he has run for more than forty years (figure 6.11). He is the only Mussoorie photographer to have resisted the shift to color photography. He continues to make black and white portraits on 120 film (with a Yashica double-lens reflex camera) in the style he adopted at the beginning of his career (figures 6.12a and 6.12b).

At first the photographs look naïve, like only slight refinements on the work of the street photographers. They are resolutely frontal, simply lit and staring. The subjects, a varied cultural mix of poorer townspeople and farmers from nearby villages, look into the camera with a disconcerting intensity and openness. Taken as a body of work, Sharma's photographs are an extraordinary gallery of Indian faces, varied in type, but by no means "types." As in all good portraiture, each picture denies us access to a life, but in doing so each also attests to a life.

Sharma's method requires people to sit for three to four minutes. This is not the perfunctory photography of the street photographers nor the instantaneous photography of Gun Hill, but neither is it like the careful

6.11. R. S. Sharma at the door of his studio, Mussoorie, 1988.
Photograph by David MacDougall.

staging done by Bhumbra or the lengthy holding of a pose that makes so many people in nineteenth-century daguerreotypes look dead. The timing seems about right to allow the subjects to collect themselves, to take seriously the moment of photography, but not to lose their energy in waiting. If this is part of Sharma's talent, then it is a very unobtrusive one. Sharma himself is reticent about claiming any gift beyond a certain technical expertise. He does everything himself—developing, printing, framing, bookkeeping—and he is committed to black and white because otherwise, he says, "you have nothing to do with the photograph."

If one looks around his tiny studio there is evidence that Sharma could work in another style if he chose to. There are several portraits with oblique poses and softer, more conventional lighting. And surprisingly, Sharma once worked briefly in Bombay taking production stills for a film company, but he didn't like it. In Mussoorie's photographic microcosm, Sharma seems an anachronism and, stylistically, an anomaly. His prices are not necessarily the cheapest, and he portrays his subjects with uncompromising and often unflattering directness. However, he is a success. While other photographers struggle to make a living, he has a regular succession of clients. The other photographers may think him old-fashioned but they nevertheless seem to respect him.

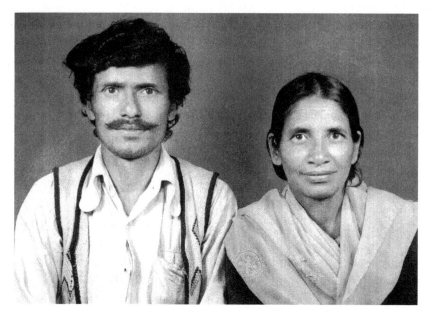

6.12a. A married couple from Garhwal. R. S. Sharma, Mussoorie, 1980s.
Courtesy of Glamour Studio.

6.12b. A married couple from Garhwal. R. S. Sharma, Mussoorie, 1980s.
Courtesy of Glamour Studio.

How are we to account for his success? There is clearly a market for his kind of photography, which at first glance appears such a contradiction of Indian conventions. One local explanation (from Indra Prakash) is that he has built up a loyal clientele over many years, mostly poor or rural people who would be embarrassed to go to an unfamiliar or more upmarket photographer. Another possible explanation is that he has simply replaced the street photographers who no longer exist in Mussoorie. Against this second view must be put the fact that the pictures he takes are not merely for identification purposes (although he takes his share of I.D. photos) but also include many double portraits of couples. These are apparently for domestic use. Nor does he engage in the kind of trick effects (through reframing and combining paper negatives) offered by some street photographers in Delhi. In the Garhwal hills beyond Mussoorie we saw one of his photographs hung high up on a wall inside a village house: a framed portrait of an old man, now dead, garlanded like the portraits in the Ram Chander shop. In its pose, energy, and clarity it displays very much Sharma's present style.

In such a setting one may also conclude that certain attributes of Sharma's photography owe as much to an Indian as a European origin. These characteristics lie in the extreme frontality and symmetry of the pose, which, although it can be found in European portrait photography (for example, in the armchair "bulldog" pose), is found less often than one might suppose. The close cropping at the sides and the neutral background, used in preference to a pictorial backdrop, isolate the figure and project it forward in a way that, combined with its lateral symmetry, has more in common with early Bodhisatvas and Tirthankara figures and the hieratic medieval depictions of Hindu deities than more recent Indian religious images influenced by Mogul and European art. The same pose can be found elsewhere in Indian photography, particularly in the nineteenth century, as well as in modern Hindu religious posters. A similar non-European style, characterized by frontality, symmetry, massiveness, and whole-body framing, has been noted in formal Yoruba portrait photography by Sprague,[25] who relates it to conventions of Yoruba sculpture. If, as in the Garhwali village, Sharma's photographs are sometimes placed in positions of honor, the pose used is appropriate to semi-sacred ancestors before whom *puja* may be performed and who, like iconic images of the gods, possess *darshan*—the ability not only to be seen but also to see those who regard them.[26]

The convergence of the worldly and the sacred in these images suggests a further explanation for Sharma's success: that in India there exist different needs and different expectations of photography among a very large class of people who are rarely photographed. Because of their lack of influence, this view often goes unrecognized and lacks prominence in mainstream photography. Despite the popular taste for the elaborate and multilayered in films, when it comes to photographs of themselves and their families, many people desire a more severe, realist approach—photographs that more vividly recall the living person.[27] The formal, frontal pose may also more fully reflect the primary function of photography as perceived by members of a peasant society—to represent the subject in a way that is regulated, unassuming, and deferential, demanding reciprocal deference.[28] Within this context, R. S. Sharma arguably provides a style of photography that is more compatible with his clients' wishes than the work of other photographers and that does not impose upon peasants and working-class people the pretensions of the bourgeoisie, as so often happens in other studios.

After looking at the work of R. S. Sharma it is also difficult not to come to the conclusion that here, for all his lack of pretension, is an unknown photographer of unmistakable power and artistic integrity. He is, for me, the most interesting photographer in Mussoorie, and perhaps his modest success simply attests to a tacit recognition of these qualities among his clients. Comparing the work of many photographers in Mussoorie, past and present, one might also not be wrong in seeing a certain unity and closure between the domestic photographs of the princely families and the "plain style" of Glamour Studio. It is a spiritual resemblance that places both of them far from the world of Gun Hill.

Notes

I am indebted to Christopher Gregory, Gary Kildea, Judith MacDougall, Christopher Pinney, Nicholas Thomas, and Paul Willemen for their comments and suggestions on earlier drafts of this chapter.

1. All quotations from Mussoorie sources are taken from tape recordings (or translations of them) recorded during the making of the film *Photo Wallahs* (1991) in July–December 1988 and October–December 1989.

2. Sontag 1977: 52.

3. Carpenter 1976: 118–21.

4. Gillen 1968: 261.

5. Geffroy 1990.

6. Pinney 1990a.

7. Ibid., p. 272. The parallel with natural science collecting is also evident in some of the language used at the time. In directing government officials to obtain the photographs for *The People of India*, E. C. Bayley, Secretary of the Government, India, specified the "photographic likeness of a few specimens of the most remarkable tribes" (Cohn 1984: 16). See figure 6.3.

8. Das 1988.

9. Gutman 1982: 141–43.

10. Gombrich 1972.

11. Price & Jamin 1988: 160.

12. Sontag 1977: 154.

13. By June 1999 the price for three photographs had increased to ten rupees, or about 25 U.S. cents at the exchange rates then current.

14. See Berreman 1972.

15. Parkes 1850: 229.

16. In 2003 I saw an even larger photographic print, measuring about two meters high by one meter wide, in Mysore Palace. It was made by Del Tufo & Co. of South Parade, Bangalore, and Mount Road, Madras. It was a photograph of the young Wodeyar prince and princesses of Mysore, taken about 1894.

17. Bazin 1967: 165.

18. That was the estimate at the time this essay was written in 1992. It is now more like forty million.

19. Bourdieu 1990b: 36.

20. *Police Public* (1990), directed by Esmayeel Shroff and starring Raj Kumar and Naseeruddin Shah, was filmed largely in Mussoorie in 1989. A major reason for shooting on location, the crew told us, was to ensure continuous access to the stars, who in Bombay would be constantly dividing their time among many productions. Christopher Pinney reports reading an interview with a film director who gave the same rationale for filming at hill stations and other remote locations.

21. However, being photographed in regional dress was also a feature of European tourism at the turn of the twentieth century.

22. See Crick 1989: 309; Errington & Gewertz 1989: 43.

23. By contrast, for nineteenth-century British residents of India "the natives" were but one item on a standard itinerary of sights to be viewed when visiting such hill stations as Ootacamund. See Hockings 1987.

24. Pinney 1991.

25. Sprague 1978.

26. Hancock 1989: 9.

27. Christopher Gregory suggests that in the worship of photographs as ancestral gods, photography in India is perceived as mediating between the living and the dead by reuniting the sign (image) with its referent (the person), which have been split by death. If H. S. Chadha takes pictures of people who appear as gods but are really thieves, R. S. Sharma takes pictures of those who appear as people but are really gods. Christopher Gregory, personal communication.

28. Bourdieu 1990b: 81–83.

7

STAGING THE BODY: THE PHOTOGRAPHY
OF JEAN AUDEMA

S EVERAL YEARS ago I bought two picture postcards dating from
around 1905. Most postcards fit into one or another generic category and give little away about the photographer who took the picture. These two, however, hinted at a witty and unconventional personality. They show an encampment in the heart of French colonial Africa, at
a place called "La Vallée de la Moundji Mayumbe." There is a tent, a
camp table, and a chair set in scrubland, with some seventeen African
soldiers, porters, and servants scattered around in various attitudes of
vigilance and relaxation. The photographs (figures 7.1a and 7.1b) appear
to be of a military or hunting expedition, or possibly an administrative
tour. In one of them, seated at the table, is a bearded European in his
forties or fifties, dressed in a uniform or safari clothing and wearing a
topee. At first glance the second photograph appears to be a duplicate of
the first, except that here the European is gone, as though vanished into
thin air. There is the suggestion of a ghostly presence still occupying the
empty table and chair. Upon closer inspection, it is clear that the chair
has been moved to the other side of the table. It is also clear that the
Africans in the scene, although in roughly the same positions, have moved
slightly between the taking of the two photographs.

Who was the European, and where had he gone? At first I thought he
might be the photographer himself, who had perhaps gone to attend to
his camera and taken the empty photograph (that is, empty of himself) as
he set up the scene. Then, when he was securely seated within it, he had
had an assistant take the second. Could this have been self-photography
in the days before the self-timer? I am now fairly certain that the European
in the picture is not the photographer. Nonetheless, the two pictures remain a puzzle. One question that arises, surely, is which picture was taken
first? Viewed separately, the two photographs are merely descriptive.
Viewed together, they suggest a narrative of sorts. It struck me as odd that
both versions had been published, for either would have made a satisfactory postcard on its own. Someone appeared to have a sense of humor.

These two postcards were the work of Jean Audema,[1] a photographer
who had already attracted my attention for other reasons. They were

7.1a. "Un Campement dans la Vallée de la Moundji Mayumbe,"
postcard by J. Audema, French Congo, ca. 1905.

7.1b. "17. Un Campement dans la vallée de la Moundji,"
postcard by J. Audema, French Congo, ca. 1905.

among a number of postcards of African scenes that I had bought from time to time over the years. Audema's name appeared on some of them, printed on the front of the card in small red or black letters in a caption reading "Collection J. Audema." Less often his signature appeared in white, apparently written on the negative. All of Audema's photographs were taken in the French Congo around the end of the nineteenth century. The postcards were printed in the French town of Nancy, at first by A.B. & Co. and from 1905 onward by Imprimeries Réunies de Nancy. About half had been sent through the post and bore postmarks ranging from 1904 to 1910, with one as late as 1920. I had bought about thirty of his cards in all—at the Paris flea market, from street stands, and from postcard dealers.[2] Clearly Audema, like François-Edmond Fortier in Senegal, had been a popular and successful photographer in his own time, at least in this genre.[3] But when I tried to find out more about him, he seemed to have vanished from public memory as completely as the European in his picture.

My main interest was in colonial photography rather than postcards themselves. However, postcards offer a particularly useful insight into colonial and settler history for what they show of public tastes, the interests of photographers, and the subjects photographed.[4] Much can also be learned from how they are captioned and what is written on them.[5] Audema's photographs had especially interested me. They possessed a stylistic originality and suggested a cast of mind that made them stand out from almost all the other colonial photographs I had seen. I was curious to know more about him. But although postcards have recently attracted considerable attention as cultural artifacts, far less is known about the photographers who produced them. That proved to be true in this case.

Like many of his contemporaries in colonial Africa, Audema produced a series of photographs showing the "native types" of the region in which he was stationed. These visual taxonomies can be traced back to the photographs of tribe, caste, and occupation produced for administrative purposes in India as early as the 1850s.[6] They have an even earlier heritage in the representations of *petits métiers* dating from the sixteenth century.[7] There was a late resurgence of the idea in August Sander's project to produce a photographic typology of the classes and occupations of Weimar Germany. Postcards showing "native types" had anthropological overtones, for the publishers realized that they could profitably appeal to the public's passion for exoticism, and often eroticism, under the guise of scientific knowledge. Yet it is likely that many of those who produced these photographs had a genuine interest in the different cultural groups and individuals they encountered. Postcards were simply one of the most immediate, popular, and lucrative forms of publication available.

Some of Audema's postcards are in what could be called the "anthropo-metric style," derived from the methods developed by Thomas Henry Huxley and John Lamprey in the 1860s for anthropological photography. Anthropometrics was based on the mistaken assumption that social evo-lution could be seen encoded in physical characteristics. The most well-known formula, a pair of frontal and profile views, still survives in police identification photographs. An anthropometric intention is apparent in some of Audema's poses, but in others it seems tongue-in-cheek, espe-cially when seen in the larger context of his photographic output. What first attracted me to Audema was that the people in his photographs seemed to possess a remarkable élan and self-confidence. This contrasted with the many colonial photographs of the period in which the subjects look embarrassed, coerced, or miserable. It pointed to a wider range of sensibilities and attitudes to be found in colonial photography than is sometimes acknowledged.

I was frequently aware, as well, of a disjunction between the images on these postcards and how they were captioned. For the most part, the cap-tions simply give the name of a place or tribal group, or sometimes both, transforming the persons seen into specimens. Many are prefaced with "Congo Français et dépendences," adding a further colonial and geo-graphical imprimature. The captions are thus informational and political in character, denying the obvious individuality of the people photo-graphed, and in fact contradicting it with the stamp of the "native type." Many are in fact described as "Type Banda," "Types N'Goundis," and so on, or they are placed in another general category such as "femme," "enfant," "guerrier," and so forth. There are a few cases in which the title and name of a notable person is given—for example, "N'gara, chef des Pandés, à Bania"—but this is rare. The images and the words attached to them are thus of a very different order, for the images present us with a person rather than a category; however, the words imply a high degree of uniformity within each ethnic group while at the same time suggesting a high degree of variation among ethnic groups. Both assumptions are obviously suspect. It is difficult to know how much the disparities between captions and images are indicative of Audema's view of things or were more fully institutionalized in administrative and publishing practice. Audema was clearly the source of most of the information printed on the postcards, but the form it took followed established postcard conventions.

It was usual at this time to pose the subjects with care before taking the picture because of the difficulty of setting up a glass-plate camera and the long exposures sometimes required.[8] However, Audema seems to have taken greater pains in this than most. Each portrait and group photograph shows forethought and a certain flamboyance. Equally interesting are the stances he has chosen for his subjects. Some of his groups possess a styl-

7.2. "Guerriers Oudombo–Region de l'Ogooué,"
postcard by J. Audema, French Congo, ca. 1905.

ishness that evokes the heroic poses of figures in historical tableaux or
the arrogance of fashion models[9] (figure 7.2). There is something very like
an untold drama going on in these images. One might well wonder if the
subjects felt some discomfort or resentment at striking these poses, but as
far as one can tell (and this must be largely a matter of interpretation)
there appears to be a degree of cooperation in the process. The confidence

of the subjects looks more like their response to the importance the photographer has attached to making the photograph and perhaps the appreciation he is showing them as his actors.

The stylistic qualities of Audema's photographs were so distinctive that I could soon spot a postcard of his among hundreds of others on a dealer's table. Although other colonial photographers placed their subjects in formal poses, few maintained his stylistic consistency. I also came to recognize some of Audema's subjects as individuals, for he made a point of photographing a number of them from different angles. These different poses would appear on separate postcards, issued and reissued over a considerable period. Among those so treated is a young Fang man identified only as "Guerrier Yenvi" with a spear, feathers in his hair, and elaborate chains and amulets strung around his body (figure 7.3). His portrait appears in several versions, not only taken from different angles but printed in different sizes on the postcards. Whether the printing variations were at Audema's behest is hard to say, but this man was clearly one of the photographer's favorites. The images of him must have been well known, for one of them served in 1910 as the basis for a series of postage stamps from Congo Français Gabon (figure 7.4).

For all the hauteur exhibited by their subjects, Audema's individual portraits have an intimacy that distinguishes them from the coldly objectified look of so many colonial studies of "native types."[10] A youth with distinctive scarification on his chest and abdomen appears on one postcard identified only as "Type Bakamba" (figure 7.5). Scarification, along with tattooing and coiffures, seems to have been a preoccupation of colonial photographers, and the number of postcards devoted to it amounts almost to a subgenre.[11] Tattooing had been known and emulated in Europe since Captain Cook's time, but scarification inspired fascination and horror and was evidently taken as an indication of the mind of the "savage" visibly inscribed on his own body. A number of Audema's postcards dwell on this type of image. But apart from the scarification of the young Kamba man, it is difficult to see why he was chosen as a subject. He is not a heroic figure, a teenager really, and hardly an ideal "tribal type."[12] There may be a degree of homoerotic interest underlying this picture, which gains support from the rather large number of photographs by Audema depicting young men as "warriors."

Audema, however, unlike many colonial photographers such as Fortier, never seems to have indulged in overtly erotic photography, such as the postcard standby of bare-breasted young African women. None of the postcards I have seen show young women with their arms raised to emphasize their breasts, nor are any of his subjects in languid reclining positions, as one often sees in other African postcards. Many of his portraits are of older or middle-aged women, not at all stereotypically erotic in character.[13] Although a number of colonial photographers were clearly

205. - CONGO FRANÇAIS. - Guerrier Yenvi

Collection J. Audema

7.3. "Guerrier Yenvi," postcard by J. Audema, French Congo, ca. 1905.

engaged in taking suggestive photographs of semiclothed Africans for the European market, the criticism that is often directed at them as a group may be misplaced and perhaps reflects a certain historical and cultural insularity. For colonists like Audema, nakedness would soon have become as ordinary as for local people. It may be politically satisfying to see all colonial photographic subjects as exploited, but it also does many of them a disservice, denying them any agency or authority at the time.

7.4. A 5-centime stamp issued by Postes Congo Français Gabon, February–March 1910, based on a photograph by J. Audema.

Several writers have made an effort to portray this history more accurately by focusing on the varied approaches of individual photographers and exploring the relationships between them and their subjects. Christraud Geary has examined the work of Anna Wuhrmann in what is now Cameroon and that of Casimir Zagourski in the Belgian Congo, both of whom made photographs that appeared on postcards. Philippe David has analyzed the massive output of Fortier in Senegal. There has also been an effort to recover the "lost" careers of African photographers who ran their own photographic businesses and produced postcards in the colonial era, such as the father and son team of N. Walwin and J.A.C. Holm in Ghana and Nigeria, the Lisk-Carew brothers in Sierra Leone, and Alexander Accolatse in Togo.[14]

Audema's Group Photographs

More interesting in some respects than Audema's portraits of individuals are his group photographs. Here his peculiar mastery of *mise-en-scène* emerges most clearly. Nineteenth-century photographers prided themselves on arranging people artfully before the camera, but for the most

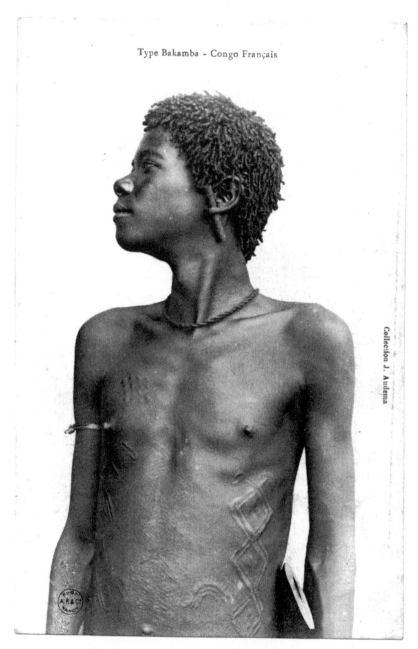

Type Bakamba - Congo Français

Collection J. Audema

7.5. "Type Bakamba," postcard by J. Audema, French Congo, ca. 1905.

part they followed tried-and-true generic conventions—the military portrait with the crisply held cigarette, the family group with the father asserting his authority, the sports team or school photo with the junior members stretched out in the front row like recumbent lions. The colonial
equivalents of these were somewhat different: the lineup photograph of
dejected "natives," the "anthropometric" studies previously discussed,
people at work as laborers or artisans, missionaries surrounded by their
happy converts, and various tasteless jokes about native ignorance and
procreation.

Audema's group photographs are, so far as I can tell, unprecedented.[15]
They are of people in small clusters facing outward, several looking up
as though forming a defiant and self-protective unit (figure 7.6). They are
often armed with spears, shields, knives, rifles, and other weapons. Their
careful arrangement sometimes suggests anthropometrics, for one may
find at least one figure in profile and one facing the camera head-on. But
in fact Audema seems more interested in achieving a balanced and varied
composition of human forms. There is a conscious interplay of diagonals,
with spears and occasionally other elements cutting across vertical lines.
Each figure has been carefully posed individually as well as positioned in
relation to the others. Many appear to have been given a specific piece of
stage "business" such as holding a spear at a certain angle. When people
are not holding objects, their limbs are relaxed in contrast to the other
figures. Unlike his portraits, which are usually photographed using a plain
white backdrop, the group photographs are situated in a specific place,
the details of the village setting clearly visible around them.[16]

In these groups, Audema has created a kind of living statuary, perhaps
inspired by classical models or French academic painting. He may also
have been influenced by the neoclassical sculpture of Rodin and such earlier figures as Jean-Baptiste Carpeaux and Albert-Ernest Carrier-Belleuse.
The exaggerated pride of his subjects, rather more rare in French sub-
Saharan photography than in British photography of East African pastoralists, nevertheless accords with the spirit of much nineteenth-century
French Orientalist art, romantically celebrating the peoples of North Africa, the Mediterranean, and the Middle East.[17] Yet there is at the same
time something not altogether serious about Audema's portrayal of the
noble savage, as if he were mocking the very formality and dignity he was
creating. Perhaps he saw it as false, or an overblown ideal. His pictures
suggest that he knew there was much more to his subjects than photographs could reveal. Was it, then, a photographic game he was playing, a
potentially well-paying one? Was it a *jeu d'esprit* in collusion with his
subjects?

Although Audema's most dramatic pictures are his group photographs
and individual portraits of young men and warriors, he shows an equal

108. - CONGO FRANÇAIS. - Indigènes du Congo Français

Collection J. Audema

7.6. "Indigènes du Congo Français," postcard by J. Audema,
French Congo, ca. 1905.

interest in formal arrangement when he is photographing more domestic scenes. He made pictures of families and ordinary villagers, as in one typical postcard entitled "Types N'Goundis, Région de Nola" (figure 7.7). The young man and woman, adolescent girl, and two younger girls in this photograph could be the members of one family or simply unrelated people assembled by Audema for the photograph. The figures have been carefully arranged by size, the height of the man to the right offset by the group of the three shorter girls lower on the left. The man's profile is repeated in the profile of one of the girls, while the others face outward, slightly away from the camera. The necklaces of the girl on the left and the woman make sharp diagonals across the picture, and their arms and leather skirts form pairs of counterdiagonals lower down. The five figures are almost but not quite touching, forming a compact and yet complex cluster. This is a far cry from the lineup pose found in so many colonial photographs, and although stiffer than many other group photographs by Audema, it still gives the impression of a collaborative effort.

Another picture, captioned "Types N'Gombès – Rive gauche de l'Oubangui," shows a senior man and two women, perhaps two of his wives (figure 7.8). The hands of the women are held in formal but relaxed positions. Their gazes cross, one looking away from and the other toward the camera. The man leans slightly into the photograph, grasping his spear. These appear to be important people in their community, unintimidated by the photographer's presence and acknowledging the photograph as their due. The same three appear in another postcard with the same caption, this time joined by seven other people.

As in the portrait of the Kamba youth, there is a personal directness in several of Audema's portraits that appears to bypass aesthetic or commercial considerations. These are more like pictures of friends or acquaintances than exotica, despite the fact that they are captioned according to the practice of the day as tribal types. Two photographs that Audema personally signed on the negatives are of a Banziri woman with a stooped posture and elaborately coiffed hair (figure 7.9). She is an older woman whose body is worn but whose face suggests intelligence and a strong character. She appears to have been photographed as much for this as for the ethnic group she represents. In both photographs Audema's signature appears on her arm, as though making a personal claim or a statement of regard. Another photograph, of a Banziri youth, is one of two portraying him (figure 7.10a). It shows him posed conventionally as a heroic warrior, whereas the other shows him looking directly into the camera with a slight smile (figure 7.10b). The second is an unusual photograph to have been published commercially. It is more like a snapshot, and like the portraits of the Banziri woman, it suggests that Audema may have had more sustained contact with the Banziri than with other groups.

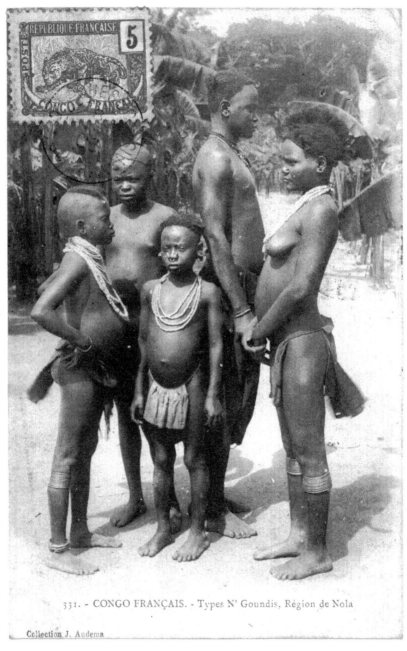

7.7 "Types N'Goundis, Région de Nola," postcard by J. Audema,
French Congo, ca. 1905.

Collection J. Audema

CONGO FRANÇAIS et Dépendances
Types N'Gombès - Rive gauche de l'Oubangui

7.8 "Types N'Gombès – Rive gauche de l'Oubangui,"
postcard by J. Audema, ca. 1905.

CONGO FRANÇAIS et Dépendances
Femme Banziri - Oubangui

Collection J. Audema

7.9 "Femme Banziri – Oubangui," postcard by J. Audema,
French Congo, ca. 1905.

An Elusive Life

When I first became interested in these photographs, I knew nothing
about Audema himself. This continued for some years. Until 1998 I could
find no mention of his name or his work in books on photography. Except
for the interest of a few postcard collectors, he seemed to have vanished

7.10a "Type Banziri – Bas-Kouango," postcard by J. Audema,
French Congo, ca. 1905.

7.10b "Type Banziri – Bas-Kouango," postcard by J. Audema,
French Congo, ca. 1905.

completely into the colonial past. His name was unknown at the photographic archives of the Musée de l'Homme in Paris, or at the Royal Anthropological Institute in London, or the Pitt Rivers Museum in Oxford. There was a collection of 193 of his postcards at the Eliot Elisofon Photographic Archives of the Smithsonian Institution in Washington, but little was known about his life. He was mentioned briefly in a 1998 collection of essays on postcards representing foreign cultures.[18] Two of his postcards appeared in an exhibition of the Völkerkundemuseum in Zurich and were reproduced in the exhibition catalogue.[19] One was unattributed and the other was accompanied only by his name. Four other Audema postcards appeared in Christraud Geary's *In and Out of Focus: Images from Central Africa, 1885–1960*, together with a short assessment of his work based on the Smithsonian's holdings.[20] It was only at the Centre des Archives d'Outre-mer in Aix-en-Provence that Audema's life seemed to be known in any detail, and then only as a colonial servant rather than a photographer. His file concerns his postings, his promotions, his sick leave, and so on, but nothing about his photography.[21]

Born in Montpellier on 19 August 1864, Jean François Audema started his working life as an accountant but joined the colonial service in 1894. He was made an Agent Administrateur, 2nd Class, and was immediately posted to Loango in the French Congo. He rose steadily through the administration, promoted to Chef de Poste, Chef de Station, and eventually Administrateur Adjoint.[22] He appears to have traveled widely in the colony, partly due to his attachment to the Bureau des Concessions, which supervised economic and, in particular, agricultural development. For two years he ran a model plantation at Loudema, where a wide range of crops was grown.

Audema's career seems to have been decisively shaped by his appointment as adjutant to Henri Bobichon, who held a series of high administrative posts and who in 1904 effectively became the governor of the interior of the French Congo.[23] Bobichon had been appointed by Liotard, the governor of the territory of Oubangui, to develop navigation on the Oubangui and other rivers. On one occasion, a river steamer was cut into three pieces, carried by porters around a series of rapids, and reconstructed upstream. Possibly Audema's interest in photographing river steamers resulted from his association with Bobichon. Bobichon undertook a number of increasingly important missions, and in 1903 he was charged with exploring and extending administration into the areas of the Likouala and Sangha in the vast concession of the Frères Trechot.[24] Part of Bobichon's brief was to study the local populations, and Audema's photographic activities may well have been encouraged by Bobichon as part of his duties. Trained in the army, Bobichon had a reputation as an effective if mercurial administrator who occasionally got into trouble with his superiors. Much

7.11 Portrait of Jean Audema, F. Cairol, Montpellier, France, ca. 1909.
Courtesy of the family archives of Benoît Estival-Audéma.

of his work seems to have been to bring peace to areas where rebellions had previously been met with savage repression by the colonial authorities. He respected the African population and was vigilant in curbing the abuses against them by the French companies that were exploiting the resources of the region.

Audema's colonial service ended in 1905, when he returned to France on sick leave. His illness persisted and he never returned to the Congo. He spent the last period before his retirement in 1910 attached to the Madagascar bureau. He was made a Chevalier de l'Ordre de l'Etoile d'Anjouan in 1909 and was awarded a pension for illnesses contracted in the course of his duties (figure 7.11). Within his family, Audema was considered the "eccentric."[25] He never married but was apparently a great womanizer and was known for his many female conquests. He died in 1936 at the age of 72 and was buried at his family home in Castries, near Montpellier. We know from his dossier that he spoke some conversational English. Perhaps the most curious fact about him is that he lost part of his left arm while still young. His brother Antoine accidentally wounded him with a rifle while they were playing, perched in a tree at Castries.[26] (Antoine later became a general in the French army.) This loss does not seem to have impeded his professional or photographic career, but how he managed to take all of his photographs remains a matter of some interest.

The official files in the colonial archives give hints of Audema's character but little insight into him as an artist or creative person. The earliest assessment by a superior, L. de Roll, in 1899, describes him as "a somewhat difficult personality who sometimes makes relations with the local people troublesome."[27] If one is sympathetic to Audema, it is possible to put this disgruntled comment down to his actual interest in local people and the time he devoted to photographing them. Another note in his dossier, dating from 1901, describes him as "a somewhat hotheaded officer."[28] Later, he appears to have earned a good reputation, for in 1904 he is praised by Gentil, the Commissaire Général in Brazzaville, for his zeal and devotion in developing agriculture in the colony and in particular setting up the model plantation at Loudema. A small number of Audema's postcards attest to this interest, showing various plants and trees. By 1906 he is described as "loyal, with much common sense, who knows how to make himself liked and obeyed." His moral character is not questioned, and he is credited with "serious intelligence" and "excellent judgment." Close to his retirement, there is a suggestion of his creative abilities in a note from the lieutenant-governor, who describes him as "a good officer, very gifted, who is well able to carry out his plans."[29]

In some respects, Audema's photographic career parallels that of Fortier, probably the most prolific producer of postcards in French West Africa. Both traveled widely in their regions, but whereas some postcard publishers commissioned or purchased photographs taken by others, Audema's and Fortier's "collections" are primarily their own work. How Audema started making postcards, and what his dealings were with publishers and printers, is still not known.

Judging by the different versions of Audema's postcards that appeared, and the long period over which they were reprinted and circulated, his photography was well received and widely disseminated in the early years of the century. Postcards provided one of the only outlets for many photographers' work at this time, for the use of photographs in magazines and newspapers was still in its infancy. Postcards also ensured that the photographs were widely seen, both in terms of actual numbers of viewers and geographically. The period from 1900 to 1910 was the heyday of the picture postcard and coincides exactly with Audema's output. It has been estimated that a typical print run of postcards would have been about three thousand, with some cards reprinted many times over. As Peterson points out, in 1909–10, 866 million were mailed in Great Britain alone, and this says nothing about those that were purchased but never sent.[30] In France it is estimated that 8 million postcards were printed in 1899, increasing to 60 million in 1902 and 123 million in 1910.[31] In the context of colonialism, postcards were one of the most important sources of information (and misinformation) for the general public about how colonized people looked and behaved, as well as creating and reinforcing many of the stereotypes of empire. Even among the colonizers themselves, a series of "native types" of the sort produced by Audema would have served to sharpen impressions of the different regions and peoples under French control.

At the end of the nineteenth century, picture postcards such as Audema's served several functions and impinged upon people in a variety of ways. They would have been viewed very differently by French residents in the colonies than by their friends and relatives in metropolitan France. It cannot be assumed that attitudes in the colonies were more or less racist than attitudes at "home," but the nature of this racism would have been different. In France it would have been more romantic and tinged with exoticism. The colonists saw Africans under more intimate circumstances but at the same time belonged to a settler society determined to maintain its power and sense of superiority. Postcards passed from Africa to Europe, sending ambivalent messages about these attitudes. The picture postcard was a relatively new phenomenon, its roles multiple and not yet clearly defined. It was just beginning to become an artifact of travel and tourism, which it was destined to become almost exclusively once its other roles—as a medium of communication, of advertising, of instruction; as a way of printing private photographs; and as an object for collectors—were abandoned or displaced by more attractive alternatives.

At this time, the picture postcard was part of a more restricted spectrum of visual media than was soon to become available, and its power to shape public perceptions was therefore considerable. Photography was being practiced, but only by professionals and dedicated amateurs. Compared to today, families would have owned only a few photographs. Books and magazines were beginning to include photographs, but sparingly. Cinema was in its infancy. The postcard craze followed closely on the heels of the stereograph craze, and to some extent the didactic function and tone of the stereograph, depicting faraway places and peoples, was also adopted by the postcard. Even earlier, large albumen prints had been made for sale to travelers and collectors to paste into their scrapbooks. The importance of these photographic prints has generally been underestimated, for in many respects they were the direct forerunners of the picture postcard. They were produced in large numbers by local photographers in such far-flung places as Colombo and Port Said and were sold through local stationery shops and chemists. Others were produced by travelers with a talent for photography such as Francis Frith, Felice Antonio Beato, and Samuel Bourne. Like postcards, they were often numbered and captioned. Many were in fact later turned into postcards.

Audema and His Subjects

In the absence of diaries or letters, it is impossible to know from Audema's photographs precisely what his feelings were toward his subjects or his relations with them. Photographers have been adept at both concealing and revealing the motivations behind their work, perhaps especially so within the context of colonial power relations. But overall, Audema's published work, which may have numbered several hundred different postcards,[32] gives an impression of interest in, and involvement with, the people and varied cultures he encountered. If nothing else, this is indicated by the care he took in documenting them. Although people's bodies were, in a formal sense, his main subjects—he took pleasure in their postures, their arrangement, their decoration, and their physiques—there is not the sense of a fascist aesthetics, as Susan Sontag has remarked upon in the African photography of Leni Riefenstahl.[33] Fascist aesthetics subordinates individuals to a dream of an idealized community and body culture.[34] Although Audema presents his subjects in heroic stances, as Riefenstahl does in her books (and indeed in her films, *Olympia* [1938] and *Triumph of the Will* [1935]), there is no suggestion that these men and women belong to a master race or that they possess some primeval power. Their heroism perhaps lies more in the fact that they have survived colonialism than that (as Sontag puts it) they are "awaiting the final ordeal of their proud heroic community, their imminent extinction."[35] This is not *Götterdämmerung*, at least not yet.

The fascist aesthetic is all about the triumph of power and the ecstasy of submitting to power. This power is often seen as primitive, reaching back to a time before modern civilization—in the case of the Nazis, to Teutonic myth; in Riefenstahl's adulation of the Nuba, to a pure and elemental African society before its contamination by outsiders. As Sontag observes, it repudiates anything intellectual, skeptical, or individual. "What is distinctive about the fascist version of the old idea of the Noble Savage is its contempt for all that is reflective, critical, and pluralistic."[36]

There is little evidence of this sensibility in Audema's photography. In his portraits, if less so in his group photographs, he appears more interested in individuals and in cultural diversity than in any notion of a transcendent African ideal. He photographs people as much for themselves, with their imperfections and distinctive personalities, as for their exemplification of tribal characteristics. When he creates a dramatic scene, it is almost a scene of resistance. He also appears to understand the depth and value of local traditions of which, as a colonial outsider, he must inevitably have limited knowledge. Finally, there seems, at least to me, to be an ironic edge to his work, slightly derisive of the colonial enterprise.

Although most of Audema's photographs are of Africans, shown either singly or in groups, his output covers a larger range of subjects than this and gives a more comprehensive view of the French colonial world in which he took part. From my sample of approximately 160 of Audema's postcards, it is possible to divide his work into a number of different categories or genres:

1. "Native types" (individual portraits of both men and women, with subcategories focusing on scarification and "warriors")
2. Formal groups (men, women, and mixed groups of men and women)
3. Village scenes (some showing local customs or craft production)
4. Special identities (soldiers, chiefs, etc.)
5. Europeans, most often seen in encampments while on administrative tours
6. Administrative posts, plantations, and local industries
7. Towns and public buildings
8. Landscapes and vegetation
9. River steamers

Audema's collected photographs suggest constant travel as he moved around the colony with Bobichon on tours of duty, meeting new people and checking on local administrative and commercial activities. The photographs of different African groups and isolated colonial habitations are knitted together by his photographs of temporary camps and river steamers. The steamers, in particular, seem to epitomize those described in the writings of Joseph Conrad and André Gide in the Belgian Congo (figure 7.12). The rivers on which they traveled were the lifelines of the colonial enterprise. Such was the diversity of local cultures that the French Congo would have been seen by the colonists as a vast panorama of "tribal types." There seems little doubt that Audema also saw it this way.

Since the late eighteenth century, the travel literature of African exploration by such writers as Mungo Park, David Livingstone, and Paul Du Chaillu had prepared the ground for a public eager to see the "reality" of far-off places in photographs, a desire that albumen prints, then stereographs, and finally postcards were to fulfill. The early travel books were illustrated with lithographs and engravings, but the contrast between even lifelike drawings and photographs was compelling. People felt that for the first time they were seeing not just travelers' impressions but something

7.12 "Le Vapeur *'Brettonet,'* de la Cie des Messageries Fluviales
du Congo à Brazzaville," postcard by J. Audema, French Congo, ca. 1905.
Courtesy of the Eliot Elisofon Photographic Archives, National Museum
of African Art, Smithsonian Institution, Image no. EEPA 1985–140051.

"stenciled off the real" (as Sontag has put it),[37] however staged the photographs may have been.

Audema's audience would have included both French visitors and their
relatives and friends in France, to whom they sent the postcards. In this
sense, these were "public" postcards, as Albers and James have defined
the term, as distinct from postcards made for a smaller circle, such as
church missionary societies.[38] However, the range of Audema's photographs also suggests a more local French colonial audience and perhaps
an administrative purpose in their documenting of outposts, tours of duty,
and local industries. There is a postcard showing Mme Bobichon at a
place called Ouesso (Haute-Sanghua) surrounded by Africans and
Frenchmen holding elephant tusks, with her husband, Henri Bobichon,
standing behind her. Audema himself appears in another postcard captioned "Une chasse à l'éléphant," his rifle apparently clasped under the
stump of his left arm, two dead elephants in front of him (figure 7.13). It
may be the only published image we have of him. (But see also the formal
portrait of him, figure 7.11, made by a Montpellier photographer and
friend of the Audema family, in which the injury to the left arm is disguised.) We do not know who took this hunting photograph, although it
was probably Audema's assistant. The brutality of the scene contrasts
with a photograph taken by Audema of a young elephant at the edge of

Congo Français
274. - Une chasse à l'éléphant

7.13 "Une chasse à l'éléphant." Jean Audema appearing on one of his own postcards, French Congo, ca. 1905. Courtesy of the Eliot Elisofon Photographic Archives, National Museum of African Art, Smithsonian Institution, Image no. EEPA 1985–140040–02.

a river, gently holding an African man by the waist with its trunk. This postcard is captioned "L'Ami de Banziville." It is one of the few Audema postcards in which a sentiment of affection is openly expressed, both in the caption and in the image itself.

Other Audema postcards document encampments, the ways in which Europeans were carried by porters in hammocks, their hunting exploits, and the canoes they used on the rivers. There is a photograph of an ivory buyer in Brazzaville surrounded by Africans holding tusks. There is a full-length portrait of a French soldier of the colonial army, but also one of a Senegalese soldier in the same army. In a similar spirit, Audema records the changes occurring in the local African population, with one postcard showing a "Femme Banziri civilisée" wearing a long white dress and another of several African men grouped around a sewing machine, one of them in a suit and tie (figure 7.14). There is no condescension in this photograph. Rather, it is an image of modern Africans affirming their own commercial interests and autonomy.

Although Audema devoted most of his attention to photographing Africans, his choice of other subject matter indicates a desire to document the colonial world in greater breadth. It also reveals his versatility as a photographer, for each subject is approached in a slightly different manner. His landscapes emphasize the luminosity of sky and water against

7.14 "Un Tailleur Loango (Congo Français)," postcard by J. Audema, French
Congo, ca. 1905. Photograph probably 1894–95. Courtesy of the Eliot Elisofon
Photographic Archives, National Museum of African Art, Smithsonian
Institution, Image no. EEPA 1985–140100.

dense vegetation. His photographs of African villages stress their architecture and give a good sense of their domestic spaces. In these pictures the villagers, although carefully placed, are more naturally posed and have none of the assertiveness of those in his group photographs. His pictures of plantations and local industries reveal the scruffiness of enterprises hastily carved out of the jungle, in contrast to the order and decorum of the public buildings that he photographed in Brazzaville.

A Colonial Eye

Where does Audema's curious corpus fit into the history of the colonial postcard? In some ways it can be seen as thoroughly conventional. To many critics it no doubt bears all the usual fingermarks of oppression and racist ideology: the power to control a subjugated people, the pretense of scientific inquiry, the ruthlessly objectifying gaze. Audema's postcards fall into genres and depict scenes shown on many other postcards of the period. There are the staged groups of warriors (seen on postcards from North America to Oceania to South Africa), the possibly bogus family groups, and the displays of individuals as tribal specimens. Any variation must be read within this context and take into account how the photographer, as an individual, responded to the assumptions of his times.

Two of the major studies of colonial postcards—Malek Alloula's *The Colonial Harem* and Nicolas Peterson's study of postcards in Australia[39]—are more concerned with drawing general conclusions from postcards as a form of historical evidence than with the work of individual photographers. Peterson's aim is to discover what themes are encoded in postcard images of Aboriginal people in the first two decades of the twentieth century. It is assumed that certain attitudes of the time are reflected in the choice of images and their handling, since the postcard market responds to popular cultural, political, and aesthetic values as well as playing a part in shaping them. Peterson draws upon a very comprehensive database of commercially printed postcards and a smaller one of postcards printed in more limited numbers on photographic paper. Within this postcard corpus he is able to explore a number of issues relating to gender, the family, economic activity, and settler-indigenous relations. Among the observations that emerge from the study is that commercially printed postcards presented a very different image of Aboriginal family relations than postcards printed on photographic paper, which were usually made for a much smaller circle of relatives and friends, often under church auspices. While the latter suggested the possibility of a successful adjustment to settler society, the former reflected a public perception that Aboriginal family life was breaking down, justifying the role of the state in removing Aboriginal children from their families.[40]

Alloula, an Algerian poet, examines a much more limited category of postcards—those portraying Algerian women from about 1900 to 1930—which he sees as but one expression of a larger French Orientalist "phantasm" combining oppression, exploitation, and sexual desire. For him these postcards are a form of symbolic violence against Algerian society—indeed, a rape and a theft—and the photographers are monsters, seeking revenge for their exclusion from that society by creating a counterfeit world of Algerian women's lives. They cover their guilt by secretive and devious means. Any impression of authenticity in the photographs is a trick designed to make us believe the photographers' lies more fully. As this is a "collective phantasm," the individual photographers are unimportant (indeed, are never discussed or differentiated). What is more, the postcard itself is held to be the "degree zero" of photography, its very mediocrity and ubiquity creating a further opportunity to mislead. "The exotic postcard is a vulgar expression of colonial euphoria just as much as Orientalist painting was, at its beginnings, the Romantic expression of the same euphoria."[41]

Within such an argument subtle differences can serve only to reveal different forms of deceit, what Alloula calls a "rhetoric of camouflage." The one postcard he actually admires can only be an exception that occurs by "an unexpected happenstance," proving the general rule. Although in this case he says the photographer creates "a sort of masterpiece of the genre," no credit is given to the photographer, whose success is attributed to the "law of numbers."[42] Clearly, Alloula's text approaches colonial photography from a position that is personally and historically very different from that of most other critics. It is an act of resistance and, as W.J.T. Mitchell points out, a "counter-magic, a contrary incantation."[43] Alloula himself describes it as his exorcism of the colonial gaze. But even as a countertext, Alloula's analysis cannot be immune from the accusation that it stereotypes the photographer as much as the photographer stereotypes the subject.

It is worth examining how Audema's photographs compare with Alloula's model of the colonial postcard. The setting of almost all the postcards discussed by Alloula is the studio. It is the studio that the photographer requires to create his (we must assume it is a "he") false image of Algerian women's domestic lives, for he has no access to the reality of it, just as he must employ prostitutes to simulate respectable Algerian women. "The photographer's studio will become, then, a pacified microcosm where his desire, his scopic instinct, can find satisfaction."[44] In this respect, Audema's—and the majority of colonial postcards—differ from Alloula's selections. Alloula is examining a special case in which the representation of the life of the colonized must be achieved by an excess of fictional means. He would perhaps argue that photographs taken outside the studio are equally duplicitous,[45] but in many of Audema's pictures one at least sees village settings—perhaps accidentally (which may guarantee a certain authenticity), perhaps because he wanted us to see them for their own sake. The fact that many colonial postcards are of landscapes and village settings without people prominent in them tends to reinforce the second view.

Alloula comments on one postcard of three young women that the "forced smile" of one of them "is there to further emphasize the illusory complicity that the photographer steals from his models."[46] Supposing this were true (that the appearance of complicity is necessarily illusory), it is still questionable that one could tell this by looking at the photograph. In Audema's photographs the evidence for complicity rarely depends upon a smile. It depends in fact upon the *artificiality* of the scene rather than its verisimilitude. The very theatricality of these photographs, and the care taken in posing them, is the best indication we have of a collaborative production. As for Audema's portraits, there is little to support the idea that the smiles, where they exist, are forced or stolen. In the case of figures 7.10b and 7.14, the idea that they result from coercion must rely on the larger assumption that the actors were very adept at concealing their feelings. Discussions of the smile in colonial photographs are burdened with a desire to read them simultaneously as expressions of oppression and resistance. The smiling subject is being induced to smile, but the smile is also a weapon of the "returned gaze," confronting the photographer and the colonial apparatus.[47]

In contrast to this, it is worth examining one of Audema's finest photographs, a portrait of a woman described in the caption only as "Femme Coumbé – Congo Français" (figure 7.15). Here the smile is so gentle as to be hardly a smile at all, but it is nonetheless present in the mouth and eyes. The woman stands confidently facing the camera. There is nothing forced or tense about it, only a slightly humorous expression as if looking back at an equal. The woman is neither beautiful nor exotic, although a certain beauty of character illuminates the portrait. The unassuming simplicity of the photograph conveys the dignity of the subject. As in the photograph of the Banziri woman (figure 7.9), Audema has signed his name on the negative, together with the date 1899.

Apart from a few intimate portraits such as this, it is the formal staging of Audema's photographs, rather than their naturalism, that remains the strongest argument for distinguishing his photography from that which Alloula describes. For Alloula, the chief subterfuge of the colonial photographer is to present the studio situation as reality. Beyond this, the very vapidity of the postcard ensures that its contents will be taken at face value. "Because it has erased the traces, and above all the direction, of its *mise-en-scène*, the colonial postcard can successfully keep up this mirror trick (tautology), so that it presents itself as pure reflection, something it definitely is not."[48] But only the most naïve viewer could ever interpret

7.15 "Femme Coumbé – Congo Français" postcard by J. Audema,
French Congo, ca. 1905. Photograph 1899, courtesy of Benoît Estival-Audéma.

Audema's group photographs as pure reflections of reality. They are by
their very nature avowals of the opposite. It is here that Audema takes a
decisive step away from both the false spontaneity attempted by some
photographers and the determinedly objectivist stance of nineteenth-century scientific photography.

Audema strikes me as an eccentric figure in the history of colonial photography. Like Everard im Thurn, who photographed the indigenous people of British Guiana at the end of the nineteenth century, his photographs
stand out for the sense they give of a personal involvement with the subjects.[49] Unlike most of his contemporaries in Europe and the colonies,
who regarded Africans as curiosities, Audema seems alive to the beauty
of his subjects as individuals rather than merely as exotic types. But there
is something more. Unlike im Thurn, whose interest seems straightfor-
wardly humanitarian, Audema brings to his photography a quality of
mind that is both creative and quirky. Audema, the showman, is mounting
a drama that is dryly subversive from behind his job as a colonial servant.
To what extent he did this consciously, or as part of his official duties, we
shall perhaps never know.

There must be many forgotten photographers just as interesting as
Audema. He may not have been nearly as unusual as this brief excursion

suggests. If that is so, and there is more variation among colonial photographers than we have come to believe, we may have to replace our ideas about the practices of the period with a more nuanced analysis than most critics have so far accorded them. In any case, we owe it to those colonial photographers who were prepared to take risks to pay some attention to their vision. That may require looking at their work more carefully, even if this means shedding our preconceptions about the banality of the postcard and haunting the stalls of the postcard dealers.

Notes

I am indebted to Benoît Estival-Audéma (grandnephew of Jean Audema), Roger Benjamin, Lynne Thornton, Nicolas Peterson, Jeffrey Ruoff, and Christraud Geary for their assistance in the preparation of this chapter. Thanks also to Nicolas Peterson, Judith MacDougall, Rosamund Dalziell, and Marianne Gullestad for reading and commenting on earlier drafts.

1. I have chosen to spell Audema as he himself had it printed on his postcards, and as it appears on his tombstone, although some members of the family spell it with an acute accent on the "e"—as Audéma.

2. The majority of the postcards shown in this chapter are from my own collection. Three are from the collection of the Eliot Elisofon Photographic Archives at the National Museum of African Art, Smithsonian Institution. One belongs to Benoît Estival-Audéma.

3. A good deal is known about Fortier, thanks to Philippe David, who has studied his life and photographs closely. (See David 1986–88.) There is a growing body of scholarly research on postcards as social and cultural artifacts and as a source of historical information. See, for example, the extensive body of research on postcards portraying Native Americans by Patricia C. Albers and William R. James (1988, 1990). For work on African colonial postcards, see David 1978, 1986–88; Prochaska 1991; and Geary 1990, 2002.

4. Peterson argues that "The vast majority of postcards were (and still are) commercially produced by people seeking to make a profit. . . . As such it can be presumed that they are a distillation of the images of most contemporary interest, so that some cultural significance resides in the themes selected, the relative proportions on each theme, and the imagery" (1985: 167–68).

5. There is at least one study of the written messages on picture postcards (Baldwin 1988). Other commentators on postcards often note the disjunction between what is written on postcards and what they portray.

6. See Pinney 1990a, 1992c. See also Edwards 1990 for a discussion of the idea of the human "type" in ethnological photography.

7. See Prochaska 1990: 375, 408–9.

8. By the 1890s exposure times in sunlight could be very short indeed. Nevertheless, one occasionally sees postcards from this period with blurred human figures, indicating an exposure of a half second or more.

9. Certain of the more naturalistic poses used by Audema and some other colonial photographers in their village scenes seem related to the ways in which "primitive" people were portrayed in the "life groups" of nineteenth-century museums (influenced in their turn by Victorian waxworks and *tableaux vivants*) and in the reconstructed villages of colonial expositions. See Hinsley 1991, Griffiths 2002.

10. Christopher Pinney remarks upon the same qualities in G. Western's portraits made in India in the 1850s. "Western's images have an intensity and fragility whose absolute atypicality leaps at the viewer. There is nothing casual or unengaged about these images; rather they have an intimacy that seems to spring from some deep knowledge of the sitters, who are clearly equal participants in these portraiture events" (Pinney 1997: 31). Pinney goes on to compare Western's photographs to Nadar's, which depart from the formulaic approach of other French portrait photographers such as Disdéri.

11. See Christopher Wright's essay on Francis R. Barton's photography of tattoos in Papua New Guinea (Wright 2003).

12. Christraud Geary interprets this image in another way, as one of an "anthropometric" pair. In a second postcard, the same youth is seen facing the camera head-on. See Geary 2002: 19.

13. Christraud Geary (2002: 55n17) notes that Audema's postcards are still widely sought after by collectors, indicating a persisting interest in "his exotic and erotic images." Although the exoticism is clearly there, I have found few, if any of his pictures that seem intentionally erotic. Perhaps Audema here suffers unfairly from association with other photographers.

14. For an overview of this research, see Geary & Webb 1998: 163–77. For a more extensive discussion of African photographers and their work, see Geary 2002: 103–23. Scholars such as Christraud Geary, Philippe David, and Vera Viditz-Ward have made important contributions to the history of early West and Central African photography by drawing attention to the work of such figures as Alphonse Owondo in Guinée, W. S. Johnson in Sierra Leone, George S. A. da Costa in Nigeria, Gerhardt Lutterodt in Ghana, and Herzekiah Andrew Shanu in the Belgian Congo. One might also point to the "rediscovered" careers of several photographers of more recent times who began working in Bamako, Mali, in the 1940s and 1950s: Seydou Keïta, Félix Dialo, and Malick Sidibé.

15. One can find examples of similar group photographs among those published by Fortier of Dakar and other colonial photographers. What is distinctive about Audema's photography is the extreme to which he carried these conventions. Although one of the most common practices when photographing Africans in the colonies was to line them up in front of the camera, there were also more carefully posed village scenes. These were no doubt inspired both by museum exhibits of "life groups" and by the village displays created at colonial expositions. Photographers such as Robert Visser, Leray, and "P. A." who also worked in the French Congo, arranged their subjects carefully but less dramatically than Audema. Nonetheless, there is a formal resemblance. It is probable that the photographers working in the French Congo were aware of one another's work. Their self-conscious approach to posing seems to have been more common here than in other colonies, suggesting the emergence of a local photographic style.

16. Patricia C. Albers and William R. James, in their articles about picture postcards of Native Americans, make the point that the use of a plain background removes the subjects from their historical context, making it easier to project symbolic and metaphorical readings upon them. This practice tended to reinforce romantic and stereotyped readings. See Albers & James 1988, 1990.

17. See R. Benjamin 2003.

18. See Geary & Webb 1998: 150.

19. See Kümin & Kumschick 2001.

20. See Geary 2002: 28–29.

21. For information on Audema's career and life, I am indebted to personal communications from Benoît Estival-Audéma, Jean Audema's grandnephew; Jeffrey Ruoff, a film scholar and filmmaker; and Lynne Thornton, an art historian who has taken an interest in Audema's photography.

22. I am grateful to Jeffrey Ruoff for looking up some of these details in the files of the Centre des Archives d'Outre-Mer in Aix-en-Provence.

23. Serre 1988: 40. Although acting as governor, Bobichon apparently only held the title of Commissaire Spécial at this time. He was appointed Commissaire in 1906.

24. Ibid., pp. 39–40.

25. Personal communication from Benoît Estival-Audéma.

26. Ibid.

27. From *Bulletin Individuel des Notes*, 1899: "Un caractère un peu difficile qui rend les rapports avec les indigènes quelquefois pénibles." Dossier AEF/c/1043/Audema.

28. From copies of Audema's service record at the Archives Nationales des Pays D'Outre-Mer, provided by Benoît Estival-Audéma (personal communication). The entry reads: "Je n'ai pas encore une opinion absolument arrétee [*sic*] sur Audema qui me parait [*sic*] un agent un peu casse-cou."

29. From notes copied from Audema's service record at the Archives Nationales des Pays d'Outre-Mer, provided by Benoît Estival-Audéma (personal communication). The entry reads:

1906, 11 ans 9 mois de service
Notes du commissaire special
Santé: assez bonne
Intelligence et jugement: serieuse intelligence, excellent jugement
Connaissances administratives: suffisantes
Instruction génerale, Appreçiation des connaissances accessories: bonne instruction génerale
Valeur morale: très bonne
Caractère: loyal, a beaucoup de bon sens, sait se faire aimer et·obéir. Parle corectement, écrit bien, très actif

From Audema's service dossier EE/II/4193/18 at the Centres des Archives d'Outre-Mer, copied by Jeffery Ruoff (personal communication). The entry reads in part: "*Bulletin Individuel des Notes*, 1909; notes du Lieutenant-Gouverneur 'C'est un bon fonctionnaire, bien doué, qui peut bien faire s'il le veut,' le 6 septembre 1908.

30. Peterson 1985: 166.

31. Prochaska 1990: 375.

32. Many postcards at this time were issued in numbered sequences or "collections," partly to feed the hobby of postcard collecting, which had blossomed early in France, with numerous clubs and magazines devoted to it (Prochaska 1990: 376). The series numbers in the Collection J. Audema run up into the 500s, but postcard series numbers are notoriously unreliable and do not necessarily indicate the actual number of cards published in a series or the number of cards by individual photographers. The same cards often appear with and without series numbers, as is the case with Audema's postcards.

33. Riefenstahl 1973, 1976, discussed in Sontag 1980.

34. Sontag 1980: 87–90.

35. Ibid., p. 87.

36. Ibid., p. 89.

37. Albers & James 1990.

39. Peterson's study is still in progress and will result in a book. He has so far produced several articles on the subject, including "The Popular Image" (1985) and "The Constructions of Aboriginal Femininity in Early Twentieth Century Photography" (1991).

40. Reported by Peterson in an unpublished conference paper, "The Aboriginal Family, Gender, and the State in Turn-of-the-Century Photography" (1997).

41. Alloula 1986: 29. It seems to me that Alloula draws too sharp a line between photography for postcards and photography as documentation or as art. Many of the images that ended up on postcards also appeared in a variety of other contexts. Many had never been produced with postcard publication in mind.

42. Ibid., pp. 28, 35, 130n17.

43. Mitchell 1994: 308.

44. Alloula, 1986: 14.

45. In fact, he observes at one point: "The countryside is another reservoir of types for the exotic postcard" (129n9).

46. Ibid., p. 34.

47. See Geary & Webb 1998: 58–60; Lutz & Collins 1993: 198.

48. Alloula, 1986: 28.

49. See Tayler 1992.

PART IV

THE ETHNOGRAPHIC IMAGINATION

8

THE VISUAL IN ANTHROPOLOGY

The Visual as Metaphor

ANTHROPOLOGY HAS had no lack of interest in the visual; its problem has always been what to do with it. This problem is historically related to another anthropological problem: what to do with the person—the sentient, thinking being who belongs to a culture but, from the anthropologist's point of view, can often reconstitute very little of it. As anthropology developed from an armchair discipline to a study of actual communities, it seemed somehow strange that the person, the object of the anthropologist's attention, should remain largely invisible to the anthropological audience. An early remedy was to bring exotic people to museums, lectures, and such popular venues as world's fairs and colonial expositions. In a sense this gave a gloss of scientific respectability to the existing practice of displaying indigenous people as curiosities at circuses and other entertainments.[1] Ishi, the last of the Yahi, spent his final years at the University of California's Museum of Anthropology as Kroeber's informant and a kind of living exhibit. Franz Boas helped organize the Anthropological Hall at the World's Columbian Exposition of 1893 in Chicago, where fourteen Kwakiutl were displayed.[2] Senegalese swam in the fountains of Paris during the Exposition Ethnographique de l'Afrique Occidentale of 1895.[3]

This provided visibility, but the anthropologist couldn't finally put a Wolof potter or Trobriand gardener into an ethnological monograph. A better alternative to importing people was to put photographs of them in the monograph and show films of them at lectures, as Sir Walter Baldwin Spencer did with his films of the Aranda at Melbourne Town Hall in 1902. "What I would like to show would be the real native," he wrote to his friend Lorimer Fison, but by this time he meant only uncensored photographs of naked men and women.[4] In any case, as anthropologists had discovered earlier, the body in question, removed from its usual surroundings, was often singularly uncommunicative about culture. The anthropological "body" in fact included much more, extending outward from the person to include the social group, the physical setting, the fields and pas-tures, the dwellings, and implements and other possessions. Photographs and artifacts helped fill this gap and took some of the pressure off the living person, who could now be assumed to exist at the fieldwork site.

If anything, the absence of the person strengthened the importance of the visual, which through photographs, films, and museum artifacts began to replace it. But the problem remained that there was something disquieting about visual images. They appeared to show everything and yet, like the physical body, remained annoyingly mute. The visual world was like the husk you removed to get at the conceptual and verbal worlds inside, but having done so you couldn't in good conscience throw it away. Visible objects, having exerted great fascination as the products and indicators of culture but failing as expositors of it, began to acquire a new function (in museums) as metaphors for anthropology. And as metaphor, the visual flourished.

Victorian photographs of hunting expeditions often displayed tigers and antelopes in decorative heaps, the artifice enhancing the prestige of the hunter. Early museum exhibits displayed their artifacts in similarly symmetrical and intricate patterns of positive and negative space. This created an ornamental effect not unlike the bones of the dead stuck in the plaster of Roman catacombs. At the Pitt Rivers Museum in Oxford some objects were organized solely by shape, although a functional or evolutionary relationship was sometimes suggested. The aesthetic merits of individual artifacts, and their evidence of ingenuity and workmanship, became part of a larger aesthetic and spiritual design. The great halls of the Musée de l'Homme and the American Museum of Natural History communicated a religious aura of science celebrating humankind, much as paleolithic caves once celebrated the animal world. Here the visual stood in for an absent humanity, as church architecture stood in for the invisibility of God.

For a general public imbued with ideas of social Darwinism, the visual appearance of exotic peoples was the most obvious way of placing them on a scale between civilized man and animal. Pictures became a substitute for more abstract or esoteric knowledge, which in any case was now beginning to contradict evolutionary theory ("primitive" languages, for example, were now recognized as highly complex). Features such as nakedness and the use of animal products (feathers, skin, hair, and bones), communicated by means of photographs and visible artifacts in museums and magazine illustrations, became symbolic indicators of how close people were to nature.

These indicators were turned back upon anthropology in books (as in H. Rider Haggard's *King Solomon's Mines* [1885]) and in early films, as popular culture created its own literary and theatrical savages. In the first decade of the twentieth century the stereograph and picture postcard fads were reaching their peak. The Keystone *Stereoscopic Encyclopedia* of 1906, a guide to its first boxed set of six hundred "views," contains 154 references to "racial geography, peoples of all lands." By 1907 the H. C. White company was capable of producing fifteen thousand stereo view cards per day.[5] In 1909–10, 866 million picture postcards were posted in Great Britain alone.[6] A prominent postcard genre was photography of indigenous people in native dress (or nakedness), many borrowing from the photographic systems of T. H. Huxley, John Lamprey, and other scientists a self-consciously "anthropometric" style. The dioramas of museums, usually showing animals but sometimes including models of "primitives," imitated the framing of photographs and aspired to the trompe-l'oeil of stereoscopic views.

As anthropology developed in the colonial context, the visual had further primacy as a way of organizing society by types. Like the collecting of artifacts and botanical samples, photography provided a new way of creating human models, against which further examples could be compared and classified.[7] For administrative purposes it was often more important to identify someone as a member of a group than to know much about the group itself. Visual clues, as Berreman notes, help people identify members of other groups, but (at least in the Indian context) people "are more knowledgeable about those superior to themselves in status and power than about those inferior."[8] In the latter case, visible signs may be more important in defining people in relation to oneself than in relation to each other. The visible emphasizes what one is not. For the colonizers as well as the colonized, a concept of purity and impurity was an underlying principle of social segmentation. Manipulating human categories reinforced the colonizers' sense of difference as well as their sense of power. In India, the passion for anthropometry and photographic cataloguing of ethnic and occupational types—encouraged according to Pinney by India's extraordinary heterogeneity[9]—was nevertheless no more than a subset of the larger anthropological and imperial project of typing the whole world. Such forms of measurement may have paid meager returns in terms of actual knowledge but they had the satisfying look of knowledge. Popular culture mimicked this knowledge: picture postcards from around the world bore such captions as "Type indigène," "Guerrier Tanosy," and "A typical well proportioned Zulu woman."

Natural science, which used illustrations extensively in compiling its taxonomies, provided an early impetus for anthropology to study the visual aspects of culture. Anthropology was inspired by zoology, botany, and geology to describe the world visually, and there was a corresponding emphasis upon those aspects of culture that could be drawn or photographed. Travelers, as well, considered it incumbent upon them to record ethnographic information. Nineteenth-century ethnographies and books of exploration are filled with line drawings of implements, body decorations, costumes, jewelry, and architectural details.

Photographs were a prominent feature of ethnographies until the 1930s but become progressively scarcer in later works. Hattersley's *The Baganda at Home* (1908), for example, contains 80 photographs. Junod's *The Life of a South African Tribe* (1912) contains 112 illustrations, most of them photographs. Rattray's *Ashanti* (1923) contains 143. But by 1965 an ethnography such as Spencer's *The Samburu* contained only four, and his *The Maasai of Matapato* of 1988 none at all. Some of the possible reasons for this decline have been summarized by Pinney,[10] but the decline itself has perhaps masked the fact that visual anthropology—as an anthropology of the visual—appeared early and has a long heritage. If visual anthropology later became less focused on content than on method (ethnographic filmmaking and photography), it is perhaps partly because such interests were soon hived off into studies of primitive art, technology, and folklore.

But there were other reasons, too. Grimshaw argues that the end of the nineteenth century ushered in a shift in attitudes toward the visual in which the assumed coherence and superiority of European civilization's vision of the world was finally shattered by the Great War.[11] While this shift may have changed the role of the visual in anthropology, it did not immediately diminish it. The panoptic view of humanity was gradually replaced by a notion that the life of any people could be expressive *of itself* through images, as in the early films of Lumière and of the 1898 Cambridge Anthropological Expedition to the Torres Strait. These films emphasized simple "showing" over "telling."[12] Thus at this time seeing was apparently still construed as a way of knowing, as it had been earlier in the century. A demonstration of fire making (such as that in the Cambridge Torres Strait footage) could act as a template for the process, allowing it to be reproduced, rather like following an instruction manual. Visual recording "saved" the event in some reified sense, a view that was still being voiced by Margaret Mead in 1975 when she wrote of behavior "caught and preserved" by film "for centuries."[13] Interpretation could be provided later; the crucial thing was to salvage the data.

Visible Culture and Visual Media

The early interest in visual anthropology, which began with such enthusiasm, gradually faded into perplexity. Félix-Louis Regnault's dream of an ethnographic film museum[14] and A. C. Haddon's view of the film camera as "an indispensable piece of anthropological apparatus" has been replaced in recent years by Kirsten Hastrup's view that, compared to anthropological writing, film is "thin" description[15] and Maurice Bloch's belief that anthropologists who dedicate much time to film have "lost confidence in their own ideas."[16] There are of course alternative views, but the history of visual anthropology suggests that most anthropologists have never known quite what to do with the visual. Vast archives of record footage remain unseen and unused. Sophisticated analysts of other societies profess ignorance and alarm when it comes to analyzing the structure of an ethnographic film. To anthropology the visual often seems uncommunicative and yet somehow insatiable. Like the tar baby, it never says anything, but there is always something more to be said about *it*. Words, on the other hand, speak out and thus define their own terrain.

Despite such sentiments, activities in visual anthropology are once again increasing, filling some of the roles once promised for it. But here we must make a key distinction. What activities are encompassed by visual anthropology? There is, on the one hand, the visual anthropology that studies visible cultural forms. On the other is the visual anthropology that uses the visual media to describe and analyze culture. In Sol Worth's terms, this is the difference between "using a medium and studying how a medium is used."[17] The two will sometimes overlap—the study of visible systems sometimes demands visual communication—but the first form is essentially an extension of traditional anthropological concerns into new subject areas. The second proposes a much more radical break with anthropological modes of discourse.

As an anthropology of visible cultural forms, "visual anthropology" is now broadening its scope in two ways. It is expanding to embrace indigenous media production as a parallel strand of cultural representation; and amongst academic anthropologists it is beginning to pay attention to a range of cultural forms that have received only patchy anthropological attention before: historical photographs, news photography, sports events, comic books, postcards, stereographs, body decoration, indigenous painting, "tourist art," home movies, family snapshots, itinerant theater, vernacular architecture, children's drawings, political regalia, court ceremony, gesture and facial expression (although these have a longer history of study), advertising, costume and personal adornment, industrial design, and so on—in short, any of the expressive systems of human society that communicate meanings partially or primarily by visual means. We may attribute part of this broadened view of culture to Barthes's exploration of "mythologies" in the 1950s, which revealed a complex world of hidden sign-systems. Like those earlier anthropological findings in remote cultures that stimulated a cultural critique of our own, the discovery of new meaning systems in Western society has led to a reexamination of visual systems in what were once called "traditional" societies, particularly in their historical engagement with the West.

Indigenous media production presents a more complex case, for it is perceived by anthropologists within two different frames of reference: first, as an evolving cultural form like many others (e.g., Australian Aboriginal acrylic painting), and second, but more importantly, as a self-conscious expression of political and cultural identity, directed in part at countering representations by others. For indigenous people, the visual media can serve as an instrument of political action (as among the Kayapo) or cultural reintegration and revival (as among the Inuit), or as a corrective to stereotyping, misrepresentation, and denigration (as among many Native American groups).

The model of visual anthropology that indigenous media implicitly opposes is the canonical ethnographic film, framed in intercultural terms—a film made by one cultural group (usually Euro-American) attempting to describe another (usually of the Third or Fourth World). Such a definition increasingly applies to ethnographic films made *within* Western society, since the subjects are almost always from a class or subculture different from that of the filmmakers. However, Ginsburg has argued that much indigenous media production has a broader educative purpose, both within and outside an indigenous community. As a result there is a crossing of cultural boundaries between subjects and potential audiences as well as a project of mediating "ruptures of time and history" in the communities themselves.[18] This provides some common ground between indigenous media and ethnographic filmmaking.

Further arguments have been put forward for considering indigenous media "in relation to a broader range of media engaged in representing culture,"[19] in part because indigenous media production itself is rapidly changing. Its producers are increasingly addressing international audiences and situating themselves at the cultural crossroads, where there is a constant flux and interpenetration of cultural forces. Indigenous media is also entering the mass media and vice versa. The indigenous person, along with the ethnic and diasporic person, is no longer contained within a social enclave, nor necessarily considers himself or herself a bonded representative of a cultural and political group.

All these factors place indigenous media producers and artists in an intercultural and intertextual position. Their work is both a product of and commentary on contesting cultural identities. Ginsburg further suggests that this expansion has implications both for what is represented and how it affects representation. It creates a "parallax effect" that, by displacing the traditional view of ethnographic film, may in the end invigorate it.[20] Nichols, writing in a similar vein, is perhaps not merely being ironic when he implies that as ethnographic filmmakers are becoming increasingly marginalized, they would do well to identify more closely with other marginalized peoples.[21]

As anthropologists discover new subjects—either in established visual cultural forms or in evolving uses of the visual media—they may well redefine the terrain of anthropology. As indigenous groups take greater control of the visual media they may well alter traditional anthropological representations of themselves. But in neither of these cases does visual anthropology pose a fundamental epistemological challenge to what has been called "the anthropological project." They merely make anthropology more sensitive to the politics and possibilities of visual representation. The more substantive challenge to anthropological thought comes not simply from broadening its purview but from its entering into communicative systems different from the "anthropology of words." In this, it revives the historical question of what to do with the visual.

The few steps that have been taken in this direction have tended to be isolated and idiosyncratic, and as is often the case in a developing discipline, the pioneers have often been outsiders (such as Flaherty and Marshall) or rebels (such as Bateson and Rouch). Jay Ruby's comment—"if non-anthropologists can produce credible ethnographic films then why should anyone interested in producing films about culture bother being trained as an ethnographer?"—reflects a widespread view that innovators must also satisfy the conservative mainstream.[22] Even when new directions have been opened up by formally-trained anthropologists, the results are often misconstrued. As Paul Stoller notes, "Jean Rouch is well known for his technical innovations in film but not for the contributions his films make to theories of ethnographic representation."[23] For others, Rouch's films are acceptable only because their ethnographic content exists in addition to the different *kind* of anthropological understanding they make possible cinematically. This is perhaps to be expected, since most works of visual anthropology aim to do far less. Nor is it likely that visual anthropology will be worthy of serious consideration *as anthropology* so long as it confines itself to illustrative uses of film, or tries to translate anthropological concepts into images, or grafts models of television journalism onto anthropological subjects. All of these forms remain wedded to earlier forms. None commit themselves to different ways of "speaking."

It seems clear that visual anthropology now urgently needs to consolidate itself within a theoretical framework that reassesses anthropological objectives. A fuller use of the properties of the visual media will entail significant additions to how anthropologists define their ways of knowing, which is to say that categories of anthropological knowledge will have to be seriously rethought, both in relation to science and to the representational systems of film, video, and photography. The potential of ethnographic film can no longer be thought of simply as a form of filmic ethnography, as Ruby has sometimes defined it.[24]

Visual media make use of principles of implication, visual resonance, identification, and shifting perspective that differ radically from the principles of most anthropological writing. They involve the viewer in heuristic processes and meaning creation quite different from verbal statement, linkage, theory formation, and speculation. As Gilbert Lewis has noted, they also have quite different ways of placing stress and contextualizing detail. "The painter can elaborate details without sacrificing the general effect. The picture may still retain its unity and simplicity in spite of the mass of details. You see it as a whole. But when a passion for details is displayed in literature the effect is quite different. After a long academic tradition of learning from the printed page, the ways in which we can represent the lives of others are changing."[25] Above all, the visual media allow us to construct knowledge not by "description" (to borrow Bertrand Russell's terms) but by a form of "acquaintance."[26]

Although there is a crucial difference between using and studying the use of the visual, there is an important link between them. The study of collective visual representations itself generates new questions about how anthropology can communicate about them. Do visual systems require certain forms of visual analysis and communication? Do they suggest distinctive patterns of understanding? A greater awareness of visual systems directs our attention towards a range of cultural domains that have long remained at the margins of anthropology, not least because they are linked to visual sign systems more familiar to other disciplines, such as art history. Visual anthropology may offer different ways of understanding, but also different things to understand.

Enlarging Anthropology

In recent years there has been mounting anthropological interest in emotion, time, place, the body, the senses, gender, and individual identity. Although the importance of many of these areas of study was recognized long ago, they have often been relegated to the disciplines of psychology, philosophy, medicine, linguistics, and history. One of the difficulties of exploring and communicating understandings about them has been in finding a language metaphorically and experientially close to them. One of the reasons for the historical primacy of the visual has been its capacity for metaphor and synesthesia. Much that can be expressed about these matters may best be expressed in the visual media.

Use of the visual media for this purpose may not necessarily require the development of a specialized visual language ("a framework of anthropological visual symbolic forms which are conventionalized into a code or argot"), as Jay Ruby argued in 1975, but (as he also argued) it does require a shift away from making films *about* anthropology to making anthropological films.[27] This, however, is likely to produce changes in what has been considered anthropological, as well as in how film (or photography or video) is used. The subject matter may no longer lend itself to objectified scientific description, and visual anthropology may no longer fulfill conventional criteria for creating data, articulating theory, or describing methodology. But rather than rejecting existing documentary and fictional forms outright, visual anthropology is more likely to adapt them or use them in new combinations. Existing forms provide a common basis of cultural experience and points of reference between filmmaker and viewer, however much any given work may depart from them—just as written anthropology depends upon the conventions of expository and scientific writing developed over several centuries before anthropology emerged as a discipline. As Stoller comments, "radically empirical" visual anthropologists such as Rouch will "mix their genres, sometimes employing narrative style, sometimes employing plain style, sometimes blurring the lines between fact and fiction."[28]

Anthropological writing in recent years demonstrates a shift toward new cultural categories and concepts of knowledge. This is evident in the experimental ethnographies described by Marcus and Cushman[29] and in the revision of anthropological assumptions about the meaning of fundamental institutions such as ritual.[30] It is also evident in theoretical writing, which has begun to make use of a lexicon newly charged with bodily experience. The language of postmodern anthropology is filled with such words as "congeal," "slippage," and "rupture." At the limit such writing suffers the consequences of its own innovation and self-absorption, leading its readers into obscurity. It may also demand of readers a more active and interpretive style of engagement. But essentially it reveals dissatisfaction with earlier models and a straining at the boundaries of anthropological understanding—a need to pass beyond received conceptions of representation to what Tyler has called "evocation" and Barthes has called "figuration."[31] This is the experiential field that film and other visual media at least offer anthropology.

Here it is necessary to insist that visual anthropology is not about the visual per se but about a range of culturally inflected relationships enmeshed and encoded in the visual. Just as anthropology can read some of these in the visual, so too it can use the visual to construct works that give a richer sense of how culture permeates and patterns social experience. These works may bring into play familiar ways of engaging with visual media, such as realist strategies of narrative identification and description, or less familiar forms of juxtaposition and montage that address the viewer on multiple levels. They may make greater demands on hermeneutic processes than anthropological audiences are used to exercising, using ways of making cultural representations that are no longer simply declarative.

If we consider for a moment only the world of visual symbols, these new works may attempt to construct sets of relationships that resemble those of poetry in the verbal domain, since such cultural complexes must be grasped as totalities rather than piecemeal. If we consider the visual as offering pathways to the other senses and to experience more generally, then what may be required of the viewer will often combine psychological or kinesthetic responses with interpretive ones. For example, a work that invites us to enter into a visual narrative as a participant may also require us to place that experience within the context of how the experience has been created for us, and what indications there are of the visual anthropologist's own engagement with the situation at the time. The anthropologist may never be able to articulate this fully outside the matrix of the work itself.

Sometimes an anthropological understanding may be afforded chiefly through metaphor. Mimesis alone is rarely enough, because purely experiential responses across cultural boundaries can be profoundly misleading. It is unlikely, for example, that the viewer of a film will grasp the meaning of a ritual that has over the years been "inscribed in [the] very bodies" of the participants, as Christina Toren puts it."[32] Metaphor in film (as in life) can be the concretizing of the self and experience in other things, not as simile or analogy but as bodily extension. As Michael Jackson argues, "To emphasize the psychological or social aspects of metaphor construction and use is unhelpful as long as it implies a dualistic conception of human behaviour. . . . My argument is that metaphor must be apprehended [as] . . . a true interdependency of mind and body, Self and World."[33] This collapsing of meaning is taken for granted in idioms of spoken language. It can be an even more powerful form of construction in visual media, as is clear in such "documentary" films as Wright's *Song of Ceylon* (1934) or Franju's *Le sang des bêtes* (1949) and the work of fiction filmmakers such as Antonioni. Indeed in film, metaphor is almost always present, in the sense that environments and images of objects are persistently associated with feelings, actions, and states of mind.

No doubt part of the attraction of the visual to early anthropology lay in its very contradictions—its promise of more than it delivered. In this respect, the visual (whether as museum exhibit, photograph, or film) acted as it has in other contexts, promising commodities (as in advertising) or sexual fulfillment (as in pornography) but holding these in an unconsummated suspension. Pinney (following Christian Metz) has observed that the stillness and suspension of the photograph resemble "the glance in childhood which fixes the fetish."[34] What was paradoxical about visual imagery, as against written text, was its apparent plenitude, which flooded the observer with concreteness and detail yet revealed little in the absence of a surrounding discourse. Just so, the advertised product speaks only within a cultural discourse of fashion and desire, the pornographic image within a narrative of improvised fantasy.

To the anthropologist who knew the cultural context, the visual image spoke volumes, but that power was also a source of danger. An uncaptioned photograph was full of undirected potential. Unlike written descriptions, which always provided some sort of context, a photograph could be supplied with any sort of meaning by the viewer—from competing scientific discourses or unwelcome popular ones such as racism. It all too easily escaped from professional control. Similar fears are heard today from anthropologists who deem certain films to be dangerous to the public (or their subjects) through what they fail to show or to say. There is a moral imperative against allowing viewers to jump to the wrong conclusions.

The declining use of photographs in monographs may well be put down to this cause, in concert with a shift away from evolutionary anthropology's omnivorous appetite for detail toward more holistic descriptions of cultures. The same threat of undisciplined interpretation may have been responsible for ethnographic films of the same period developing primarily into illustrated lectures, in which a text provided the supporting framework for the images. If anthropologists had felt confident enough to contextualize the contents of their films by any other means, they might well have done so, but this was often regarded with suspicion as "art." Thus we see the visual in anthropology kept in safe bounds, like a bomb with the detonator removed.

There are certain emblematic moments in the history of visual anthropology: the transition from chronophotography to cinema in 1895, the simultaneous appearance in 1922 of *Nanook of the North* and Malinowski's *Argonauts of the Western Pacific*, the day in the 1950s (perhaps apocryphal) when Jean Rouch lost his tripod in the Niger. Another such moment was the appearance in 1942 of Gregory Bateson and Margaret Mead's book *Balinese Character*—or rather, it might have been. It is interesting to speculate whether much that is happening now in visual anthropology might not have happened sooner if the famous Bateson-Mead project had taken a different turn. As it was, this innovative project, which had the potential to revolutionize visual anthropology, fell short of doing so. It neither legitimized visual research methods in anthropology nor turned film and photography into a channel of anthropological discourse and argumentation.

The reasons for this conclusion, and even its validity, deserve fuller examination than is possible here, but there are some provocative clues. The edited films that emerged from the project in the 1950s are unrelentingly didactic, with Mead's voice constantly guiding us and, at one point, telling us, "You will have to watch very carefully to follow any of this at all."[35] In part, this approach can be explained by American "educational film" conventions of the time; but by asking viewers to find what they are told they will find, it may also indicate an intellectual predisposition of the research itself. In support of this is the account given by Bateson, which suggests that the photographs were subordinated to and seen very much in the context of Margaret Mead's prior written interpretations of the events.[36] A conversation between Bateson and Mead in the 1970s reveals a fundamental split in their objectives, indicating that Bateson had wanted to conduct the enquiry by means of filming, but Mead had wanted to film first and analyze later. One can imagine Bateson applying the exploratory approach of *Naven* to a film or photographic project, but not in this collaborative context. *Balinese Character* finally falls between two divergent conceptions of photography—one an extension of the mind, the other an extension of the eye.

> MEAD: [The] effort was to hold the camera steady enough long enough to get a sequence of behavior.
> BATESON: To find out what's happening, yes.
> MEAD: When you're jumping around taking pictures . . .
> BATESON: Nobody's talking about that, Margaret, for God's sake.
> MEAD: Well.
> BATESON: I'm talking about having control of a camera. You're talking about putting a dead camera on top of a bloody tripod. It sees nothing.
> MEAD: Well, I think it sees a great deal. I've [tried to work] with these pictures taken by artists, and really good ones . . .
> BATESON: I'm sorry I said artists; all I meant was artists. I mean, artists is not a term of abuse in my vocabulary.
> MEAD: It isn't in mine either, but I . . .
> BATESON: Well, in this conversation, it's become one.[37]

Many anthropologists still feel caught between the possibility of conceptual advances from visual anthropology and the more conservative paradigms of a positivist scientific tradition. There is continuing interest in studying such virtually untapped archival resources as the Bateson-Mead corpus and in using visual media for education. Both of these objectives are enhanced by world networking and the possibilities of multimedia. What remains unresolved is whether the visual can attain a more productive role in anthropology as a medium of enquiry and discourse.

The epistemological and methodological implications of such a shift are substantial. They involve putting in temporary suspension anthropology's dominant orientation as a discipline of words and rethinking certain categories of anthropological knowledge in the light of understandings that may be accessible only by nonverbal means. In exchange, visual anthro-

pology offers the possibility of new pathways to anthropological knowledge, as in understanding the transmission of culture and in newly identified areas of cultural construction. Foremost is the need to build an
intellectual foundation for visual anthropology by enabling a shift from
word-and-sentence-based anthropological thought to image-and-se-
quence-based anthropological thought. Visual anthropology can never be
either a copy of written anthropology or a substitute for it. For that very
reason it must develop alternative objectives and methodologies that will
benefit anthropology as a whole.

Visual anthropologists themselves have been notoriously reluctant to
explain the anthropological value of their work, partly because they feel
no need to justify it, but also because it is very difficult to justify it in the
usual anthropological terms. Rouch's films fail miserably as demonstra-
tions of "scientific method," and if they theorize about their subjects, the
theories cannot be reduced to a verbal précis. On the other hand, some
anthropologists conceive of visual anthropology in such highly proscrip-
tive and ideal terms as effectively to define it out of existence. Existing
work is either tipped into the rubbish bin of naïve science (untheorized
records) or naïve amateurism (untheorized impressions). Other visual
works that might be considered as anthropology are said merely to resemble it, through a kind of mimicry.

But visual anthropology is not going to appear miraculously some day
in the future. It is being created now, even if we do not always recognize
it. There is already a substantial body of visual work that deserves to be
examined more closely for what it has achieved. Ákos Östör made this
point in 1990 when he wrote: "It is time to lay aside the old debate about
visual anthropology failing or succeeding in the quest for full-fledged disciplinary status, or about film finally becoming worthy of scientific anthropological inquiry. It is time to begin analysing and interpreting
films."[38] Instead of campaigning for the creation of a mature visual anthropology, with its anthropological principles all in place, we would be
wise to look at the principles that emerge when fieldworkers actually try
to rethink anthropology through use of a visual medium. This may lead
in directions we would never have predicted from the comparative safety
of theory.

Notes

1. See Hinsley 1991, Poignant 1992, Street 1992, Davis 1993.
2. Hinsley 1991: 348–50.
3. Shown in a Georges Demeny film shot in 1895. See *A Cinema Programme
of 1896.*

4. Cited in Cantrill & Cantrill 1982: 37.

5. Darrah 1977: 50–51.

6. Peterson 1985: 166.

7. Edwards 1992b:7.

8. Berreman 1972: 573, 575–77.

9. Pinney 1990a: 261.

10. Pinney 1992: 81–82.

11. Grimshaw 1997.

12. Ibid., pp. 9–10.

13. Mead 1975: 4.

14. See Rouch 1975: 85.

15. See Haddon 1900; Hastrup 1992: 15.

16. See Houtman 1988: 20.

17. Worth 1981: 190.

18. Ginsburg 1991: 102–5.

19. Ginsburg 1994: 6.

20. Ibid., p. 14.

21. Nichols 1991.

22. See Ruby 1994: 168.

23. Stoller 1992: 204.

24. Ruby 1975; 1989: 9.

25. Lewis 1986: 414–15.

26. Russell 1912: 46–59.

27. Ruby 1975: 104–11., esp. 109

28. Stoller 1992: 217.

29. Marcus & Cushman 1982.

30. See Bloch 1974, G. Lewis 1980, Jackson 1989, Piault 1989.

31. Tyler 1987: 199–213; Barthes 1975: 55–57.

32. Toren 1993: 464.

33. Jackson 1989: 142.

34. Pinney 1990b: 43.

35. Mead's commentary in *Childhood Rivalry in Bali and New Guinea* (1952).
See Filmography.

36. Bateson & Mead 1942: 49–50.

37. Bateson & Mead 1977: 79.

38. Östör 1990: 722.

9

ANTHROPOLOGY'S LOST VISION

JOHN GRIERSON is often credited with inventing the term "documentary film" when he wrote of the documentary value of Flaherty's *Moana* (1926).[1] According to Jean Rouch, "ethnographic film" originated at a conference organized by André Leroi-Gourhan in 1948.[2] At the time, however, the term designated not so much a genre of filmmaking as films of general interest to anthropologists. The notion of "visual anthropology" had existed in some sense since the 1850s, but the words only began to be used when they appeared in the title of a book in 1975.[3] In that same book, Colin Young coined the term "observational cinema." Perhaps even now some new film form lies dormant, waiting only for a name.

Of the several terms I have mentioned, visual anthropology may be regarded as either a highly specialized activity or a more broadly inclusive one, depending on one's point of view. This may indicate a problem of focus connected with the variety of roles that have historically been assigned to it. It would be satisfying to think of visual anthropology as a discipline that had evolved systematically, beginning with line drawings and paintings, incorporating still photographs in the nineteenth century, adding motion to its repertoire at the turn of the century, and then ripening into one of the accepted dialects or "discourses" of contemporary anthropology. It would be encouraging to think it had achieved enough stability to be "rethought," as the title of one book put it in 1997, or that it had enough coherence to have "principles," as another did in 1975.[4] However, this is far from the case.

At one point the growth of visual anthropology into a mature discipline looked possible. I would place the date around 1898, a few years after the invention of cinema and the same year in which Alfred Cort Haddon (or more probably his assistant Anthony Wilkin) made the first ethnographic films in the field. By then anthropological photography was already well established, with rules on how to go about it drawn up by Thomas Henry Huxley and John Lamprey. There were serious debates about what to photograph, as well. When Everard im Thurn presented his photographs taken in British Guiana to members of the Anthropological Institute in 1893, he suggested that anthropological photography should be "not of the mere bodies of primitive folk . . . but of these folk regarded as living beings."[5]

Some time after this, perhaps even as late as World War I, a curtain seems to have come down on visual anthropology. Although there were sporadic photographic and filming efforts by anthropologists such as Walter Baldwin Spencer and Franz Boas, and by non-anthropologists such as Edward S. Curtis and Robert Flaherty, interest waned and, as Luc de Heusch pointed out in 1962,[6] anthropologists gradually stopped publishing photographs in their books. In visual terms, anthropology had entered a dark age. It was not that anthropologists stopped looking and seeing, or even that they stopped taking photographs—Malinowski took many, and if anything the practice probably increased among fieldworkers—but actually showing photographs was no longer considered an important way of producing anthropological knowledge.[7] Since then visual anthropology has had an erratic and quite unorthodox history.

There is some uncertainty about why this happened. Was it because photography and cinematography were considered too difficult and costly, or because anthropologists had lost faith in vision as a source of knowledge? In the view of Anna Grimshaw, Martin Jay, and others, with World War I "confidence in sight as the noblest of the senses and a privileged source of knowledge about the world was finally destroyed."[8] Or was it that images were considered vulgar—the stuff of entertainment and magazine supplements? As Alison Griffiths observes, "the cinematic medium's unsavory associations with cheap popular amusements undoubtedly discouraged some professional anthropologists from taking up the medium."[9] Or was it that anthropological research had become dependent on the words of informants, reinforcing it as a discipline of words, as Margaret Mead maintained?[10] Or was it that anthropological interests had made a decisive shift away from the visible world of material objects to the invisible world of beliefs and abstract relations?

Of these explanations, the last has been the most powerful but also the most perplexing. For along with the turn to such invisible matters as kinship were rising interests in observable social behavior. The eclipse of visual anthropology seems to have coincided with a period when participant-observation in fieldwork was in fact being established as the cornerstone of anthropological practice. In any case, interest in the invisible was far from new to anthropologists. Before Frazer there had been considerable interest in mythology, religious beliefs, and animism, as can be seen in Edward Tylor's writings. This was also the era of interest in psychology and rising interest in its links to social anthropology. Among early fieldworkers, two of Haddon's associates, W.H.R. Rivers and William McDougall, were psychologists, and Malinowski was among the first to dignify the concept of the native's point of view. It would have been hard to find a method better suited to observing and recording social behavior, or what the "native" actually saw and experienced, than film. Yet if anything, anthropologists increasingly distanced themselves from the new medium. They appear to have turned a blind eye to it just when it seemed to have the most to offer them.

The most plausible explanation may be twofold, involving historical timing and the formation of professional attitudes. When the shift to more abstract thinking was occurring in anthropology, film was still too undeveloped to be of much use in examining social relationships, and by the time it was ready to do so, anthropologists had already consigned it to the narrower roles of note-taking and public education. Film and photography were thus pushed to the two extremities of the discipline—to the earliest stage, where conclusions were yet to be formed, and to the final stage, where they were already being popularized. Films perhaps fell too easily into the category of "life groups" and illuminated dioramas, which by this time were well established in natural history museums.[11] Even Franz Boas, who was centrally involved in the development of museums and an innovator in anthropological photography, had at best an ambivalent attitude toward the medium.[12] Visual anthropology would eventually emerge from its isolation in the 1950s, after shifts in documentary and fiction filmmaking—and anthropology itself—had prepared the way for it to be taken up again. But the gap of four decades had by then left its mark on the discipline.

The Dark Age

The period of anthropology's transformation from an armchair pursuit to an empirical science coincides with the period between cinema's invention at the end of the nineteenth century and its transformation into an expressive medium in the 1920s. This timing had unfortunate consequences for the development of visual research methods. When film was still in its infancy, anthropology was already making the transition from collecting accounts and material artifacts to more systematic studies based on fieldwork. The Cambridge Expedition to the Torres Strait in 1898 is often cited as the beginning of the new era, in which several of the expedition members, including W.H.R. Rivers and Charles Seligman, were later to play an important part. The expedition's leader, A. C. Haddon, was quick to seize on the new technology and recommend it to colleagues such as Walter Baldwin Spencer, who used it in central Australia in 1901. Museums supported similar endeavors in other parts of the world, and showing films publicly soon helped to defray some of the costs of anthropological expeditions.

Like the earliest filmmakers (Thomas Edison and Louis Lumière), Haddon and Spencer could do little more with a camera than set it on a tripod, point it at something of possible interest, and turn the crank. No doubt this is essentially what we still do today, but we have the great advantage of imagining the outcome as a sophisticated form of communication, with a hundred years of cinematic experimentation and convention to guide us. For early audiences, cinema provided an almost magical illusion of reality. For us it has become less magical in a technical sense but possibly more so in its potential for exploring the intricacies of human experience. But to reach this point it was not enough to invent the camera—the cinema had to be invented as well. Even today the difference is not widely understood. For many people, how films work on them is largely a mystery. Nor does achieving greater sophistication bring an end to the matter. It is one thing for a filmmaker to be able to string shots together competently in some kind of logical order; it is quite another to do so in a way that constructs a new reality—a time and a place and people interacting within that setting. And having done that, it is yet a further step to be able to reveal the feelings and relationships of the people one is showing.

As anthropology became professionalized, it developed its own discursive voice, adapting earlier missionary and travel writing to a more abstract style outfitted with a specialized scientific vocabulary.[13] The anthropological questionnaire, combined with new fieldwork practices, led to a standardization of categories within which to fit the new knowledge. The styles varied, but the method of participant-observation, which replaced gleaning information from missionaries and local administrators, put the anthropologist firmly at the center of the new ethnography. He or she was not merely an intermediary between the society studied and the anthropological audience but performed a kind of digestive process on the experiences of fieldwork, out of which emerged a new object. This process was later to be described as a translation of culture.[14]

From social philosophers, anthropologists obtained much of their terminology, including "ethnology" and "sociology." From explorers and novelists they borrowed styles of narrative description, and from literary essayists occasional notes of humor and personal reflection. However, the discursive voice that they increasingly adopted was that of the natural scientist reporting back to a professional society. This came equipped with techniques for converting the active into the passive voice, the past into the ethnographic present, and the "I" of first-person observation into the more impersonal "one." Later on, a kind of objective subjectivity emerged in the use of the impersonal "you," as in Evans-Pritchard's "If you suffer a serious misfortune you will immediately suspect witchcraft."[15]

This is not to suggest that early anthropological writing styles were altogether derivative, but to draw attention to the emergence of a powerful new form of presentation against which visual images must often have appeared troublesome or unnecessary: troublesome because they tended to bypass the anthropologist's mediating and interpretive role, unnecessary because they merely reiterated less pointedly what the anthropologist had already seen, digested, and reported upon. Perhaps, too, they now appeared outdated, reflecting earlier anthropological preoccupations with material artifacts and racial types. The human body had gradually ceased to be a site of meaning. In the new anthropology, the knowledge that mattered was no longer an expression of physical form but a set of mental constructions. Photographs and films were not amenable to much further elaboration; they remained brute facts. They provided evidence of the anthropologist's professional activities in the field, but this required little more than polite acknowledgment.

Anthropologists had certainly not stopped looking, nor did they discount the importance of vision. However, their response to the disjunction between their writing and their seeing, although it varied in style, resulted in much the same thing. For some, discussing the intricacies of a legal system or a kinship structure could be accomplished with little visual description. For others it was an invitation to sharpen their descriptive skills. Critics have pointed out the visualism and the importance of literary models for Malinowski's and Firth's prose, and Geertz has discussed "the intensely visual quality of Evans-Pritchard's style," describing it as a "slide show."[16] On the other hand, this verbal display might well be regarded less as a celebration of photographic values than a way of making photographs unnecessary. Although Evans-Pritchard used quite a few photographs in his books, they stand in an uncomfortable and in some respects subversive relation to his texts.[17]

Through various adaptive maneuvers, anthropological writing gradually subsumed and bypassed the visual. In some cases, visual images came to be regarded as simple extensions of words. Anthropologists often showed lantern slides as part of their lectures. When ethnographic films were shown, the program was much the same. Baldwin Spencer's first screenings of his Aranda films in 1902 were part of a public lecture series, advertised as "illustrated by lantern slides, cinematographic views, and phonograph records."[18] Visual images not only needed verbal exegesis, they were to be surrounded and enfolded in words. The anthropological voice thus accommodated itself to photography both by simulating some of its qualities and subordinating it to verbal accounts. Exactly the opposite was occurring in cinema, where intertitles were subordinated to images and the whole was accompanied by music rather than speech.

By the 1920s photography had become a sideline among anthropologists, and ethnographic filmmaking the activity of a few scattered enthusiasts. There was no longer much call for the anthropometric documentation that had flourished when anthropologists were trying to link racial and occupational "types" to social evolution. Meanwhile, ethnographic filmmaking had changed little since Haddon's and Baldwin Spencer's day, except that anthropologists were no longer doing it. If one looks at ethnographic film in Australia up until the 1940s, one finds that the practitioners were a mixture of amateur ethnologists, missionaries, journalists, dentists, doctors, businessmen, and travelers.[19] The only institutionally based anthropologist-filmmaker was Norman B. Tindale, for some years curator of anthropology at the South Australia Museum. For the most part, the films that were made consisted of loosely related scenes of hunting, food preparation, tool making, and religious ceremonies. Although some of these achievements were considerable and were carried out under difficult conditions, they inevitably reflected the weakness of a field in which there was no professional training and few theoretical guidelines. One looks in vain for the academic excitement that had surrounded discussions of ethnographic photography and film in the nineteenth century. Neither now offered a model for professional publication that could compete with the journal article and the ethnographic monograph. Visual anthropology had become a technique of supplementary documentation, and not a very interesting one at that.

Anthropologists in Flatland

One of the problems facing anthropology from the very beginning was that films and photographs did not explain or summarize matters—they expanded upon them almost without limit. If anything, they were too full of specific and unmediated information. This perhaps held attractions for certain devotees, or museum curators with insatiable appetites, or entrepreneurs who could exhibit films to the public, but to most anthropologists it was this very literalness that was disconcerting. Films of things looked remarkably like the things themselves. By contrast, scientific activity consisted not in the faithful reproduction of reality but in collecting data, building up a theoretical framework, and publishing conclusions. It was difficult to see how film could assist in these tasks.

Robert Flaherty's *Nanook of the North*, when it appeared in 1922, inspired no imitators among anthropologists, unlike Malinowski's *Argonauts of the Western Pacific*, published in the same year. One is tempted to ask why this was so. It demonstrated, after all, an entirely new use for film—not merely a record of activities, nor an instructional tool, but a doorway one could step through imaginatively into the life of another people. One reason may be that Flaherty had no disciples, either among filmmakers or anthropologists. Perhaps also, the demonstrable humanity of Nanook and the details of his daily life were not for anthropologists the most pressing scientific issues of the day. Even though Malinowski was advocating immersion in another culture as a way of understanding it, this was a prescription for fieldwork rather than for professional publication. As Malinowski's own photographs suggest, he did not see photography as a systematic way of exploring another society, or even a way of allowing others to experience it more vividly.[20]

A further reason may be that Flaherty's achievement was in many ways more radical than anyone realized at the time, despite the acclaim surrounding the film. Its apparent simplicity, even naïveté, masked a fundamentally different approach to understanding other cultures, a focus on the individual that would only flower in anthropology several years later in the Culture and Personality school. It was produced by a period of long-term fieldwork that resembled Malinowski's but had an added dialogic and collaborative dimension. Flaherty's film also proposed a narrative approach to ethnography quite unprecedented in the anthropology of the time. Like the "life history" ethnographies published many years later, the film suggested that narrative might be one of the only ways of grasping how social forces actually converge upon an individual in society.

Some of Flaherty's potential imitators may also have been discouraged by his considerable cinematic skills and his commitment in resources and time. Although the narrative and cinematic techniques he used were in some ways less radical than those being developed by D. W. Griffith, they were nonetheless new departures for nonfiction film and not easily copied by others. Moreover, they were quite different in character from the narrative effects that Malinowski, inspired by Frazer and Conrad, was trying to develop in his writing, which were designed more to evoke scenes he had observed than the experiences of others. Films for most anthropologists were still perceived as slide shows with motion. Filmmaking was the production of one picture, and then another picture. It would have required a great conceptual leap to envisage using such scenes as a way of restructuring the viewer's imagination.

For scientists perhaps more than for others, film represented an extension of the pragmatic mode of nineteenth-century still photography, which had long been used to document a variety of natural objects, one of the first being the moon in 1840.[21] The separation between viewer and photograph and between camera and object—made manifest in the case of the moon—was consonant with the scientific view of photography as an optical-chemical process that produced a material image, in contrast to the popular or "primitive" view that a photograph somehow magically embodied its object. This materialist attitude expresses itself in the "flatness" of much early photography and film, which had developed in concert with nineteenth-century modes of industrial production and technical drawing.[22]

Anthropological photography had reached an early high-water mark in anthropometry, as advocated by Thomas Henry Huxley and John Lamprey as early as 1868, and in the chronophotographs of human and animal locomotion made by Muybridge, Marey, Anschütz, and Regnault soon after. Typically, the subject was viewed on one plane against a flat background, sometimes in silhouette, the only other feature being a grid or scale for measurement. The familiar anthropometric trope of a pair of frontal and profile photographs is still with us today in police mug shots. The profile view is suggestive of a medical cross-section. Scientific photography of this period carries with it the implication of a world comprehensible in two dimensions, reducible to a kind of geometry. There is a clarity of intention, if not much utility, in these photographic pairs, as if they represented, on the one hand, completeness (frontality), and on the other (the profile) progress toward some final destination beyond the frame. It is perhaps not coincidental that the conventional image of the Rise of Man is a line of figures in profile, gradually becoming more erect.

If the anthropometric pair is the most memorable image of ethnographic photography, the "line-up" photograph of full-length figures is almost as familiar. This approach to the human body is not just an artifact of wide-angle lenses or the laborious process of setting up a glass-plate camera. It seems linked as well to a conception of the person as presenting two symbolic surfaces, the frontal primary because it is the site of expression, nourishment, and procreation, as represented in the face, breasts, and genitals, and the dorsal, representing indifference, negation, even shame. More than simply enabling clear identification, frontality and full body length seemed intended to sum up the person in some fundamental sense.

Photographs of individuals were also taken to typify entire communities. In the imperial context, anthropological and administrative objectives often became intermixed, as tribes and other groups were classified according to occupational and physiognomic types, each represented by a photograph of a single person with an identifying caption. Pinney has shown how in India caste took on a new political meaning after the "Mutiny" of 1857, since it was believed that "caste was not merely an index of status but had formed the basis of opposition to alien rule. . . . To discover political allegiance so clearly mapped in the physiognomy of the citizen was an administrator's dream."[23]

There is another sense in which nineteenth-century anthropological photographs were "flat." Many indigenous groups, forcibly dispersed, shot, and reduced by disease, were widely believed to be dying out, both biologically and culturally. If not already doomed, they were perceived as people without a future—or rather, as people whose future was preordained to be a memory. In any case, the project of salvage anthropology—snatching the last records of "dying races"—collapsed past and present, leaving no room for a future. These populations were in a sense "already" dead, destined for little more than a small panel in the frieze of human history.

One common view of the early cinema of Thomas Edison and the Lumière brothers is that it was also flat. Events were filmed on a single plane facing the camera, as if on a stage. There was but a single fixed shot for each film and, as a result, no shift in point of view. The camera was usually placed at eye level. The protagonists made entrances from the left or right of the frame. Film, in short, was conceived in terms of a theatrical experience rather than the perspective of an actual person living in a three-dimensional world. As in still photography, there was an implicit separation between camera and subject, viewer and viewed.

This of course is not entirely true. Even the famous *L'arrivée d'un train* at Le Ciotat station—one of the first Lumière films—was shot at an oblique angle down the platform, suggesting the experience of a prospective passenger. However, even if not always true in every case, the observation is true to the spirit of these films, which were presented as a series of pictorial "views," or like specimens in a museum showcase.[24] Even early fiction films, such as Georges Méliès's *Le voyage dans la lune* (1902), although visually extremely inventive, presented the viewer with flat, cut-out figures and effects. According to anecdotal accounts, what most amazed the viewers of early films was not seeing human beings represented, or even their actions, but the sudden invasion of the theater by the randomness of the outside world, as seen in the complex movements of waves, leaves, and smoke.[25] As Edgar Morin rightly observes, it was not to see reality that people crowded into the cinema hall, but to see the image of reality.[26]

Early ethnographic films share many of the features of what is often called "primitive" cinema. The surviving films of the Cambridge Expedition to the Torres Strait show the subjects filmed frontally, as though performing on a stage, occasionally making entrances and exits from the sides of the frame. The flatness in these films is as much intellectual as visual. The aim is to isolate one aspect of human activity—a ritual, a demonstration of fire making, a few dances. If these are not literally labeled, they stand in much the same relation to the spectator as labeled material artifacts or photographs of them. Where there are signs of individuality or emotion, these are clearly superfluous to the purposes of the film. As in nineteenth-century photographs of human "types," the apparent discomfort of the subjects in these and many other early films is not necessarily a sign of the insensitivity of the anthropologist but of a more generally institutionalized scientific attitude. This was particularist in character, directed toward discrete features of social life rather than toward the more integrated view of culture that was to emerge some decades later.

If we are to understand anthropology's aversion to images for much of the following century, we must see it in the context of this early flatness. Photography and film produced objects to be held at arms' length. The cinema was not yet a medium of communication, much less an expression of thoughts and feelings, or the creator of a new subjectivity in the audience. Nor was there any immediate desire among social scientists to make it so. If the new nineteenth-century visual technologies promised a radical departure from the viewing practices of the *camera obscura*, each of these technologies also required the elaboration of a new aesthetic. Strategies for producing audience identification with individuals on the screen were yet to be developed in the cinema. Anthropologists certainly had close relationships with some of their informants, but few would have considered them, as Flaherty did, the proper focus of their studies. Although fieldworkers such as Haddon, Spencer, and Malinowski made photographs and even films, few would have seen visual media as expressive in the way that writing was. At this stage, ethnographic film remained a technology holding out little more promise than an improved typewriter or a better way of taking notes.

Visual Anthropology's Other History

Visual anthropology has by now acquired the semblance of a history, although far from a definitive one.[27] It is, as I have suggested, a history of cross-purposes and frustrated starts, but it is more conventionally seen as a story of progress toward greater sophistication and more varied forms. According to this view, visual anthropology began as documentation, absorbed elements of documentary cinema to produce ethnographic films, which then developed various didactic, observational, participatory, and reflexive approaches. In its most recent incarnation it has rediscovered still photography, assimilated indigenous media production, and even appointed itself the custodian of all forms of visual culture.[28]

Underlying this account is the assumption that visual anthropology has followed the trajectory of mainstream anthropology—in both accepting and questioning approaches modeled on the natural sciences and later in adopting various psychological, narrative, political, and phenomenological perspectives. As part of this, it has become increasingly self-conscious and has evolved its own metacommunicative discourse. Thus each of its shifts is seen as following more general movements in anthropology's intellectual history.

In contrast to this processual view, I would propose a different and more erratic history, focusing on tendencies that were present from the beginning but were often overlooked or discounted in the years that followed. In this account, the indifference of anthropologists to visual methods is linked more to disciplinary habits than to larger theoretical principles. Furthermore, some of the innovations of visual anthropology, such as its interest in text construction and reflexivity, anticipated rather than followed those of anthropology proper. Although a visual approach sometimes failed because it clashed with dominant anthropological paradigms, more often it simply seemed irrelevant.

Despite this, I believe there was always a flickering of interest in the possibility of a visual anthropology, perhaps for what it promised that anthropological writing could not. The activities of a few unorthodox anthropologists and ethnographic filmmakers kept these interests alive. Much of what interested them—the embodied experience of individuals, the relation of people to places and material objects, the performative aspects of social life—have now become part of the anthropological mainstream. Perhaps one day these concerns will be seen as having been central to visual anthropology's potential from the very beginning.

We have recently seen the emergence of a complex set of interests in anthropology focusing on how culture is constantly being reinvented in the interactions of daily life. These processes are increasingly understood as embodied rather than abstract, variable across individuals and subgroups, and expressed in a panoply of patterns and symbolic forms involving material objects, the emotions, and the senses. Today culture is more often defined as a dynamic aspect of human relationships rather than a set of governing principles. Although one can find traces of anthropology's various "schools" in visual anthropology (from early evolutionary theory to structural-functionalism to hermeneutics), one also finds a persistent undercurrent of other preoccupations. This "other" visual anthropology sets aside the notion of the camera as a recording instrument in favor of a more intimate kind of intervention.

One can see this in certain eccentric approaches to ethnographic still photography at the end of the nineteenth century and also later, in the work of such widely different filmmakers as Flaherty, Bateson, Jean Epstein, Luis Buñuel, and Basil Wright, whose practices straddled the worlds of documentary, ethnography, the avant-garde, and commercial cinema. There are further oddities such as *Grass* (1925), made almost accidentally as part of the preparations for a fiction film, and the strange collaboration of James Agee and Walker Evans in their book *Let Us Now Praise Famous Men*, which, at least in Agee's case, can be regarded as an obsessively subjective experiment in ethnography. This aberrant trend continued more vigorously after World War II in the work of Georges Rouquier, Jean Rouch, John Marshall, Robert Gardner, and others.

As these names suggest, it is possible to look at the history of visual anthropology within two very different frameworks. Within the first it is a subsidiary activity of anthropology, useful for documentation, teaching, and popularization. Here visual media have played a useful if minor role in recording changing cultures and providing detailed data for the study of ritual, material culture, dance, facial expression, body movement, and other specialized projects. They have also served to bring anthropology to a wider public through print publications, films, and television. Some who take this position in fact consider visual media to have had a great but underutilized potential for anthropology. If only anthropologists had treated ethnographic film (or video) as a scientific instrument, they feel, instead of a means of popularization, its promise might finally have been realized. They share a sense of being outflanked by an inauthentic visual anthropology that has more to do with making films about anthropological subjects than conducting anthropological research.[29] Non-anthropologists tend to be seen as interlopers. As well as declaring that anthropologists had failed negligently to film the world's cultural diversity, Margaret Mead complained that certain filmmakers were "wrecking everything that we're trying to do."[30]

Within the second framework, which takes developments outside the discipline more seriously, one discovers a quite different visual anthropology. Here, the practice is seen as marginal to the discipline for the very reason that it has constituted a radically different way of approaching human societies. Its pioneers have therefore almost of necessity been non-anthropologists such as Flaherty and Marshall, or rebel anthropologists such as Bateson and Rouch. It is consistent with this more comprehensive view that Rouch should have declared two non-anthropologists, Flaherty and Dziga Vertov, to be the "fathers of anthropological film" and (in sharp contrast to Margaret Mead) filmmakers to whom "we owe all of what we are trying to do today."[31]

What Flaherty and Vertov brought to visual anthropology was in fact a challenge to the notion that the filmmaker (and the audience) stood outside the world of the subject, as though separated by a pane of glass. Their approaches contested both the conceptual and physical flatness of this encounter. In their attempts to take the viewer closer to the world of the subject, films had to become part of a larger, three-dimensional imaginative conception, instead of objects to be inspected or windows to be looked through. One of the consequences of this was to acknowledge the importance of the camera's shifts in point of view, in contrast to the ideally static and objective stance of scientific observation. Another was to engage the viewer's imaginative participation in piecing together the world created by the film. Flaherty's achievement was to draw the viewer into a social world defined by human relationships, interactions, and sequences of events. Vertov's was to invade the physical space of that world more aggressively through his use of the camera, drawing attention to the mechanisms behind the filming process. In Flaherty, Rouch recognized his own desire to portray the social experiences of others, in Vertov his own playfulness and provocative questioning of representation itself. In each he saw a filmmaker who participated in the life he was filming and was able to communicate something of that encounter to the viewer.

Far from developing in concert with written anthropology, visual anthropology can therefore be seen as a more autonomous and dissident enterprise—an enterprise that has only begun to converge with orthodox anthropology as the agenda of anthropology itself has gradually widened. But visual anthropology, especially ethnographic filmmaking, has also had to clarify its own objectives and develop its own ways of carrying them out. In this it has borrowed much from other forms of cinema. Where visual anthropology has diverged most sharply from anthropological writing has been in its approach to the particularities of social experience, which it often addresses by narrative means. And although theory is part of the external superstructure of most anthropological writing, it is almost always implicit in a visual work. Writing tends to present its conclusions in propositional form, whereas film presents not conclusions but events and suggests their possible causes, cultural predispositions, and ramifications. Where anthropological writing can provide overarching descriptions and marshal lists of examples, visual "description" is limited to a narrower view, but often one of more fine-grained and integrated detail.

Certain kinds of anthropology have obviously been more suited than others to the discursive properties of visual media. These include approaches requiring extensive audiovisual description, such as ethnomusicology; studies of ritual, gesture, and expression; studies focusing on art, artifacts, aesthetics, and visual culture; and those stressing the agency of individuals or their social experience. Thus, some properties of film have held an appeal for anthropologists engaged in a particular range of studies—for example, film's capacity to portray social structure at an intimate level, invoking both its norms and practical implementation. Film was also to attract interest for its capacity to communicate the experience of individual social actors, as was being sought through ethnographic life histories and, more generally, in a focus on indigenous perspectives. The narrative possibilities of film were of interest to anthropologists who were trying to describe how individuals negotiated their way through conflicting social pressures and expectations. Recently, visual media have become increasingly useful for showing how social processes are objectified in material objects, bodily expression, and performance. Visual anthropology also comes to the fore in exploring how environments shape social experience—and how social environments are themselves constructed.

Clearly, film had its attractions for at least some anthropologists. But were early ethnographic filmmakers such as Flaherty, or even later ones such as Ian Dunlop, John Marshall, and Timothy Asch, actually producing new anthropological knowledge? Or, as some critics contend, were they merely mimicking the fieldwork practices of anthropologists and producing films on stereotypical anthropological subjects?[32] The question is important but probably flawed, given that the answer would necessarily depend upon whether one adopted a less or more inclusive definition of anthropology. What the question opens up more usefully is a debate about anthropological knowledge itself, in its institutionalization and relation to theory. Is there such a thing as visual knowledge? What is the relation between knowing in the abstract and understanding subjectively the ins and outs of the specific case? Can knowledge exist in the absence of someone knowing it, or must it be resurrected at each "reading"? If the answers to such questions are still emerging, then it is possible that the pioneers so warmly regarded by Rouch were sometimes producing knowledge that had not yet become anthropological, and that in duplicating anthropological field methods they were also helping to invent them.

Learning How to Look

The conceptions of visual anthropology prevailing around 1975 were clearly mapped out in Paul Hockings's landmark collection, *Principles of Visual Anthropology*. Not only were no commonly held "principles" apparent, but the articles fell into two distinct groups: those that saw film as a method of acquiring data for research and those, such as Rouch's, that saw it as a way of generating new kinds of anthropological knowledge. The publication of the book marked a transitional moment for visual anthropology, for it provided a mirror in which its various practitioners could see themselves and consider the future of the discipline. It contributed significantly to the rethinking of visual anthropology. Earlier, there had been two equally important moments, the first the 1898 Cambridge Expedition to the Torres Strait and the second the appearance of *Nanook of the North* in 1922. These enunciated quite different approaches. By the 1930s the split between them had become very evident in Gregory Bateson and Margaret Mead's innovative Balinese project.

The Balinese project of 1936–38 (which included work in New Guinea) was a turning point in visual anthropology. For the first time, anthropologists were inspired to apply visual media to something other than the visible features of culture, such as ritual or technology. Although the project studied external behavior, its object was to see how this reproduced an inner world of cultural attitudes and social relationships. In the end the project produced some 28,000 photographs and 22,000 feet of 16mm film, leading eventually to two books, a number of journal articles, and seven edited films.

The overall aim of the project was to explore the relationship between parents-child interaction and the development of Balinese character. This was to be studied through direct observation and photography; however, photography played a less prominent role at the start than later on in the project. Bateson and Mead had very different ideas about how to approach this research. That they collaborated at all, and so well, is a matter of some amazement. Bateson's first plans for the project sound rather like a variant of Flaherty's among the Inuit. "An attempt will be made to film a few very short scenarios with plots. . . . The scenarios will be based either upon native myth or, preferably, upon incidents in the lives of specially studied individuals. The natives will be induced (if possible) to take a major part in the planning of these scenarios."[33]

Bateson's interests lay in developing somewhat further the ideas about schizmogenesis and cultural ethos that he had postulated in *Naven* (1936). He hoped to use 16mm film to investigate how emotion was communicated through gesture and body movement, and how the Balinese dealt with potentially polarizing social forces. Although Mead's interests also focused on the expression of emotion, she regarded photography primarily as an objective recording and note-taking device that would provide theoretically neutral material for analysis. Along with her interest in trance states, which appeared to be culturally institutionalized in Bali, she wished to make longitudinal studies of child development, extending the range of her earlier Samoan research.

In many respects Bateson's and Mead's interests overlapped, but their conceptions of how to use the camera were quite different. For Bateson, filming was to be an analytical tool—a way of making sense of complex social interactions. The process of filming was to be actively investigative. For Mead, filming was primarily a form of documentation to back up direct observation and act as a check on the possible biases of the observer. As well, photography increasingly became for her a way of illustrating her conclusions.

The Balinese project thus combined a conception of scientific photography that had prevailed in anthropology since the nineteenth century with a new approach that envisaged it as a way of investigating the complexities of social experience. Forty years later, Bateson and Mead were still debating the difference. Bateson believed a camera should be an extension of a process of thought, a way for the filmmaker to explore a subject and for the viewer to follow that exploration. For him, actively looking and merely seeing (or recording) were two different matters. "I'm talking about having control of a camera," he told Mead later. "You're talking about putting a dead camera on top of a bloody tripod. It sees nothing."[34]

If *seeing* implies a passive form of vision that scans a subject or preserves it in some impersonal sense, *looking* implies a more selective, intentional activity, a search for or an investment of meaning. To look with a camera is to see with some purpose and leave a trace of that process in the resulting images. Nothing is easier, of course, than to read the wrong intention into a photograph. In still photography the signs of intention may only emerge from a large group of images taken by the same photographer. And for many people, the photographer's intention does not much matter: they are more concerned with the photograph's content or, at a more sophisticated level, with its broader ideological and cultural implications. For Barthes it was often both—the detail that aroused his interest, as well as the expression of culturally encoded messages.

Seeing and looking with a camera are finally matters of degree, for strictly speaking there is no image made without intention, even by a bank's surveillance camera. For the critic, the task is often one of interpreting the level of conscious intention with which the camera is used, or the intention of the intention—to what extent the author's interest is consciously made manifest in the work or is erased from it. The casual viewer may read the author's interest more simply as a style or a conventionalized attitude toward the subject. The requirements of genre can easily mask any traces of authorship. Nineteenth-century portrait photography was so standardized that only a strong creative sensibility such as Nadar's stands out among the tens of thousands of Daguerreotypes that were produced.

The linear time structure of film adds to photography a further frame of reference for interpreting a filmmaker's interests. It provides an underlying narrative of the choices made by the filmmaker. Shifts between different points of view, different degrees of proximity, and movement within the shot all serve as indicators of the filmmaker's relationship to the subject, intellectually, physically, and emotionally. Occasionally, even a very early "primitive" film, such as *Duke of York Opening First Federal Parliament* (made in Melbourne in 1901),[35] can give us evidence of the filmmaker's eye and mind behind the camera. As the Duke and Duchess of York and their entourage walk along a pier toward a boat that will take them away, the camera pans with them and then suddenly moves sharply to the left and reframes on an empty part of the pier, into which they duly walk. In this move is a clear change of intention, perhaps in the first instance to prevent the royal couple getting ahead of the panning motion, but more probably to prepare a new scene for them to enter—an early intimation of film editing.

Learning to look with the camera, rather than merely see with it, took ethnographic filmmakers a long time, because it first had to be understood that a camera could be handled with more than the general intention of being aimed at a subject. Perhaps this was not unlike the ancient discovery that producing different sounds in a sequence creates music. The desire to use the camera interpretively was also—within science, and often outside it—in competition with the notion that the camera was itself possessed of a perfect vision and will to truth—an expression of God's optical laws or, as Henry Fox Talbot put it, "the pencil of Nature." It was in some such sense that Margaret Mead would declare many years later that the camera "should act as an automatic correction on the variability of the human observer."[36]

This use of a camera implied instrumentation of a kind that extended the natural capabilities of the eye, in exceptional cases through the use of telephoto lenses or slow motion or highly sensitive film stocks. Mead equated the camera with the cyclotron and the electron microscope. The more common scientific analogy was that of a window through which one could see the world, the image Alberti had used to describe single-point perspective. "Because we have film," wrote E. Richard Sorenson and Allison Jablonko in the 1970s, "we may make windows, however small, through which we can review past events."[37] "Looking," by contrast, required not an improvement in instrumentation but a refiguration of thought and space.

The Cinematic Imagination

Paul Hockings notes that in W.H.R. Rivers's monograph, *The Todas* (1906), there are two very different kinds of photographs: the first, stiffly posed frontal images of individuals against picturesque backgrounds, taken by professional photographers resident in Ootacamund, the second, "more amateurish and probably by Rivers himself."[38] The former evoke a sense of timelessness, which Hockings speculates may have been inspired by Frazer's vision of "a lost mythic past."[39] The latter document certain rituals, including a secret calf sacrifice. Here the camera is used in a more spontaneous manner. It is closer to its human subjects and seems more at one with the spaces they inhabit.

In discussing Rivers's contributions to anthropology, Anna Grimshaw cites Ian Langham's observation that Rivers felt anxiety over what he believed to be his loss of the ability to think visually, a faculty he considered prelinguistic and "protopathic."[40] She takes this as a sign of his modernism, reflecting his desire to express abstract social relations in visible form, as in his invention of the kinship diagram.[41] The kinship diagram was meant to evoke a complex, relational view of human society rather than a schematic or mechanistic one, such as might have been created by earlier anthropologists, or by structural-functionalists such as Radcliffe-Brown. If Grimshaw's interpretation is correct, we have in Rivers the paradox of a meticulous fieldworker who was nevertheless troubled by the opacity of fieldwork records, someone who sought to reach through them to a more multidimensional kind of understanding. The kinship diagram incorporates this paradox as a map for a new way of seeing.

Grimshaw links Rivers indirectly with the great innovators of early cinema, D. W. Griffith, Sergei Eisenstein, and Dziga Vertov. The kinship diagram brings to mind what in cinema is called the "180-degree line" rule. This rule, often presented as obligatory in filmmaking manuals, regulates the positions of the camera and subject with relation to the viewer in three-dimensional space. It is based on the premise that although "reality" may be broken down into separate shots in the cinema, it must nonetheless remain relationally coherent. By not allowing the camera to cross a 180-degree line drawn through the actors, the filmmaker reinforces in the viewer's mind that the actors have maintained their relative positions, even if one or another of them is not actually present in the frame.[42] Thus, like the kinship diagram, the 180-degree line rule provides a framework for seeing social reality from different positions within a larger conceptual schema. This represents a significant intellectual step beyond the single, universalizing perspective of earlier photographic and cinematic record-making, in which it was felt necessary to maintain all the directional coordinates within the frame. The two conceptions, and perhaps Rivers's own oscillation between them, are nicely reflected in the two types of still photographs that he eventually published. From the evidence Hockings presents, one should perhaps conclude that Rivers was not so wanting in visual imagination as he feared.

In these photographs one can see, first, the presence of a confident, Olympian (or Frazerian) attitude toward anthropological knowledge, and second, a more provisional and contingent one. The pictures of the calf sacrifice look more like film frames than still photographs. They seem to prefigure the emergence of an imaginative shift in anthropology, analogous to what was soon to occur in the cinema. I mean to suggest by this a fundamental change in how knowledge of the world is constructed, from an approach consistent with documenting a social reality that is fully "known" in the abstract, to discovering a more ambiguous and piecemeal one at close hand. If Rivers' treatment of shell shock victims of World War I can be taken as a metaphor for this, the shift would not be unlike his experience of encountering emotionally shattered men who still had the appearance of simple soldiers. While hostilities were breaking out in Europe, Malinowski was among the Trobrianders, experiencing the similarly dissociated shock of encountering another culture and observing that "I'll have to find my way in all this."[43]

Certainly for many anthropologists, as for many scientists and artists, the change in perspective was accelerated, if not indeed created, by the spiritual and intellectual trauma of the Great War, expressed most vividly in the visual chaos of the trenches.[44] If the response sometimes took the form of an alienation of vision and the other senses, it could also lead to a more sophisticated understanding of how vision intersects with the different experiential registers of language, mind, and body. If modernism involved the questioning of surface appearances, it also celebrated the expressiveness of the visual sense. When anthropologists more or less stopped using visual images, it was not necessarily for the reason that they had lost the power of visual imagination but that they had not yet found the means to make visual expression commensurate with their new-found experiences.

The shift toward a "cinematic" imagination among anthropologists has not been confined, or necessarily even linked, to the scientific uses of film—indeed, in many respects, these specialized uses have been antithetical to it. Such uses could even be regarded as a "compensatory" clinging to nineteenth-century models of natural science.[45] In this connection, one thinks of such projects as the *Encyclopaedia Cinematographica* in Germany, designed to create a comprehensive collection of examples of human behavior. If "cinematic" qualities have emerged in anthropology and other disciplines, it should not be assumed automatically that they have been inspired (or contaminated) by the cinema—that would be too great a claim—but rather that these disciplines have experienced a shift in parallel with what occurred in cinema itself. George Marcus has noted modernist strategies in recent ethnographic writing that resemble certain principles of cinema, notably *montage*.[46] It is possible, however, to find traces of such tendencies much earlier in the history of anthropology. Although these have appeared erratically, depending upon the anthropological interests of the day—and although there has been little synchrony with similar developments in visual anthropology—"cinematic" ways of thinking have nevertheless been present in both.

What I have called the "cinematic imagination" involves, as one of its key characteristics, a desire to create an interpretive space for the reader or spectator. In Malinowski's *Argonauts of the Western Pacific*, the imagination, as Robert Thornton puts it, " 'fills in' the lacunae of both experience and description. It is this imaginative potential that allows the reader to connect the words and phrases of the text itself to the more general images which it evokes."[47] Structuring a work in this way involves a multi-positional perspective that acknowledges the fragmentary nature of experience and, by extension, the constructed nature of human knowledge. It also involves a displacement of the reader/spectator from the margins of the work toward its center, turning him or her into what Nick Browne has called a "spectator-in-the-text."[48] This is a stance fundamentally different from that of the laboratory scientist, who seeks to maintain a separation between observer and observed, between self and object. Rouch has described vividly the sense of crossing that boundary when he writes of the filmgoer suddenly finding himself "walking in towns or across terrain that he has never seen before but that he recognizes perfectly."[49]

This possibility was not immediately apparent to filmmakers. It emerged gradually as a new way of employing the camera, in some cases utilizing protocinematic techniques already invented by writers. Novelists from Stendahl to Flaubert had already marked out multiple points of view for readers of a scene, and scenes that were sketched in a few swiftly observed details. In its invitation to the reader, this modernist strategy differed radically from the notion of looking at a finished picture, even taking into account the capacity of painting and photography for *trompe l'oeil* and linear perspective. Instead of presenting its object as a totality, it presented it as a set of constituent elements within an imagined or abstract space. This possibility was inherently available long before film was invented. It required not so much a set of cinematic conventions as the ability to project oneself imaginatively into another consciousness, building a coherent world out of separate glimpses—much as neuroscientists tell us human vision constructs the world around us not by seeing it all but by selective sampling.

The cinematic imagination invites infilling and extrapolation just as other discursive methods invite their own kinds of interpretative and creative elaboration. There are, for example, ironic forms of humor that make us bridge incompatible frames of reference and double meanings. Through humor we sometimes find an improbable logic in otherwise unfathomable human relationships. In early anthropological photography there are, as we have seen in the case of Rivers, a few instances of the cinematic imagination already at work. Other photographs of the period occasionally go beyond mere pictorial documentation. They evoke social encounters and more complex points of view. Donald Tayler has noted the unusual intimacy that infuses many of the photographs of the British colonial administrator and ethnologist, Everard im Thurn, in contrast to the typical objectification of native people as racial or cultural types.[50] A similar nonconformity is apparent, but in quite a different spirit, in the work of Jean Audema, a colonial photographer who specialized in recording native peoples of the French Congo at the turn of the century. Several of Audema's pictures appear to be jokes (see chapter 7). In others an ironic "anthropometric" style is superimposed upon people posed in defiantly grandiloquent attitudes. These photographs evoke a sense of dignity and a collusion between photographer and subject rarely found in similar photographs of the period. It was tendencies of this sort, indicating a desire for further complexity, that eventually produced cinema out of mere cinematography.

Martin Jay has described the "scopic regimes" of modernity as not uniform and harmonious but a "contested terrain" of different historical traditions.[51] One could argue, following Jay, that the confident "seeing" of the Victorian era was neither unalloyed nor always dominant. According to most histories of visual representation in Europe, the prevailing mode of vision in recent centuries originated in the Cartesian separation of mind and body, imagining the mind as a darkened inner space in which experience could be independently inspected. This inner space was not unlike the inside of a *camera obscura*, with a pinhole or lens at one end through which the world projected its image. A flattened image was the logical outcome of the objectifying gaze of Italian Renaissance perspective, which constructed visual representation (be it in painting or, later, photography) as a three-dimensional scene projected on a two-dimensional surface. The result was variously compared to a window, screen, canvas, mirror, or photographic plate. However, according to Jay and other art historians, this general conception was already being challenged in seventeenth-century Dutch painting by a preoccupation with the particularity of objects, and in the eighteenth by the convolutions and fantasies of the Baroque.[52] These were more fragmented and personally inflected ways of looking, less concerned with putting a controlling frame around vision.

The viewer of a film is involved imaginatively with physical objects in a way quite different from someone who views an image through a window or sees it framed by an objectifying scientific discourse. And yet, scientific discourse played a part in producing this embodied vision by drawing attention to the physiological processes of perception. Jonathan Crary describes the dynamic role of medicine and biology in generating a new model of sight, which he believes began to overturn formal perspectival vision early in the nineteenth century.[53] This insertion of the body into the process of seeing—its *processing* of vision, both physically and imaginatively—can be taken as a possible starting point for the cinematic. Although Crary's dethroning of the *camera obscura* as the dominant model of sight may be overemphatic, it points to how a more physically contingent conception of vision could gain a foothold in the nineteenth-century consciousness.

New technologies, perhaps even more than biology and physiology, may have been responsible for a growing awareness of the senses as a key to both the constructedness of perception and the potential for alienation from it. Like inventions such as the telephone and the phonograph, the camera transformed the conditions of immediate experience, making present the images of people who were physically absent and depriving vision of its accompanying sounds and other sensations. Although the separation of the senses created by the new technologies was capable of producing feelings of disorientation and loss, it was also responsible for a new acuity. Images lacking sound and projected on a screen allowed one to see the world with fresh eyes, as though secretly taking reality unawares. It called attention to the material autonomy of objects and human bodies, but it called equally insistently for a reintegration of the senses, an objective that was to be partially fulfilled in the 1920s with the introduction of the sound film. There is an illuminating passage in Proust, cited by Siegfried Kracauer and explored further by Sara Danius,[54] in which the narrator sees his beloved grandmother as he has never seen her before. This is precipitated by hearing her voice over the telephone at the post office in the town of Doncières. The sound evokes both distance and "the most tender proximity," but above all the day when his grandmother will be dead. (The passage interestingly foreshadows Roland Barthes's contemplation of photographs of his dead mother in *Camera Lucida* [1981].) He returns to Paris and upon entering the room in which his grandmother sits reading, sees her as he supposes she would appear to a visiting photographer, stripped of the personal qualities he loves, which have for him always masked her actual physical appearance. "The process that automatically occurred in my eyes when I caught sight of my grandmother was indeed a photograph." He becomes, in his imagination, a photographic plate: "I saw, sitting on the sofa beneath the lamp, red-faced, heavy and vulgar, sick, vacant, letting her slightly crazed eyes wander over a book, a dejected old woman whom I did not know."[55]

Proust's reflections on such experiences foreshadow Walter Benjamin's and John Berger's discussions of the mechanical and decontextualizing effects of photography, as well as the fascination of the surrealists with the materiality of photographic vision, and Dziga Vertov's exhilarated cry: "I am the 'cine-eye,' the mechanical eye; I am the machine that will show you the world as only the machine can see it."[56] Yet far from driving photographic reproduction into the realm of abstraction, these perceptions underline its gnawing presence at the nerve ends of human experience.

One might say that the "stereoscopic imagination" was a necessary precursor to the development of the cinematic imagination. (Crary considers stereo photography, after photography itself, the most important new visual technology of the nineteenth century.[57]) What distinguished stereoscopy was both technical and aesthetic. It produced a distinct break from single-plane, monocular photography. The eyes and brain were led to create a field in depth by mimicking binocular vision, which ordinary photographs suggested only to a very limited degree. But stereoscopy also created a new aesthetic in which the object of the photograph (and, in a sense, the viewer, too) was fragmented and decentered. Single objects were part of an integrated complex of objects at different planes, which both receded from and invaded the space of the viewer.[58] Each plane could thus be regarded as a separate possible locus of perception, and indeed when viewing stereographs one's eyes shift from one plane to another, creating a number of virtual photographs within the frame. Most importantly, the viewer is physically implicated in the scene as an observer positioned spatially in relation to every other object.

Stereoscopic photography was invented in the 1840s, long before cinema, but reached its zenith about the time that cinema was invented at the end of the nineteenth century. Viewing stereo photographs was widespread, an experience few people are familiar with today. Stereographic photographers traveled the world and created a new form of popular ethnography under the rubric of human geography. This was quite different in spirit from nineteenth-century anthropometry, and different again from the images of exotic peoples being disseminated on picture postcards during the same period. Stereographs, or stereoscopic "views," were produced in numbered series and boxed sets devoted to particular regions or industries, a practice that resulted in certain subjects being shown not only in three dimensions but from multiple perspectives.[59] The photographers undoubtedly had these sequences of images in mind when they made their photographs, suggesting a kind of protocinema.

In another important respect, stereo photography prefigured the cinema. Although stereo photographs could be viewed through a system of mirrors, or from glass plates in a large cabinet, the usual way of viewing them was as paper prints in a handheld stereoscope of the type invented by Oliver Wendell Holmes in 1862. Although this could be done in a family setting with other people, or even as a group activity with several stereoscopes, it was in many respects a solitary experience, as cinema often is. The hood of the stereoscope blocked off the outside light so that one's eyes entered a darkened chamber, often padded with velvet. The invention of cinema may have hastened the demise of stereo viewing, but stereo viewing may well have prepared the public for the new imaginary spaces of cinema.

Vision Regained

Ethnographic filmmakers have been so few that, despite their many differences, their paths have often crossed. One of the most curious of Jean Rouch's films is an homage to Margaret Mead, *Margaret Mead, Portrait of a Friend* (1977), a series of long takes in which he talks to her in her office at the American Museum of Natural History, follows her through some of its storerooms and exhibition halls, and then bids her good-bye as he moves away through Central Park. It is a surprising and sometimes awkward tribute, for fundamentally their views could not have been more different. The film is evidence of Rouch's omnivorous appetite for spiritual mentors, who have included Vertov, Flaherty, Mauss, Bateson, Griaule, and Ivens. Mead, who had dared to use film in the field as early as 1936, had earned a place in the tradition, and Rouch's respect. The two were also allied by their public championing of ethnographic film, even if Mead's reputation as a popularizer may in fact have alienated more anthropologists from film than it attracted. Both had come to ethnographic film almost by accident, but in contrast to Mead, Rouch had thrown himself into filmmaking from the moment he got a camera.

While Rouch was making his first film on the Niger River in 1946–47, Robert Flaherty was making his last film in the bayous of Louisiana. Rouch always acknowledged his debt to Flaherty, but its exact nature is unclear. The title of one of his few essays on the subject, "Our Totemic Ancestors and Crazed Masters" (1995b), suggests deference mixed with admiration for Flaherty's eccentricity and risk-taking.[60] There is also respect for the wisdom of those older figures who, like the West African *griots*, have gone before and tell stories from the past. Rouch sees Flaherty in a heroic, historical light, and perhaps himself as well. In the essay he quotes the words of an old Dogan man, Anaï: " 'It's no more the time of old people, it's the time of young people; it's no longer the time of young people, it's the time of old people.' It's his idea that old people are necessary to the young; that the generations are like waves, and that at first when the wave has not yet formed it's the duty of the young people to listen to what the old have to say, then to roar forward into a surf, and to die on the sands."[61]

For Rouch, Flaherty was as important an inventor of fieldwork methods as the professional anthropologists of the early twentieth century. He was one of the inventors of "participant-observation" and was "doing ethnography without knowing it."[62] To Rouch, Flaherty's actual historical position outside anthropology is irrelevant. In fact, Rouch considers himself as much an outsider as Flaherty, despite his formal training in anthropology, for it is his view that most of the achievements in ethnographic film have come from outsiders and "amateurs."

> I consider myself an amateur [like Flaherty]. I was an amateur in anthropology too, studying only what I wanted to: possession rituals, funeral rituals, and something about migration. Richard Leacock did exactly the same thing. John Marshall, one of the most extraordinary anthropological filmmakers, is the best example of this attitude; even though while at the Peabody Museum in Harvard University he was constantly under pressure to complete an advanced degree and cease being a mere amateur.[63]

Rouch's special respect for Marshall is based on the common ground of a shared vocation and a certain shared rebelliousness. In many ways, these two are also closer in their visual sensibilities than any of the other major figures in ethnographic film. As the two leading pioneers of the 1950s, they can be seen as jointly responsible for the restoration of vision to anthropology after its long period of neglect.

What Rouch and Marshall brought to ethnographic film, and where they differed in important respects from Flaherty (and most of their other predecessors), was in their particular grasp of the perceptual and mental processes of the spectator. Flaherty had appealed to the viewer through his narrative strategies, his obvious affection for his subjects, and his detailed and often expansive view of settings and events. Rouch and Marshall wanted to draw the viewer even more fully into the physical and psychological fabric of the events themselves. If Flaherty was content to have us watch Nanook or the youth in *Moana* with a certain sympathy, Rouch wanted us to become involved with his subjects as he himself was involved—to see them through his experience as a participant as well as an observer.

Rouch's participatory camera is evident from his earliest films onward. In *Bataille sur le grand fleuve* (1951) the images and sounds of the hippopotamus hunt, and Rouch's excited voice, surround the viewer with an immediacy missing in the walrus hunt of Flaherty's film. Rouch plunges into the action, re-creating not only the kinesthetics of physical involvement but also the psychological atmosphere of the hunt. This second element was to become increasingly important in his films, particularly those focusing on performance and spirit possession, an example of which appears in *Bataille* when the Sorko villagers interrogate the spirit of the river as to the probable success of the hunt.

Rouch has said that "to make a film, for me, is to write with one's eyes, with one's ears, with one's whole body." It is to have the freedom to be anywhere at any moment, as one has in a dream.[64] Thus Rouch's filmmaking ideal reproduces the dreamlike or trancelike state of film viewing, but without the passivity of a dream. Perhaps more than any other filmmaker, his approach to film attempts to unite the perspectives of maker and viewer. In the making of the film—seeing it through the viewfinder and editing it to a large degree in the camera—Rouch becomes its first and most appreciative audience. One of his articles, published in *Le Monde* in 1971, has the title "Je suis mon premier spectateur."

Tourou et Bitti (1971) perhaps best typifies this stance. The title is taken from the names of two famous drums of the Sorko, played during a dance of possession during which the villagers of Simiri ask the spirits of the bush to guard the coming harvest against locusts. It begins with Rouch, with the camera, walking into the village. Then follows a very long take in which the movements of the camera respond to the movements of the dancers. The camera is both an observer and a participant, shaping the space around it geographically and temporally. Through it, we as observers also come to inhabit this three-dimensional world. Rouch's films, perhaps more vividly than any others, convey a sense of the life that surrounds the filmmaker, even what lies behind his back.

Ethnographic films sometimes give the impression of following in the wake of other genres, belatedly applying their ideas and techniques. But Rouch and Marshall brought something fresh to cinema, born of their experience of living in other societies. Apart from a heightened sensitivity to detail, this experience impressed upon them their position as outsiders and their dependence upon others, which was to be translated into a profound attachment to those who accepted them and taught them new ways of existing in the world. Despite their very different temperaments, one sees in Rouch and Marshall a common urge to celebrate their hosts. They approach cinema as a way of painting these new-found worlds around themselves, not from an avant-gardist or autobiographical perspective but out of respect for the wholeness and self-sufficiency they have discovered. For Rouch this process is always an adventure. For Marshall it is an act of dedication and humility.

Conceived in the immediacy of personal experience, Rouch's and Marshall's films contest the usual notion of documentary films as "discourses of sobriety" (Bill Nichols's phrase) or even as works of academic or cinematic professionalism. They are not created as the polished products of research but as an ongoing research process in themselves. The usual professional relationship with the audience is also put aside in favor of what Rouch would guilefully call his "amateurism." It is a sentiment that clearly resonates with the personal cinema of Chris Marker and Ricky Leacock and even, at a certain remove, with that of Nanni Moretti and Andrei Tarkovsky. And surely in the background hover the rebellious spirits of Dziga Vertov and Jean Vigo.

Marshall began his filmmaking career by conscientiously filming technical processes such as the making of hunting nets and poisoned arrows, the task given him by his father, Laurence Marshall, during their family expeditions to southwestern Africa in the early 1950s. He soon became more interested in filming scenes of social interaction, and it was at this time that he made a discovery that was to reshape his way of using the camera. It marked a radically different approach to ethnographic film than that held by most anthropologists, including such earlier influential figures as Franz Boas and Marcel Griaule. Like Rouch, he had come to the realization that a film is a structure created largely in the mind of the viewer, and that what appears at any moment on the screen forms only a small part of this more extensive imaginative composition. "I wanted a way to enter ordinary events and film the social worlds within. I needed more than a wide-angle lens to broaden my vision. . . . I began to learn how little we see of the reality around us through the window of a camera, and that most of the content in a film is either unseen or invisible. . . . Invisible content is most of the reality that surrounds the camera."[65]

From this he developed his notion of "slots," which he was later to define as "where unseen content is stored in our memories, or anticipated by what we see and hear, while we watch a film."[66] Part of this content was created by the narrative of the film—the events that preceded each moment and projected a set of possibilities into the future. More significant, however, was the visual continuum that surrounds every shot in a film, that both exists in reality at the time of shooting and that the filmmaker keeps constantly alive in the mind of the viewer in creating sequences of shots. These forms of diachronic and synchronic knowledge become the framework that supports and situates what one is actually seeing. It may seem obvious that when one is filming people, their lives continue even when the camera is not on them. But it is up to the filmmaker to bear this in mind and make this unseen activity part of the scene as a whole. "Unlike a still camera, a movie camera always creates a continuous context of pictures around itself when it moves. The context generates a kind of rudimentary language around the frame of the camera or the screen. . . . The scene will be wider than the frame."[67]

In Marshall's ethnographic cinema, in contrast to mere ethnographic footage or record-making, the filmmaker's eye is a participant in the midst of evolving events, one often intimately allied to the consciousness of the people he is filming. Many of the resulting scenes (such as *The Meat Fight* [1958/73]) are conceived as small dramas, centering on the kinds of structures that Victor Turner at this time was describing as fundamental to resolving breaches in the social order.[68] "When a family was sitting and talking, I would get my camera close to the person listening while I filmed the person speaking. Rather than standing back to take a middle shot, or choosing angles and distances that reflected my ideas and projections, I would pretend to be different members of the group while I shot the other participants."[69]

For Marshall, as for Rouch, "the relationship between what is happening on and off the screen is what film language is all about."[70] The new aim of Marshall's ethnographic cinema was thus to draw the viewer into what he called "the little worlds inside events"—not as a recipient of information but as a participant in a creative act of joining the seen with the unseen.

Marshall felt he had stumbled upon something new, but in many ways he was simply applying certain long-established cinematic principles to ethnographic filmmaking. He himself later said that, having started making films at the age of seventeen when he knew nothing about it, he painfully reinvented techniques that had been known to other filmmakers for decades.[71] But this cannot have been wholly true, for few other cinematographers had ever worked as he did, in the midst of spontaneous events. Nor was Marshall insulated from cinema culture, and it is clear that he drew upon it. Like others of his generation—and perhaps especially those raised in middle-class Boston and New York families—he would have been saturated with films, including many from Europe and other countries. His concept of "slots"—and his use of such terms as "distances" and "angles"—was anticipated by the theoretician Béla Balázs when he described the strategic placement of the camera: "The camera carries the spectator into the film picture itself. We are seeing everything from the inside as it were and are surrounded by the characters of the film."[72]

If Marshall brought nothing fundamentally new to cinema—except, like his countrymen Leacock, Pennebaker, and Wiseman, a commitment to handheld, synchronous sound filming—he did, like Rouch, bring something new to ethnography. His and Rouch's achievement was not so much to restore anthropology's lost vision as to introduce a new kind of ethnographic seeing. More than Flaherty, more than documentary filmmakers such as Basil Wright or Georges Rouquier, more than the Italian neorealist filmmakers, their cameras saw events from within the physical spaces of their subjects. This was often achieved by a kind of subterfuge, smuggling themselves into social positions where cameras had never been before. But this, in turn, involved the even more radical step, for anthropologists, of shaping their interpretation at the very moment of the encounter with their subjects. In effect, they were fashioning their anthropological statements in the same breath as they obtained their "data." This takes its purest form in films like *Tourou et Bitti* and some of Marshall's Pittsburgh Police films, such as *Three Domestics* (1970), in which long segments of activity are analyzed within a single shot. But it is also apparent in more highly edited sequences, for as Marshall points out, when he is filming at the height of his powers, although the resulting sequence may be edited, there is very little waste.[73]

Epilogue

Rouch's and Marshall's work, while important in itself, also acted as a catalyst for visual anthropology. It tempered the mistrust of many anthropologists who had never taken ethnographic films seriously, and it revealed the banality of most "educational" films. There was suddenly a space for a new kind of non-didactic ethnographic film. This was felt both indirectly through the intellectual and stylistic possibilities the films opened up and more directly through the influence of one filmmaker upon another. Although Marshall has rejected the approach of his film *The Hunters* (edited between 1954 and 1956, released in 1958) compared to his shorter event-based films, he has perhaps underestimated its historical importance. The film was a focal point in the filmmaking careers of Robert Gardner and Timothy Asch, and it influenced many others. Rouch, for his part, inspired a generation of young filmmakers and created a network of personal relationships that included fellow researchers at the CNRS (Centre National de la Recherche Scientifique), filmmakers in West Africa, the National Film Board of Canada, and members of the French New Wave.[74] The sheer energy of his work, and his resistance to criticism, created a new force outside the world of academic anthropology. (As Godard once put it, "Rouch doesn't give a damn anyway. He never listens."[75]) Similarly, the protection offered by Laurence Marshall's family expeditions and the Film Study Center at Harvard University allowed Marshall to pursue alternatives to the demands of American educational filmmaking, as well as to the sorts of film records being produced by others, such as films on food technology being made by Samuel Barrett at the University of California.

Rouch's and Marshall's films brought a liberating spirit to anthropology, and a set of new interests. While anthropological writers were pursuing increasingly schematized forms of analysis and exposition (the experimentation would come later), Rouch and Marshall were engaged in a mimetic analytical process. Their approach could also be described as one of amplification from within rather than reduction from without. If one were looking for a trait that distinguished Rouch and Marshall from most anthropologists of the period, it would have been their indifference to drawing boundaries. They were more interested in the creativity than the limitations of their subjects' lives. While many anthropologists were struggling to find cultural coherence, Rouch and Marshall were often, perhaps unconsciously, challenging the "culture concept." Marshall's interest lay in the dynamics of interpersonal relationships and agency, Rouch's in the zones where "cultures" meet, matters that were to be taken up more enthusiastically in the anthropology of the 1980s.

In practice, this meant that Marshall and Rouch were often concerned with unstated tensions and resonances in society—between the said and the unsaid, the theory and the act, the real and the imaginary. In Marshall's films there is an emphasis on rhetoric, gesture, and expressive silence, as in *An Argument About a Marriage* (1969) and *A Joking Relationship* (1966). Rouch's films stress the ambiguities of postcolonial and cross-cultural encounters that would later receive fuller attention from anthropologists and historians in subaltern studies (e.g., Appadurai 1981, 1996; Bhabha 1994). These concerns emerge in the double lives of Hauka initiates in *Les maîtres fous* (1955), the cross-cultural encounters of the

Nigerien travelers in *Jaguar* (1954/67), and the racial tensions explored in *La pyramide humaine* (1961). The film medium contained its own imperatives but also, no doubt, made it easier for Marshall and Rouch to depict individual lives rather than larger social structures. On the other hand, it was often the individual life that threw the rest of the society into sharper relief. The protagonists of *Moi, un noir* (1957) and *N!ai: The Story of a !Kung Woman* (1980) are seen through the dual perspectives of how they appear to others and as they often wish themselves to be. In the life histories projected by these films one sees individuals situated more precisely amid historical and transnational processes than was usual in functionalist ethnographies. This is true as well of the subgenre of ethnobiographical films created by Jorge Preloran in Argentina.

This implicitly expanded view of culture, as seen through individuals, arises not so much from a different kind of participant-observation as from a different conception of anthropological knowledge. The particularities of culture (and nature) observable to a camera are often strikingly different from those noted for inclusion in a text. In 1935 Malinowski wrote in *Coral Gardens and Their Magic* that "were it possible for [the ethnographer] to reproduce large portions of tribal life and speech through the medium of a sound film, he might be able to give the reality of the culture in much greater fullness."[76] He goes on to remark on the great cultural specificity of language, as against the more transcultural properties of the visible aspects of human life. In the second volume of *Coral Gardens* he devotes some three hundred pages to the uses of language in Trobriand gardening, for, as he says, "throughout our enquiry we are trying to overcome the limitations of ethnographic apparatus and get beyond the fieldworker's notebook to the reality of native life."[77] By providing what he calls a "double account"—the language used, and a description of its physical context—he believes that "the material thus illuminated from two sides will stand out, so to speak, stereoscopically."[78]

The different capabilities and affinities of film and text are evident in the greater emphasis Rouch and Marshall place upon the performative aspects of social life, in both formal and informal contexts. Styles of self-presentation, and the ritualized and rhetorical aspects of small actions, were already important in ethnographic films when Erving Goffman and Edward T. Hall were drawing attention to such topics. But if their films can be said to have added a different dimension to ethnography, it is perhaps most clearly seen in their use of narrative and their emphasis on the senses and the sense of place. Although these tendencies are partly attributable to characteristics of the cinema rather than Marshall's and Rouch's own interests, films such as *The Hunters* and *La chasse au lion à l'arc* (1957–65) represent a shift in ethnographic perspective away from the conventional, third-person voice of scientific inquiry. In these films it is the filmmaker's voice that is dominant, but very soon, with the availability of portable synchronous sound, it will be the voices of the protagonists. Here narrative imparts a legendary quality to the proceedings. Later it will give a better sense of how individuals perceive their surroundings and the choices open to them.

One of Marshall's films shot in 1957–58, *!Kung Bushman Hunting Equipment* (1972), shows in meticulous detail the preparation of poisoned arrows and other pieces in the !Kung hunting kit. Although it is ostensibly a film about material culture, it projects with an almost surreal, preternatural clarity the presence and textures of the items being handled. As in some of Rouch's films about magic and possession, the sensory qualities of the material world are presented as defining aspects of the subjects' consciousness and are given added anthropological weight. Although the film is limited to a few specific objects, it reflects the wider preoccupation of ethnographic filmmakers, from as early as Flaherty onward, with physical surroundings. In anthropological writing the natural world is, in a sense, subsumed by the cultural world: it is the material upon which culture is inscribed or the environment that sustains it. The new wave of ethnographic films that began to emerge in the 1950s and 1960s transformed these earlier interests in material culture into an interest in the subjective experience of material things. Ian Dunlop's *Desert People* (1966), for example, is superficially about the technologies of living in the desert, but it is more fundamentally about the personal experience of moving through the desert landscape, taking note of the surrounding objects, and the particular importance of the desert floor.

Once ethnographic filmmakers had begun constructing their films as experiences rather than informational accounts, they became increasingly aware that cinema is to a large extent involved in the recreation of the places within which people orient themselves. Places and objects possess a familiarity that is integral to a person's sense of self. It was this realization that began to fill out the profile of social experience only hinted at in earlier ethnographic films. As in such ethnographies as Fred Myers's *Pintupi Country, Pintupi Self* (1986) and James Weiner's *The Empty Place* (1991), it is a topic that has become the explicit subject of a number of recent films.[79]

It remains to note some of the historical connections between Rouch's and Marshall's work and the new sensibility that emerged in ethnographic filmmaking in the 1960s and 1970s. Rouch's colleagues and associates at the CNRS and the EHESS (École des Hautes Études en Sciences Sociales) included a number of filmmakers who would later work in Africa, such as Marc Henri Piault (*Akazama*, 1986) and Jean-Pierre Olivier de Sardan

(*La vieille et la pluie*, 1974). Another colleague, Colette Piault, began filming in Africa but soon turned her attention to rural Greece (*My Family and Me*, 1986). In the next generation, Eliane de Latour carried forward Rouch's interest in West African institutions and his intimate style of cinema with such films as *Les temps du pouvoir* (1984) and *Contes et comptes de la cour* (1993). Rouch's collaboration with West Africans, as the protagonists of his films and as film technicians, had an indirect influence on African fiction filmmaking, with at least one of his collaborators, Oumarou Ganda (Edwin G. Robinson's alter ego in *Moi, un noir*) becoming a professional director (*Cabascabo*, 1968). Michel Brault, who came to France to work with Rouch on *Chronique d'un été* (1961), returned to Canada to produce *Pour la suite du monde* (1963) and other ethnographic films. Rouch's films and methods also influenced Brault's colleague, Pierre Perrault, and the innovative Challenge for Change program at the National Film Board of Canada.

John Marshall, in addition to working with Asch, Gardner, and others at the Harvard Film Study Center, collaborated with Frederick Wiseman as co-director and cinematographer of *Titicut Follies* (1967), the first of Wiseman's influential cycle of films on American institutions. Wiseman's films and Marshall's series on the Pittsburgh police are close cousins, as are many of the films of Leacock, the Maysles brothers, and D. A. Pennebaker. It is difficult to sort out who influenced whom, but Marshall's most innovative work came earlier and undoubtedly shaped his generation's ways of thinking about ethnographic film. Robert Young, with whom Marshall traded ideas about cinematography, became the most impressive contributor to the Netsilik Eskimos series (1963–68) directed by Asen Balikci and was one of the first cinematographers after Marshall to film a hunting-and-gathering society using the new handheld synchronous sound equipment. The resulting footage was extremely influential in the way in which it portrayed informal, everyday activities and served to promote the kind of ethnographic cinema that Marshall had initiated some years earlier.

A new generation of university-trained ethnographic filmmakers inspired by Rouch, Marshall, Wiseman, and Gardner was soon to emerge from programs at Harvard University and the University of California at Los Angeles. Colin Young, the founder of the UCLA program, developed the field further in Great Britain at the National Film and Television School. The work of his students provided new models for British television, which was beginning to produce its own ethnographic films in the 1970s. Marshall's influence can thus be seen to extend to the *Disappearing World* television series and to such later work as that of Melissa Llewelyn-Davies (e.g., *The Women's Olamal* [1984] and *Diary of a Maa-*

sai Village [1985]). These innovations were institutionalized in the program of the Granada Centre for Visual Anthropology at the University of Manchester, developed by the anthropologist Paul Henley, another of Young's former students.

Rouch's and Marshall's work can now be seen as a radical strand of anthropological discourse running parallel to that of mainstream anthropology, and not the subordinate activity it was imagined to be by many anthropologists at the time. It produced a form of ethnography that was often difficult to assimilate to existing conceptions of scientific knowledge, despite what some of its partisans, such as Margaret Mead, might have wished. Emphasizing the lives of individual social actors rather than more structural or holistic accounts of culture, it has continued to produce a stream of films that, although often uneven, have demonstrated an important alternative to anthropological writing. At their worst these films verge on the exoticism of travelogues, or the didactic style of television journalism, or both together. At their best they provide new perspectives on the affective dimensions of social experience, which anthropological writing can only hope to approach through radical moves of its own. At their most provocative they raise questions about the properties of culture and the feasibility of cultural translation.

Such questions are part of contemporary anthropological thought, eliciting varied responses. For the visual anthropologist, the answers are often found in a performative approach rather than an expository or exegetical one. The best films touch on experiences at the outer limits of verbal analysis, involving material that Gilles Deleuze has called "non-language-material"—"a material not formed linguistically even though it is not amorphous and is formed semiotically, aesthetically and pragmatically."[80] At the heart of a certain impatience with visual anthropology may lie misconceptions about film that have seeped over from the habits of anthropological writing and semiotic film theory—a desire to clothe images with the properties of language rather than recognizing in them the more material properties accessible to consciousness. Visible images, as Deleuze stresses, are not equivalent to utterances; before they can be transformed by language, they must be accepted materially in themselves.

As it gained credibility, Rouch's and Marshall's work was bound to create what W.J.T. Mitchell has described as "turbulence" at the borders of the larger discipline. Well into the 1970s, when it was evident that ethnographic cinema was actually challenging the assumptions of scientific knowledge, critics were still trying to set up rules for the policing of the genre.[81] Several of those who had championed the use of film in anthropology now found that they had been supporting the least productive aspects of it. It was the very qualities they had ignored or dismissed in film that were proving more important. What had been regarded as more or less incidental to the medium—its ability to evoke places and embodied experience, for example—had become its intellectual strengths. For better or worse, a new kind of vision had been created by ethnographic film.

Notes

1. But the term probably goes back to the earlier French use of the word *documentaire*. See Hardy 1966: 13.

2. Rouch puts the date at 1948. Jean Thévenot puts it at 1947, when Leroi-Gourhan and Henry Reynaud at the Musée de l'Homme established a "Bureau internationale du film d'ethnologie et de géographie humaine" (Liotard, Samivel & Thévenot 1950: 34).

3. See Hockings 1975.

4. See Hockings 1975, Banks & Morphy 1997.

5. Im Thurn 1893: 184.

6. de Heusch 1962.

7. Geertz (1988) makes a point of E. E. Evans-Pritchard's use of photographs and the visual qualities of his writing, but it was the writing that proved influential. See also Wolpert 2000.

8. Grimshaw 2001: 41. See also Jay 1991.

9. Griffiths 1996: 35.

10. Mead 1975: 5.

11. See Griffiths 2002: 41.

12. See Jacknis 1984.

13. See Thornton 1983.

14. Talal Asad ascribes one of the first formulations of this concept to Godfrey Lienhardt's 1954 paper, "Modes of Thought" (Asad 1986: 142).

15. Evans-Pritchard 1937: 29.

16. Geertz 1988: 64.

17. See Wolpert 2000.

18. Griffiths 2002: 163.

19. The dentists included Brooke Nichols and T. D. Campbell. H. K. Fry was a doctor, O. E. Stocker a businessman who worked closely with Tindale, and the travelers and amateur ethnologists included William J. Jackson, Francis Birtles, Charles P. Mountford, and Frank Hurley.

20. See Young 1999.

21. The first photograph of the moon was taken by John William Draper in 1840.

22. Crary (1988) argues that an increasingly embodied conception of photography emerged in the nineteenth century (see below). While this may have been the ultimate import of scientific research into vision and the other senses, it is doubtful that it altered individual scientists' attitudes so directly.

23. Pinney 1990a: 267.

24. Tom Gunning (1990) has called this a "cinema of attractions" because it continued the tradition of separate spectacles offered at music halls and public fairgrounds. This should not, however, be confused with Eisenstein's earlier theory of the montage of attractions.

25. See Vaughan 1999: 5–6. Oliver Wendell Holmes had already noted this particularity of photography with wonder when he wrote that "there is such a frightful amount of detail, that we have the same sense of infinite complexity which Nature gives us" (1859: 743).

26. Morin 1956: 23.

27. Several books discuss early ethnographic still photography, of which the most comprehensive is Edwards (1992); the "prehistory" of ethnographic film in museum exhibits and "primitive" cinema (Griffiths 2002); and particular approaches to visual anthropology (Stoller 1992, Loizos 1993, MacDougall 1998, Grimshaw 2001). There have also been efforts to define the field as a whole (Heider 1976, Ruby 2000) and to broaden it (Worth 1981, Banks & Morphy 1997). One of the earliest overall accounts of ethnographic film is Emilie de Brigard's chapter in Paul Hockings's collection, *Principles of Visual Anthropology* (1975). Another excellent and more recent account is Marc Henri Piault's *Anthropologie et cinéma* (2000a).

28. For an expression of the last view, see Banks & Morphy 1997.

29. See, for example, Rollwagen 1988, Ruby 2000.

30. Bateson & Mead 1977: 78.

31. Rouch 1995: 217, 1975: 86.

32. See Banks 1992, Ruby 1975, 2000.

33. Cited in Sullivan 1999: 5.

34. Bateson & Mead 1977: 79.

35. A film of approximately ten minutes shot in Melbourne by the Salvation Army Limelight Department.

36. Cited in Sullivan 1999: 4.

37. Sorenson & Jablonko 1975: 147–48.

38. Hockings 1992: 185n1.

39. Ibid., p. 185.

40. Grimshaw 2001: 40–41.

41. Ibid., pp. 34–36.

42. This is also known as "maintaining screen direction." In effect, if the director breaks the rule and allows the camera to cross the 180-degree line, and a cut intervenes, the actors will suddenly appear to be facing each other from opposite directions, implying that they have either reversed positions or that one of them is looking away from the other. The 180-degree rule was a mainstay of "classical" Hollywood and European production and is taught in filmmaking textbooks. It began to be seriously challenged by films of the French New Wave directors. For a diagram of the 180-degree line principle, see Bordwell 1985: 110. The British director Alexander Mackendrick, in his notes collected in the book *On Filmmaking* (2004), called the 180-degree line the "axis."

43. Malinowski 1967.

44. See Jay 1991.

45. Ibid.

46. Marcus 1990.
47. Thornton 1985: 13.
48. Browne 1975.
49. Rouch 1975: 89.
50. See Tayler 1992.
51. Jay 1988: 4.
52. See Jay's summary of the arguments of Svetlana Alpers and Christine Buci-Glucksmann (1988: 12–18).
53. Crary 1988: 29–44.
54. Kracauer 1960: 14–15; Danius 2002: 13–17.
55. Proust 1982: 141–42, 143.
56. Cited in Rouch 1995a: 82.
57. Crary 1990: 116.
58. Stereographic photography has a planar quality, but I think Crary is mistaken in asserting that when we view stereographs "we perceive individual elements as flat, cutout forms arrayed either nearer or further from us" (1990: 125). This is perhaps the first, quick impression, but after one has looked at a stereoscopic image for some minutes the objects regain some of their roundedness. The time this takes is due to the mind gradually sorting out the complex binocular information presented to it.
59. See, for example, the Underwood & Underwood (later Keystone) series on Japan, or on rice cultivation in the Philippines.
60. This "essay" was actually an oral account, transcribed and later submitted to Rouch for correction.
61. Rouch 1995b: 217.
62. Rouch 1975: 86.
63. Rouch 1995b: 226.
64. Fulchignoni 1981: 7.
65. Marshall 1993: 39.
66. Ibid., p. 83.
67. Ibid., p. 41.
68. Turner 1957.
69. Marshall 1993: 42.
70. Ibid., p. 127n3.
71. Ibid., p. 20.
72. Balázs 1952: 48. Balázs emphasizes the high degree of selectivity involved in choosing particular shots for a scene from all the others that are possible. "Even if I am present at every shot, if I look on as every scene is enacted in the studio, I can never see or feel the pictorial effects which are the results of camera distances and angles, nor can I become aware of the rhythm which is their outcome. For in the studio I see each scene and each figure as a whole and am unable to single out details with my eye" (1952: 46).
73. Marshall 1993: 45.
74. However, it was not always easy to see Rouch's films, many of which existed only in separate picture and sound tracks at the Musée de l'Homme. I first saw several of his films at the Colloquium on Ethnographic Film at UCLA in April 1968, and later that year I organized a Jean Rouch Film Festival at Makerere

University in Kampala. This was only possible because the French embassy in Uganda took an interest in the idea and was particularly helpful in obtaining prints. So far as I know, this was the first retrospective of Rouch's films to be held in East Africa.

75. Godard 1972: 134.

76. Malinowski 1935: II, vii.

77. Ibid., p. 45.

78. Ibid., p. 3.

79. As precedents for this, and more recent examples, see Robert Flaherty's *Louisiana Story* (1948), Clément Perron's *Day After Day* (1962), Eliane de Latour's *Contes et comptes de la cour* (1993), my *Doon School Chronicles* (2000), and Jean Lydall's and Kaira Strecker's *Duka's Dilemma* (2001).

80. Deleuze 1989: 29.

81. See, for example, Ruby 1975, Heider 1976, Rollwagen 1986.

10

NEW PRINCIPLES OF VISUAL ANTHROPOLOGY

I N 1975 A BOOK appeared that was to prove highly influential. It brought together a number of papers from the Ninth Congress of Anthropological and Ethnological Sciences held in Chicago in 1973, and it bore the ambitious title *Principles of Visual Anthropology*. The book subsequently became a cornerstone of the subdiscipline of visual anthropology. It sold widely, and in 1995 its editor, Paul Hockings, brought out a heavily revised and expanded second edition. The title had been a brilliant choice—or a masterful piece of wishful thinking—for it referred to a field that for all practical purposes did not yet exist.

Despite its title, the book did not actually set forth any principles of visual anthropology. The contents represented a scattered range of interests and points of view, from the study of proxemics to the use of feature films as cultural documents. The essays were organized into sections, but these were fairly arbitrary, and there was little evidence that the authors rubbing shoulders in the book had ever read one another's work or had even heard of one another.[1]

However, if one now reads the book closely, some common principles—or perhaps it would be better to say assumptions—can be discerned in it. One is that the nascent field of visual anthropology was at that time conceived almost exclusively in terms of ethnographic film. Visual anthropologists were supposed to be using film themselves or studying films that other people had made. There was not, as there is today, an emphasis on the wider aspects of visual culture.[2] Nor, with a few exceptions, was visual anthropology conceived as a distinctively visual form of anthropology, but more simply as the grafting of a visual technology onto existing anthropological practices.

Related to this was a conception of film as fundamentally realist and instrumental. If anthropologists were to make films, they were assumed to be making records for later analysis or trying to teach anthropology to students who had yet to venture into the field. Filmmaking was regarded as a way of either gathering data or producing an accurate copy of reality. In the first case, the bulk of the anthropological work would be done later, when the footage was subjected to analysis. In the second, most of it had already been done, and films were simply meant to illustrate existing bodies of knowledge. Among the writers articulating these approaches were Margaret Mead, Jean-Dominique Lajoux, and Timothy Asch. One or two eccentrics like Jean Rouch and Mark McCarty, who had other aims, were given space in the book, but the dominant view was that filmmaking was a kind of anthropological note-taking, or else a lesson. In keeping with the educational boom of the 1970s and the funding it generated, the mood was distinctly didactic. One of the largest sections of the book was entitled "The Presentation of Anthropological Information."

I do not wish to pursue the book and its assumptions further, much less censure them. In many ways *Principles of Visual Anthropology* is the best summation we have of the state of visual anthropology at the time, in both its disarray and its certainties. It stands at the crossroads between an anthropology still searching for the precision of the natural sciences and a new anthropology of social experience that was struggling to emerge, through writing as well as through such novel methods as photography and cinema. The book provides a springboard for examining several early attempts to construct a theory of visual anthropology.

One of the first to appear was Karl Heider's *Ethnographic Film*, published in the following year. As the title makes clear, its conception of visual anthropology remains firmly within the realm of film. However, unlike its predecessor, it attempts to pin down the "ethnographicness" of films and establish some principles for how to make them. It is not very successful in the first endeavor, since its argument is largely circular, a casualty of its realist, common-sense approach. Underlying this is a belief in the virtues of a neutral methodology. In Heider's view, a successful ethnographic film should remain uncontaminated by too-specific theoretical interests.[3] In fact, a film should aspire to the purity of the thing perceived. From this comes his insistence on holism—the inclusion of as much of the surrounding context as possible. Heider's metaphor is the human body, which should be kept intact rather than be shown in fragments or minus its arms or legs. It is a prescription that curiously echoes early objections to close-ups in films, because they produced an amputated view of the human subject.

Throughout his discussion, Heider implicitly and explicitly contrasts the purity of the ethnographer's commitment to truth with the artist's presumed commitment above all else to aesthetic pleasure—an idea that perhaps has its origins in early American Puritanism. But his critique of art is built on an even more fundamental philosophical assumption. To the rational observer, truth, from this perspective, is manifest in the world. Any system that comes between the observer and the observed is necessarily tainted.[4] Therefore, Heider says, "in order to judge the ethnographicness of a film we have the need to know how much and to what degree

reality was distorted."[5] Sadly, it seems that to this partisan of ethnographic film, *no* film must often seem preferable to most of the films one
could imagine.

Another partisan, Jay Ruby, gradually gravitated to a similar position,
although he began his career as an ardent film buff. "There was a time,"
he wrote, "when I viewed between five hundred and a thousand films
annually ... but I cannot stand watching most documentary/ethno-
graphic films today."[6] Ruby's best-known attempt to develop a theory of
ethnographic film was published in 1975, the same year as *Principles of
Visual Anthropology*. Its title was "Is an Ethnographic Film a Filmic Ethnography?" It set forth precise principles, numbered one to four. Unlike
Heider, Ruby declared that to be ethnographic, a film must be informed
by a theory of culture, and he called for the conventions of cinema to be
radically overhauled to produce films that were anthropological in their
construction, not merely concerned with anthropological subjects. Ruby
also brought to his discussion of visual anthropology an interest in the
anthropology of visual communication, inspired by the teachings of Sol
Worth. Yet despite his gestures toward the constructed nature of human
knowledge, which stood in sharp contrast to Heider's logical positivism,
Ruby revealed himself in the long term to be a frustrated positivist. His
third principle declared that "an ethnographic work must contain statements which reveal the methodology of the author."[7] It must "include a
scientific justification for the multitude of decisions that one makes in the
process of producing a film—the framing and length of each shot, selection of subject matter, technical decisions (such as choice of film stock,
lens, etc.), type of field sound collected, use of studio sound, editing decisions, etc."[8] In short, to be truly scientific, an ethnographic film should
exhaustively reveal any biases of the filmmaker that might intervene in
the accurate representation of reality. Later on, Ruby was to develop these
ideas into a veritable mantra of self-reflexivity.

Apart from the practical obstacles involved, and the fact that scholars
tend to be blind to their own blind spots, this approach, in its reverence
for scientific method, finally circles back toward Heider's quest for purity
of perception. It is as though once all the methodological and intellectual
distortions have been stripped away, one can finally arrive at some definitive form of scientific truth. But this Platonic ideal was already increasingly
at odds with current conceptions of anthropological knowledge, which
were seen to be contingent upon the relationship of the observer to the
observed and indeed, inevitably, upon the products of that relationship.

I have taken these two examples to demonstrate some of the intellectual
problems that bedeviled visual anthropology at its point of separation
from the anthropological mainstream in the 1970s. For it was at this time
that visual anthropology began to develop an institutional infrastructure

and achieve a measure of academic recognition—thanks, not least, to the publication of Hockings's book. What we see here is an emerging discipline struggling to free itself from expectations imposed upon it by anthropologists whose intellectual goals had been formed in another medium, the medium of words. The principles of visual anthropology that Heider and Ruby were trying so desperately to work out were in fact little more than mutations of the principles of written anthropology. Although well intentioned, these prescriptions were at best confusing and at worst constituted a hindrance to the development of the new discipline. By contrast, filmmakers such as Jean Rouch, who were unfazed by the academic establishment, were discovering what visual anthropology could become and—perhaps more fully than they realized—were in the process of inventing it.

It is now clear that many of the partisans of visual anthropology were trying to find some middle ground that would make the practice acceptable to the mainstream of anthropologists. The problem they faced, however, lay in how to establish principles that bridged the gap between the tried-and-true methods that anthropologists taught their students and the new (and potentially contentious) approaches and forms of knowledge that were likely to emerge from using an audiovisual medium. Perhaps inevitably, they focused on methodology rather than content, although it was the content that was ultimately the issue. Emphasizing the established procedures of data collection, hypothesis, and proof provided the safest way of demonstrating that visual anthropology could still be rigorous social science, even if, in hindsight, we can see that it actually called for new concepts.

In fact, many of the most vocal visual anthropologists seem to have remained relatively untouched by the debates that were then challenging scientific and anthropological thought, even though these debates were occurring all around them. While vigorously promoting the pictorial "turn" in anthropology, such key players as Margaret Mead, Alan Lomax, and E. Richard Sorenson seem to have been oblivious to the linguistic turn that had overtaken their discipline. To an even greater degree, there was an obliviousness to post-structuralist thought and the challenges to "normal" science being posed by Kuhn, Rorty, Habermas, Foucault, and Bourdieu. In a sense, visual anthropology was still contracting around the ambitions of an earlier generation, despite the efforts of Clifford Geertz, Victor Turner, and others to develop hermeneutic and processual anthropologies—moves that had links to the earlier work of Edward Sapir, Ruth Benedict, and Gregory Bateson.

Despite its occasional focus on specialist areas, such as body behavior and facial expression, ethnographic filmmaking was generally expected to focus on the familiar categories of the ethnographic monograph: social organization, economics, religion, ritual, politics, and so forth.[9] Some films, of course, managed to do this while at the same time exploring other, less conventional interests.[10] Ian Dunlop's film *Desert People* (1966), while ostensibly about hunter-gatherer technology, was perhaps to an even greater degree about Aboriginal conceptions of landscape and movement through it. By and large, visual anthropology was not seen as adding a significant new dimension to anthropology but instead as a different way of communicating concerns that had already been mapped out in anthropological writing. It was thus little more than an accessory, translating these concerns into visual expository form. Although Ruby professed an admiration for avant-garde approaches to visual anthropology, there were still strong traces of this more conservative view in his quest for a "pictorial representation of anthropological knowledge."[11]

Perhaps inevitably, visual anthropology failed to reorient the discipline in any significant way. It also tended to take on the character of the social science of the countries in which it existed. The folkloric tradition of central Europe encouraged the documentation of village rituals and material culture. German visual anthropology stressed the collection and classification of comparative data. British anthropology produced films describing remote, small-scale societies from a functionalist perspective. The Americans, while showing a similar interest in isolated "cultures," also had a penchant for behavioral and psychoanalytic approaches and for didactic films. French visual anthropology, supported by the national scientific research organization CNRS, treated filmmaking more as a research process than a means of documentation and publication, and it focused on the political and religious institutions of francophone West Africa.

Although visual anthropology in the past has tried to accommodate itself to the concerns of anthropological writing—and the topics this writing has addressed—it is likely that it will increasingly be shaped by studying other aspects of social reality, including topics that have often previously gone unexplored. Not only are certain social phenomena particularly suitable for study by visual means (for example, how postures express emotions), but they are also extremely difficult to approach in any other way. Visual anthropology is therefore emerging as a different *kind* of anthropology, not a substitute for anthropological writing. As early as 1923 the film theorist Béla Balázs wrote, "A new discovery, a new machine is at work to turn the attention of men back to a visual culture. . . . The gestures of visual man are not intended to convey concepts which can be expressed in words, but such inner experiences, such non-rational emotions which would still remain unexpressed when everything that can be told has been told."[12] Some thirty years later, Robert Gardner noted that "it would be better to see what pictures do well, to find their special qualities, and to use them accordingly rather than to suppose, as is done so much in visual education, that it is only a matter of time before movies make books unnecessary."[13]

It follows that if we are to develop new principles of visual anthropology, these must be built around strategies for exploring dimensions of social life different from those already defined in verbal and quantitative terms. If we ask what aspects of culture are specifically accessible to such an approach, it is often mistakenly assumed that it is those that are visible. It is therefore important to assert at once that the visible is equally a pathway to the nonvisible, and to the larger domain of the feelings, the intellect, and the remaining senses—what Edgar Morin called "the emotive fabric of human existence."[14] The individual is involved as a thinking and feeling person, but also as a body in relation to other bodies, to objects, to time, space, and place, and to the narratives of social interaction. And although film and video are commonly linked to vision, it would be more sensible to adopt Michel Chion's conception of the cinema as an integrated sound-image construction in which image and sound mutually inflect one another.[15] Photography provides a simulation of vision; but when the dimensions of sound and motion are added to it, a much fuller range of social life becomes accessible to representation and analysis.

And yet, it would be all too easy to polarize visual anthropology and anthropological writing, as if there were no overlap between them. At the very least, we must acknowledge that visual anthropology is often as much concerned with words as with images, for words are inseparable from the social transactions of everyday life. What visual anthropology allows us to do is to see how words fit into these events, along with the postures, gestures, tones of voice, facial expressions, and silences that accompany them.

Despite such overlaps, the use of audiovisual media brings about an important shift in the emphasis of anthropology, primarily to do with its content. It brings within reach a new anthropological understanding of social life-worlds and *a fortiori* the social experience of individuals. This includes much that we might put under the heading of "sensory" knowledge—that is, how people perceive their material environment and interact with it, in both its natural and cultural forms, including their interactions with others as physical beings.

Such an emphasis on material consciousness highlights what I believe to be a longstanding discontinuity between the experiencing of ethnographic films and the terms in which they are usually discussed. Reviews, books, and articles on the subject seem preoccupied with questions of information, representation, interpretation, accuracy, and bias, as if visual images were fundamentally a series of verbal propositions. But as Gilles Deleuze has quite properly pointed out, film is in many respects a prelinguistic form, bombarding us not with utterances but with objects. Before a film image is anything, it is a physical presence. It is not knowledge. It is not enunciation. It is not a translation. It is not even a code. It is, in Deleuze's terms, an *utterable* but not yet an *utterance*.[16] Like this room, or the chairs we sit in, it has been made by someone about whose intentions we can only guess. Thus, first and foremost, a film is a collection of the materials of which it is made: at the first level, photographic images on celluloid,[17] at the second, the traces of objects "seen" by the camera and the film-maker. What is our experience of these fleetingly glimpsed objects, persons, and places? To equate it with our experience of speech or writing is, on the face of it, absurd. We are in a different experiential world—one not necessarily inferior to reading a text, but to be understood differently. I believe we should not shy away from this prelinguistic aspect of film and video, or the visual anthropology that may emerge from it. On the contrary, it allows us to reenter the corporeal spaces of our own and others' lives—the manner in which we all, as social creatures, assimilate forms and textures through our senses, learn things before we understand them, share experiences with others, and move through the varied social environments that surround us.

If we were to reinvent visual anthropology from scratch, without paying much heed to the historical development of anthropology, we would be likely to come up with a very different set of parameters for the exploration of society. Apart from the distinctive way in which a visual medium addresses its audience, our work would be more likely to concentrate on the interrelations of objects, persons, time, and place than on larger social abstractions. This, of course, is a matter of emphasis: a visual discourse is never free of abstraction or generalization in its implications, or even in its intentions. The most substantive departures, however, would result from the very different fields of knowledge opened up by the sound-image.

Many of the characteristics of film viewing are also constituent elements of our experience of social reality, in its broadest sense. These include our consciousness of three-dimensional space,[18] of objects in the world and their qualities, of the encounters, both physical and social, of human beings, and of sequences of events unfolding in time. We may add to this the more proximate effects of our identification with the worlds constructed by films: our sensations of different surroundings, of bodies other than our own, and our perception of people as unique individuals, with their own emotions, thoughts, and mannerisms. As in life, our experience of other persons in films is both physical and psychological. If we are to look for a new and more appropriate approach to visual anthropology, we would be well advised to look for such areas of confluence.

It is possible at this point to posit three principles for a reconceptualized visual anthropology, several of which are perhaps by now self-evident:

1. To utilize the distinctive expressive structures of the visual media rather than those derived from expository prose.
2. To develop forms of anthropological knowledge that do not depend upon the principles of scientific method for their validity.
3. To explore areas of social experience for which visual media have a demonstrated expressive affinity—in particular, (a) the topographic, (b) the temporal, (c) the corporeal, and (d) the personal.

The first proposal is related to Ruby's call for films to become anthropological in form, rather than remain couched in the didactic conventions of "educational" film and television journalism. It recognizes that visual media, and particularly the cinema, have developed their own expressive conventions over the past one hundred years, involving the arrangement of images and sounds in time—much as music, over a much longer period, has devised ways of organizing pitch, rhythm, and timbre. These conventions are, of course, constantly evolving.

The second is a more radical step, calling for the acceptance (and creation) of forms of anthropological knowledge that do not necessarily conform to the patterns of logic and demonstration that have arisen in the natural sciences. This proposition represents a challenge to the principles that anthropology has most often espoused in its efforts to define its claims to truth and establish itself as a discipline. In seeking ways of constructing knowledge outside these areas of legitimacy, such a step also implies a shift in the contents of such knowledge.

The third principle is to identify the conceptual domains that are particularly appropriate to visual anthropology. This is not meant to limit research to these domains or establish an exclusionary zone. Rather, it is a call to anthropologists to chart a new course in visual anthropology, without fearing that they are departing from the anthropological task of studying how life is patterned and experienced in different societies. It is a call to begin using the visual media to their fullest potential, in areas that anthropological writing has often approached only with some difficulty.

In recent years, anthropologists have become increasingly aware of the significance of personal identity, the emotions, and the senses in social life—partly through their fieldwork experiences and partly because they are perfectly aware that anthropological thought progresses unevenly, constantly redefining what is relevant to itself as a discipline. Often what has been ignored has been thought to belong to the province of another discipline, such as psychology or biology; often it has simply escaped the notice of everybody. Anthropological interests also move in cycles. Perhaps fortuitously for visual anthropology, the individual social actor is now attracting as much attention among anthropologists as the corporate group, and there is, as well, a resurgence of interest in material culture and the aesthetics of everyday life. Much that might be studied within the four domains I have named therefore already falls within the present-day concerns of anthropology.

The *topographic* encompasses the anthropology of place and space; of rootedness and displacement, migration, diaspora, and memory; questions of cultural boundedness, locality, and history; colonial and postcolonial struggles for identity; and the study of social life-worlds as they are materially and culturally constructed.

The *temporal* includes the anthropology of time; the life-history mode of ethnography; aspects of indigenous narrative, myth, and ritual; "social dramas" as studied by Victor Turner; studies of the life cycle, socialization, cultural reproduction, and social change; and broader historical issues.

The *corporeal* relates to material culture studies; the anthropology of the senses; studies of sexuality, gender, movement, posture, and gesture; the forms of intersubjective behavior; and more generally, patterns of self-presentation and the rituals of everyday life.

The *personal* continues the concerns of the Culture and Personality school of anthropology; the anthropology of emotions; certain studies of perception, cognition, and learning; concepts of personhood, social identity, individual agency, family roles, hierarchy, and so on.

Well-established cinematic modes already exist that correspond to each of these categories. Strategies for evoking place and space have been developed in film that implicate viewers in the perspectives of individual social actors and their worlds, using shifting points of view, subjective framing, and devices such as the shot-countershot. These have the effect of situating viewers imaginatively within a three-dimensional social and spatial setting. Cinematic narrative techniques allow us to follow sequences of events and the processes and conflicting social forces that accompany them. Film is also well suited to expressing the unique individuality of human beings through their faces, gestures, postures, speech, and interactions with others. Similarly, it can communicate the forms, textures, intricacies, and sensory qualities of physical objects and their culturally complex configurations.

Finally, it should be emphasized that visual anthropology is to a large extent a *performative* anthropology. It is difficult to conceive of it, like anthropological writing, as a "translation" of culture that could ever result in a series of propositional statements. It is, rather, about the presentation of objects and the reenactment of experiences in the world. But for it to contribute significantly to anthropological knowledge, it will not be enough for it to produce occasional works that sum up a society or a culture in a few images, as has so often been attempted in the past. It will be increasingly important to create long-term projects that explore complex social phenomena in a particular setting from a variety of perspectives.

Looking to the future, it would be well to reexamine what we have most valued in the visual anthropology of the past. This was not, surely, descriptions of social structure better shown in diagrams, or surveys of economics and religion better discussed in prose. Nor, probably, was it lengthy records of rituals or technical processes unrelieved by interpretation, although these obviously have their devotees. It was, rather, persons whom we met, certain rooms and streets and compounds where they lived, journeys taken, dilemmas addressed, objects made and used, sounds heard, faces and conversations, fears and pleasures—in short, intimations of the kinds of knowledge that come from a close personal acquaintance with a particular society. In the past, ethnographic films were often praised by anthropologists for just these things, but their praise was also a language of dismissal. It was all about what film could do that was not really anthropology—its evocation, for example, of a place and the appearance of people, which was possibly useful as a backdrop for teaching anthropology but of little anthropological value in itself.

I think we should now turn that view on its head and assert that what were taken as the weakest contributions of visual anthropology—its ability to conjure up bodies and places and personalities—were actually its strengths. When we look back on the work of such pioneers as Vertov, Flaherty, Rouch, and Marshall, it becomes clear that the very things we hope to pursue in the future were also what inspired them.

Notes

This chapter is based on a paper presented at the seminar "Practicing Visual Anthropology—Perspectives on Audiovisual Means for Mediating Scientific Knowledge," University of Tromsø and the Norwegian Institute in Rome, April 2002. Thanks to Lisbet Holtedahl and Peter Crawford for their comments and suggestions.

1. As if to underline the loose structure, a number of the essays were shifted to different sections of the book in the second edition.

2. See, for example, *Rethinking Visual Anthropology*, edited by Marcus Banks and Howard Morphy, 1997.

3. Margaret Mead, the most prominent champion of visual anthropology at this time, who encouraged such filmmakers as Timothy Asch and Karl Heider, noted—not without some misgivings—that "all of our recent endeavors in the social sciences have been to remove bias, to make the recording so impersonal and thereby meaningless that neither emotion nor scientific significance remained" (cited in Jacknis 1988: 172). Mead took an increasingly strong stand on the virtues of camera objectivity, arguing in her introduction to Hockings's book

for "long sequences from one point of view that alone provide us with the unedited stretches of instrumental observation on which scientific work must be based" (1975: 10).

4. "Truth" appears in the index of the book; "theory" does not.

5. Heider 1976: 7.

6. Ruby 2000: xi.

7. Ruby 1975: 107.

8. Ibid., p. 109.

9. For example, Timothy Asch suggested his Yanomamo films be organized around a set of "standard categories for studying another society": Ecology, Subsistence, Social Organization, Political Organization, Cosmology and Religion, Acculturation, and Anthropological Fieldwork Methodology (Asch 1975: 414, in Hockings).

10. The Turkana Conversations trilogy, which Judith MacDougall and I made in the 1970s, focused on the conventional anthropological topic of marriage as a social and economic institution, but the films are equally concerned with problems of knowledge acquisition in fieldwork and people's conceptions of their own culture.

11. Ruby 1989: 9.

12. Balázs 1952: 40.

13. Gardner 1957: 348.

14. Morin 1962: 4.

15. See Chion 1994.

16. Deleuze 1989: 29.

17. Video images on magnetic tape reflect a parallel but quite different process and ontology.

18. Even though individual film images are two-dimensional, films construct for us a three-dimensional space.

FILMOGRAPHY

Titles are given in the original or in the form by which they are generally best known in English-speaking countries, with the original title or a translation following in brackets.

Across the Way [*Tien yli*]. 1988. Ilkka Ruuhijärvi & Ulla Taguchi [Turunen]. RT Documentaries, Finland. 52 mins.

The Act of Seeing with one's own eyes. 1971. Stan Brakhage. USA. 32 mins.

The Age of Reason. 2004. David MacDougall. Centre for Cross-Cultural Research, Australian National University. Australia. 87 mins.

Akazama. 1986. Marc Henri Piault. CNRS. France. 80 mins.

All the Time Somewhere [*Koko ajan jossakin*]. 1987. Ilkka Ruuhijärvi & Ulla Taguchi [Turunen]. RT Documentaries, Finland. 50 mins.

Always and Not Ever [*Aina eikä milloinkaan*]. 1990. Ilkka Ruuhijärvi & Ulla Taguchi [Turunen]. RT Documentaries, Finland. 56 mins.

Les amitiés particulières. 1964. Jean Delannoy. Christine Gouze Renal. France. 105 mins.

Aparajito [*The Unvanquished*]. 1956. Satyajit Ray. Epic Productions. India. 127 mins.

An Argument About a Marriage. 1969. John K. Marshall. Film Study Center, Harvard University. USA. 18 mins.

L'arrivée d'un train. 1895. Louis Lumière. Société Lumière. France. ca. 40 secs.

L'arroseur arrosé [*Watering the Gardener*]. 1895. Louis Lumière. Société Lumière. France, ca. 40 secs.

As It Happens [*Kun se tapahtuu*]. 1986. Ilkka Ruuhijärvi & Ulla Taguchi [Turunen]. RT Documentaries. Finland. 50 mins.

Au revoir les enfants. 1987. Louis Malle. Nouvelle Éditions de Films/MK2/Stella. France/Germany. 104 mins.

Bad Boys [*Furyo shonen*]. 1961. Susumu Hani. Iwanami Productions. Japan. 89 mins.

The Bad Seed. 1956. Mervyn LeRoy. Warner Brothers. USA. 129 mins.

Bataille sur le grand fleuve. 1951. Jean Rouch. Centre National du Cinéma. France. 35 mins.

Beppie. 1965. Johan van der Keuken. The Netherlands. 36 mins.

Bicycle Thieves [*Ladri di biciclette*]. 1948. Vittorio de Sica. PDS/ENIC. Italy. 90 mins.

Billy Bathgate. 1991. Robert Benton. Touchstone Pictures. USA. 106 mins.

Blackboard Jungle. 1955. Richard Brooks. Metro-Goldwyn-Mayer/United Artists. USA. 101 mins.

The Blue Angel [*Der blaue Engel*]. 1930. Josef von Sternberg. UFA. Germany. 98 mins.

Boyz N the Hood. 1991. John Singleton. Both Inc./Columbia. USA. 107 mins.

The Browning Version. 1951. Anthony Asquith. Javelin. Great Britain. 90 mins.

Bu Doi: Life Like Dust. 1994. Arhin Mishan & Nick Rothenberg. Urban Nomad Productions. USA. 27 mins.

Cabascabo. 1968. Oumarou Ganda. Niger. 50 mins.

La chasse au lion à l'arc [The Lion Hunters]. 1957/65. Jean Rouch. Les Films de la Pléiade. France. 88 mins.

Le château de ma mère. 1990. Yves Robert. Gaumont/Productions de la Gueville/TF1 Films. France. 98 mins.

The Childhood of Maxim Gorky [*Detstvo Gorkovo*]. 1938. Mark Donskoi. Soyezdefilm. USSR. 101 mins.

Childhood Rivalry in Bali and New Guinea. 1952. Gregory Bateson & Margaret Mead. Character Formation in Different Cultures Series. USA. 17 mins.

The Children Are Watching Us [*I bambini ci guardano*]. 1943. Vittorio de Sica. Scalera/Invicta. Italy. 85 mins.

Children of the Sewers. 1998. Alex McCall. Man Alive Group Ltd/Carlton Television. Great Britain. 52 mins.

Children of the Street [*Az utca gyermekei*]. 1999. Andrea Varga. Hungary. 28 mins.

Children's Island [*Barnens ö*]. 1980. Kay Pollak. Svenska Filminstitutet/Treklövern. Sweden. 109 mins.

Children Who Draw [*Te o kaku kodomotachi*]. 1956. Susumu Hani. Iwanami Productions. Japan. 38 mins.

Chronique d'un été [*Chronicle of a Summer*]. 1961. Jean Rouch & Edgar Morin. Argos Films. France. 90 mins.

A Cinema Programme of 1896. Georges Demeny. 1896. British Film Institute. France. 10 mins.

Civilization, A Personal View [television series]. Kenneth Clark. 1969. BBC. Great Britain. 13 episodes of 50 mins.

Come and See [*Idi i smotri*]. 1985. Elim Klimov. Byelarusfilm/Mosfilm. USSR. 142 mins.

Contes et comptes de la cour. 1993. Eliane de Latour. La Sept/CNRS. Audiovisuel/Aaton/ORTN. France. 98 mins.

Day After Day. 1962. Clément Perron. National Film Board of Canada. Canada. 27 mins.

Dead Poets Society. 1989. Peter Weir. Silver Screen Partners/Touchstone Pictures. USA. 128 mins.

Death in the Seine. 1988. Peter Greenaway. Erato Films/Micros Image/La Sept/Allarts TV/NOS Television. Netherlands/France. 44 mins.

Desert People. 1966. Ian Dunlop. Australian Commonwealth Film Unit. Australia. 51 mins.

The Devil's Playground. 1976. Fred Schepisi. The Film House. Australia. 107 mins.

Les diaboliques. 1954. Henri-Georges Clouzot. Filmsonor/Vera Films. France. 114 mins.

Diario di un maestro. 1973. Vittorio de Seta. RAI TV/Bavaria Film/Miro Film. Italy. 114 mins.

Diary of a Maasai Village [television series]. 1985. Melissa Llewelyn-Davies. BBC Television. Great Britain. 5 episodes of 50 mins.

Disappearing World [television series]. 1970– . Granada Television. Great Britain. Over 50 films of approx. 52 mins.

Doon School Chronicles. 2000. David MacDougall. Centre for Cross-Cultural Research, Australian National University. Australia. 140 mins.

Duka's Dilemma. 2001. Jean Lydall & Kaira Strecker. IWF Wissen und Medien GmbH/WDR Filmredaktion. Germany. 87 mins.

Duke of York Opening First Federal Parliament. 1901. Salvation Army Limelight Department, Melbourne. Australia. ca. 10 mins.

Être et avoir. 2002. Nicolas Philibert. Maïa Films/Arte France Cinéma/Les Films d'Ici/Centre National de Documentation Pédagogique. France. 100 mins.

The Exorcist. 1973. William Friedkin. Warner Brothers. USA. 122 mins.

Experiment of the Cross [*Experimentum cruces*]. 1996. Taras Popov & Vladimir Tulkin. Gala TV Productions. Kazakhstan. 52 mins.

The Fallen Idol. 1948. Carol Reed. London Films. Great Britain. 94 mins.

Fanny and Alexander [*Fanny och Alexander*]. 1982. Ingmar Bergman. AB Cinematograph/Svenska Filminstitutet/Swedish TV One/Gaumont/Tobis. France/West Germany/Sweden. 188 mins.

Le fantôme de la liberté. 1974. Luis Buñuel. Greenwich Film. France. 103 mins.

Farrebique: ou les quatre saisons. 1947. Georges Rouquier. L'Ecran Français/Les Films Étienne Lallier. France. 100 mins.

Forest of Bliss. 1985. Robert Gardner. Film Study Center, Harvard University. USA. 91 mins.

The 400 Blows [*Les quatre cents coups*]. 1959. François Truffaut. Films du Carrosse/SEDIF. France. 94 mins.

Freeze—Die—Come to Life! [*Zamri, umri, voskresni!*]. 1989. Vitali Kanevski. Lenfilm. USSR. 105 mins.

Germany, Year Zero [*Germania, anno zero*]. 1947. Roberto Rossellini. Tevere/Sadfilm. Italy. 78 mins.

The Getting of Wisdom. 1977. Bruce Beresford. Southern Cross Films. Australia. 100 mins.

Les glaneurs et la glaneuse [*The Gleaners and I*]. 2000. Agnès Varda. Ciné Tamaris. France. 82 mins.

La gloire de mon père. 1990. Yves Robert. Gaumont/Productions de la Gueville/TF1 Films. France. 109 mins.

The Go-Between. 1970. Joseph Losey. Metro-Goldwyn-Mayer/EMI. Great Britain. 118 mins.

Goodbye, Mr. Chips. 1939. Sam Wood. Metro-Goldwyn-Mayer. USA/Great Britain. 114 mins.

Gosses de Rio. 1990. Thierry Michel. Les Films de la Passerelle/R.B.T.F.-Télévision Belge/Wallonie Image Production. Belgium. 48 mins.

La goumbé des jeunes noceurs. 1965. Jean Rouch. Les Films de la Pléiade. France. 30 mins.

Grass: A Nation's Battle for Life. 1925. Merian C. Cooper & Ernest B. Schoedsack. Paramount Pictures. USA. 63 mins.

The Great Train Robbery. 1903. Edwin S. Porter. Edison. USA. 12 mins.

Haré Rama Haré Krishna. 1971. Dev Anand. Navretan International Films. India. 140 mins.

High School. 1968. Frederick Wiseman. Osti Films. USA. 75 mins.

A High Sky Summer [*Wang Schouxian de xia tian*]. 2001. Li Jixian. China Film Group Corporation. China. 87 mins.

Homework [*Mashgh-e shab*]. 1990. Abbas Kiarostami. Karun. Iran. 86 mins.

Hope and Glory. 1987. John Boorman. Columbia Pictures/Davros Films/Goldcrest Films/Nelson Entertainment. USA/Great Britain. 112 mins.

The Hunters. 1958. John K. Marshall. Film Study Center, Harvard University. USA. 72 mins.

The Ice Palace [Is-slottet]. 1987. Per Blom. Norsk Film A/S. Norway. 78 mins.

If . . . 1968. Lindsay Anderson. Memorial. Great Britain. 110 mins.

Imaginero—The Image Man. 1970. Jorge Preloran. Tucuman National University/Film Study Center, Harvard University. Argentina/USA. 52 mins.

In the Street. 1952. Helen Levitt, Janice Loeb & James Agee. USA. 15 mins.

Ivan's Childhood [*Ivanovo detstvo*]. 1962. Andrei Tarkovsky. Mosfilm. USSR. 97 mins.

I was Born, But . . . [*Umarete wa mita keredo*]. 1932. Yasujiro Ozu. Shichiku Films. Japan. 100 mins.

Jaguar. 1954/67. Jean Rouch. Les Films de la Pléiade. France. 93 mins.

Jazz [television series]. 2001. Ken Burns. General Motors/Corporation for Public Broadcasting. USA. 10 episodes, totalling 19 hours.

Jeux interdits [*Forbidden Games*]. 1952. René Clément. Robert Dorfmann. France. 102 mins.

Joe Leahy's Neighbours. 1988. Bob Connolly & Robin Anderson. Arundel Productions. Australia. 93 mins.

A Joking Relationship. 1966. John K. Marshall. Film Study Center, Harvard University. USA. 13 mins.

Karam in Jaipur. 2001. David MacDougall. Centre for Cross-Cultural Research, Australian National University. Australia. 54 mins.

The Kid. 1921. Charles Chaplin. First National. USA. 68 mins.

Kids. 1995. Larry Clark. Lions Gate Films. USA. 90 mins.

!Kung Bushman Hunting Equipment. 1957/72. John K. Marshall. Documentary Educational Resources. USA. 37 mins.

Lady in the Lake. 1946. Robert Montgomery. Metro-Goldwyn-Mayer. USA. 105 mins.

The Last Laugh. 1924. F. W. Murnau. UFA. Germany. 77 mins.

Life [*Elämä*]. 1991. Ilkka Ruuhijärvi & Ulla Turunen. RT Documentaries, Finland. 50 mins.

Life Is Immense and Full of Dangers [*La vie est immense et plein de dangers*]. 1994. Denis Gheerbrand. Les Films d'Ici. France. 55 mins.

Lorang's Way. 1979. David MacDougall & Judith MacDougall. Fieldwork Films. Australia. 70 mins.

Lord of the Flies. 1963. Peter Brook. Allen/Hogden/Two Arts. Great Britain. 90 mins.

Louisiana Story. 1948. Robert J. Flaherty. Robert J. Flaherty Productions/Standard Oil Company. USA. 77 mins.

Mädchen in Uniform. 1931. Leontine Sagan. Deutsche Film-Gemeinschaft GmbH. Germany. 98 mins.

Mahabharata [television series]. 1988–89. Baldev Raj Chopra. B. R. Films/Doordarshan. India. 94 episodes of 45 mins.

Les maîtres fous. 1955. Jean Rouch. Les Films de la Pléiade. France. 36 mins.

Malcolm in the Middle [television series]. From January 2000– . Fox Broadcasting Company. USA. 30 mins.

Manzan Benigaki. 2001. Shinsuke Ogawa. Completed by Xiaolian Peng. Kaminoyama Delicacy Benigaki Documentary Film Production/Planet Bibliothèque de Cinema (Japan). Japan. 90 mins.

Margaret Mead, Portrait of a Friend. 1977. Jean Rouch. CRNS. France. 35 mins.

Les masques de feuilles. 1961. Guy Le Moal. Paris CFE. France. 37 mins.

The Meat Fight. 1958/73. John K. Marshall. Documentary Educational Resources. USA. 14 mins.

Les mistons. 1958. François Truffaut. Les Films du Carrosse. France. 18 mins.

Moana: A Romance of the Golden Age. 1926. Robert J. Flaherty. Paramount Pictures. USA. 64 mins.

Moi, un noir. 1957. Jean Rouch. Les Films de la Pléiade. France. 70 mins.

Mouchette. 1966. Robert Bresson. Parc/Argos. France. 90 mins.

Murmur of the Heart [*Le souffle au coeur*]. 1971. Louis Malle. Nouvelles Éditions/Marianne/Vides Cinematografica/Franz Seitz. France/Italy/West Germany. 118 mins.

My Family and Me. 1986. Colette Piault. Les Films du Quotidien. France. 75 mins.

N!ai, The Story of a !Kung Woman. 1980. John K. Marshall and Adrienne Miesmer. Documentary Educational Resources/Public Broadcasting Associates. USA. 58 mins.

Naim and Jabar. 1974. David Hancock & Herb di Gioia. American Universities Field Staff. USA. 50 mins.

Nanook of the North. 1922. Robert J. Flaherty. Revillon Frères. USA. 70 mins.

Netsilik Eskimos [film series]. 1963–68. Asen Balikci & Guy Mary-Rousselière. Educational Development Center/National Film Board of Canada. USA/Canada. 9 films in 21 parts of 26–36 mins.

The New Boys. 2003. David MacDougall. Centre for Cross-Cultural Research, Australian National University. Australia. 100 mins.

1900 [*Novecento*]. 1976. Bernardo Bertolucci. Artistes Associés/Produzioni Europee Associati. Belgium/France/Italy. 318 mins.

Los niños abandonados [*The Abandoned Children*]. 1975. Danny Lyon. Bleak Beauty. USA. 63 mins.

Olympia. 1938. Leni Riefenstahl. Olympia-Film GmbH. Germany. Part I: Fest der Völker, 126 mins. Part II: Fest der Schönheit, 100 mins.

Paper Moon. 1973. Peter Bogdanovich. Saticoy. USA. 102 mins.

The Passion of Joan of Arc. 1928. Carl Dreyer. Société Générale des Films. France. 114 mins.

Persona. 1966. Ingmar Bergman. Svensk Filmindustri. Sweden. 81 mins.
Photo Wallahs. 1991. David MacDougall & Judith MacDougall. Fieldwork Films. Australia. 59 mins.
Pixote. 1981. Hector Babenco. Embrafilme/Hector Babenco. Brazil. 125 mins.
Police Public. 1990. Esmayeel Shroff. Mehta Productions. India. 145 mins.
Pour la suite du monde. 1963. Michel Brault. National Film Board of Canada. Canada. 84 mins.
Pride of Place. 1976. Kim Landseer & Dorothea Gazidis. National Film and Television School. Great Britain. 60 mins.
The Prime of Miss Jean Brodie. 1969. Ronald Neame. 20th Century Fox. Great Britain. 116 mins.
Puberty Blues 1981. Bruce Beresford. Limelight Productions. Australia. 87 mins.
La pyramide humaine. 1961. Jean Rouch. Les Films de la Pléiade. France. 90 mins.
The Quiet One. 1948. Sidney Meyers. Film Documents. USA. 67 mins.
Ramayana [television series]. 1987–88. Ramanand Sagar. Sagar Arts/Doordarshan. India. 78 episodes of 36–45 mins.
Rebel Without a Cause. 1955. Nicholas Ray. Warner Brothers. USA. 111 mins.
Récréations. 1992. Claire Simon. Les Films d'Ici/La Sept-ARTE. France. 54 mins.
Rivers of Sand. 1975. Robert Gardner. Film Study Center, Harvard University. USA. 84 mins.
The Road to Perdition. 2002. Sam Mendes. DreamWorks. USA. 117 mins.
The Rocking-Horse Winner. 1949. Anthony Pelissier. Twin Cities Films. Great Britain. 91 mins.
Salaam Bombay! 1988. Mira Nair. Mirabai. India. 113 mins.
Le sang des bêtes. 1949. Georges Franju. Forces et Voix de la France. 22 mins.
Schpaaa. 1998. Erik Poppe. BulBul Films. Norway. 70 mins.
Sesame Sreet [television series]. From November 1969– . Children's Television Workshop/Sesame Workshop. USA. 60 mins.
Seventeen. 1982. Joel Demott & Jeff Kreines. Middletown Film Project. USA. 119 mins.
Seven Up [television series]. Starting with *Seven Up* in 1963; then one program every seven years. Paul Almond & Michael Apted. Granada Television. Great Britain. Various lengths.
Shahenshah. 1987. Tinnu Anand. Tip Top Entertainment Ltd. India. 185 mins.
Shoeshine [*Sciuscià*]. 1946. Vittorio de Sica. Alfa/ENIC. Italy. 93 mins.
Sholay. 1975. Ramesh Sippy. Sippy Films. India. 200 mins.
Sigui [film series]. 1966–73. Jean Rouch & Germaine Dieterlen. CNRS. France. 8 films of 15 to 50 mins each.
Song of Cevlon. 1934. Basil Wright. Ceylon Tea Propaganda Board/GPO Film Unit. Great Britain. 40 mins.
The Spanish Gardener. 1956. Philip Leacock. J. Arthur Rank. Great Britain. 91 mins.
The Spirit of Freedom [television series]. 1990. Bernard-Henri Lévy and Alain Ferrari. Antenne 2/Tele Images/INA. France. 4 episodes of 58 mins.
Stand By Me. 1986. Rob Reiner. Columbia Pictures. USA. 87 mins.
Sunset Boulevard. 1950. Billy Wilder. Paramount Pictures. USA. 111 mins.

Les temps du pouvoir. 1984. Eliane de Latour. La Sept/CNRS/Aaton. France. 90 mins.

Tempus de Baristas. 1993. David MacDougall. Istituto Superiore Regionale Etnografico/Fieldwork Films/BBC Television. Italy/Australia/Great Britain. 100 mins.

Three Cases of Murder. 1953. Wendy Toye, David Eady & George More O'Ferrall. Wessex Films/British Lion. Great Britain. 99 mins.

Three Domestics. 1970. John K. Marshall. Documentary Educational Resources. USA. 36 mins.

Three-Five People. 2001. Lin Li. USA. 85 mins.

Thursday's Children. 1953. Lindsay Anderson & Guy Brenton. World Wide Pictures. Great Britain. 20 mins.

Tiger Bay. 1959. J. Lee Thompson. Independent Artists. Great Britain. 105 mins.

Titicut Follies. 1967. Frederick Wiseman & John K. Marshall. Bridgewater Film Co. USA. 89 mins.

To Live with Herds. 1972. David MacDougall. University of California at Los Angeles/Rice University Media Center. USA. 70 mins.

Tourou et Bitti: les tambours d'avant. 1971. Jean Rouch. CNRS. France. 10 mins.

Triumph of the Will [*Triumph des Willens*]. 1935. Leni Riefenstahl. Reichsparteitagsfilm/L. R. Studios-Film. Germany. 120 mins.

La vieille et la pluie. 1974. Jean-Pierre Olivier de Sardan. CNRS. France. 55 mins.

Village of the Damned. 1960. Wolf Rilla. Metro-Goldwyn-Mayer. Great Britain. 77 mins.

Le voyage dans la lune. 1902. Georges Méliès. Star Film. France. 14 mins.

Warrendale. 1966. Allan King. Allan King Associates. Canada. 100 mins.

The Wedding Camels. 1977. David MacDougall & Judith MacDougall. Rice University Media Center/Fieldwork Films. USA/Australia. 108 mins.

We, the Children of the Twentieth Century [*Nous, les enfants du XXème siècle*]. 1993. Vitali Kanevski. Lapsus/La Sept/DAR. St. Petersburg. France. 83 mins.

When I Got Jesus . . . with the Slingshot! [*Da jeg traff Jesus . . . med sprettert!*]. 2000. Stein Leikanger. Nordic Screen Production/Egmont Entertainment. Norway. 82 mins.

A Wife Among Wives. 1981. David MacDougall & Judith MacDougall. Rice University Media Center/Fieldwork Films. USA/Australia. 75 mins.

The Wild Child [*L'enfant sauvage*]. 1969. François Truffaut. Films du Carrosse/Artistes Associés. France. 84 mins.

With Morning Hearts. 2001. David MacDougall. Centre for Cross-Cultural Research, Australian National University. Australia. 110 mins.

The Women's Olamal: The Social Organisation of a Maasai Fertility Ceremony. 1984. Melissa Llewelyn-Davies. BBC Television. Great Britain. 113 mins.

The World at War [television series]. 1974–75. Jeremy Isaacs. Thames Television. Great Britain. 26 episodes of 50 mins.

The Year My Voice Broke. 1987. John Duigan. Kennedy Miller Productions. Australia. 103 mins.

Les yeux sans visage. 1959. Georges Franju. Champs Elysees/Lux Film. France/Italy. 88 mins.

Young Törless [*Der junge Törless*]. 1966. Volker Schlöndorff. Franz Seitz/Nouvelles Éditions de Film. West Germany. 85 mins.

Zerda's Children. 1978. Jorge Preloran. Ethnographic Film Program, University of California at Los Angeles. USA. 52 mins.

Zero for Conduct [*Zéro de conduite*]. 1933. Jean Vigo. Argui Films. France. 44 mins.

BIBLIOGRAPHY

Agee, James, and Walker Evans. 1960. *Let Us Now Praise Famous Men*. 2nd ed. Boston: Houghton Mifflin.

Albers, Patricia C., and William R. James. 1988. Travel Photography: A Methodological Approach. *Annals of Tourism Research* 15: 134–58.

———. 1990. Private and Public Images: A Study of Photographic Contrasts in Postcard Pictures of Great Basin Indians, 1898–1919. *Visual Anthropology* 3(2–3): 343–66.

Alloula, Malek. 1986. *The Colonial Harem*. Trans. Myrna Godzich and Wlad Godzich. Theory and History of Literature Series, Vol. 21. Minneapolis: University of Minnesota Press.

Alter, Joseph S. 1992. *The Wrestler's Body: Identity and Ideology in North India*. Berkeley: University of California Press.

Anderson, Carolyn, and Thomas W. Benson. 1993. Put Down the Camera and Pick Up the Shovel: An Interview with John Marshall. In *The Cinema of John Marshall*, Jay Ruby (ed). Chur, Switzerland: Harwood Academic Publishers, 135–67.

Appadurai, Arjun. 1981. *Worship and Conflict Under Colonial Rule: A South Indian Case*. Cambridge: Cambridge University Press.

———. 1996. *Modernity at Large: Cultural Dimensions of Modernity*. London and Minneapolis: University of Minnesota Press.

Ariès, Philippe. 1962. *Centuries of Childhood: A Social History of Family Life*. Trans. Robert Baldick. New York: Vintage Books.

Arnheim, Rudolf. 1958. *Film as Art*. London: Faber and Faber.

Asad, Talal. 1986. The Concept of Cultural Translation in British Social Anthropology. In *Writing Culture*, James Clifford and George E. Marcus (eds). Berkeley: University of California Press, 141–64.

Bakhtin, Mikhail. 1981. Forms of Time and Chronotope in the Novel. In *The Dialogic Imagination: Four Essays by M.M. Bakhtin*. Michael Holquist (ed). Austin: University of Texas Press, 84–258.

Balázs, Béla. 1952. *Theory of the Film*. Trans. Edith Bone. London: Dennis Dobson Ltd.

Baldwin, Brooke. 1988. On the Verso: Postcard Messages as a Key to Popular Prejudices. *Journal of Popular Culture* 22: 15–28.

Banks, Marcus. 1992. Which Films Are the Ethnographic Films? In *Film as Ethnography*, Peter Ian Crawford and David Turton (eds). Manchester: Manchester University Press, 116–29.

Banks, Marcus, and Howard Morphy (eds). 1997. *Rethinking Visual Anthropology*. New Haven, Conn., and London: Yale University Press.

Barthes, Roland. 1975. *The Pleasure of the Text*. Trans. Richard Miller. New York: Hill and Wang.

————. 1981. *Camera Lucida*. Trans. by Richard Howard. New York: Hill and Wang.

Bateson, Gregory. 1936. *Naven: A Survey of the Problems Suggested by a Composite Picture of the Culture of a New Guinea Tribe Drawn from Three Points of View*. Cambridge: Cambridge University Press.

Bateson, Gregory, and Margaret Mead. 1942. *Balinese Character: A Photographic Analysis*. New York Academy of Sciences, Special Publications 2. New York: New York Academy of Sciences.

————. 1977. Margaret Mead and Gregory Bateson on the Use of the Camera in Anthropology. *Studies in the Anthropology of Visual Communication* 4(2): 78–80.

Bazin, André. 1967. *What Is Cinema?* Trans. Hugh Gray. University of California Press.

Benedict, Ruth. 1928. Psychological Types in the Cultures of the South-west. *Proc. 23rd Internat. Congress of Americanists*, 572–81.

————. 1934. *Patterns of Culture*. Boston and New York: Houghton Mifflin.

Benjamin, Roger. 2003. *Orientalist Aesthetics: Art, Colonialism, and French North Africa, 1880–1930*. Berkeley: University of California Press.

Benjamin, Walter. 1992. The Work of Art in the Age of Mechanical Reproduction. In *Illuminations*. London: Fontana Press, 211–44.

Benthall, Jonathan. 1992. A Late Developer? The Ethnography of Children. *Anthropology Today* 8(2): 1.

Berleant, Arnold. 1992. *The Aesthetics of Environment*. Philadelphia: Temple University Press.

Berreman, Gerald D. 1972. Social Categories and Social Interaction in Urban India. *American Anthropologist* 74(3): 567–86.

Bhabha, Homi K. 1994. *The Location of Culture*. London and New York: Routledge.

Biella, Peter. 1993. Beyond the Ethnographic Film: Hypermedia and Scholarship. In *Anthropological Film and Video in the 1990s*, Jack Rollwagen (ed). Brockport, N.Y.: The Institute, 131–76.

Bloch, Maurice. 1974. Symbols, Song, Dance and Features of Articulation: or Is Religion an Extreme Form of Traditional Authority? *Archives Européenes de Sociology* 15: 55–81.

Bordwell, David. 1985. *Narration in the Fiction Film*. Madison: University of Wisconsin Press.

Bourdieu, Pierre. 1990a [1980]. *The Logic of Practice*. Stanford, Calif.: Stanford University Press.

————. 1990b. *Photography: A Middle Brow Art*. Trans. Shawn Whiteside. London: Polity Press.

Briggs, Jean L. 1970. *Never in Anger: Portrait of an Eskimo Family*. Cambridge, Mass.: Harvard University Press.

Brown, Penelope, and Stephen Levinson. 1978. Universals in Language Usage: Politeness Phenomena. In *Questions of Politeness*, Esther Goody (ed), Cambridge: Cambridge University Press, 56–310.

Browne, Nick. 1975. The Spectator-in-the-Text: The Rhetoric of *Stagecoach*. *Film Quarterly* 29(2): 26–38.

Bruner, Edward M. 1986. Experience and Its Expressions. In *The Anthropology of Experience*, Victor W. Turner and Edward M. Bruner (eds). Urbana and Chicago: University of Illinois Press, 3–30.

Buck-Morss, Susan. 1994. The Cinema Screen as Prosthesis of Perception: A Historical Account. In *The Senses Still*, C. Nadia Seremetakis (ed). Boulder, Colorado: Westview Press, 45–62.

Burch, Noël. 1981. *Theory of Film Practice*. Trans. Helen R. Lane. Princeton, N.J.: Princeton University Press.

Burton, David. 1993. *The Raj at Table: A Culinary History of the British in India*. London: Faber & Faber.

Calvino, Italo. 1993. *Six Memos for the Next Millennium*. New York: Vintage Books.

———. 2001. *Why Read the Classics?* Trans. Martin McLaughlin. New York: Vintage Books.

Cantrill, Arthur, and Corinne Cantrill. 1982. The 1901 Cinematography of Walter Baldwin Spencer. *Cantrills Filmnotes* 37/38: 27–42.

Carpenter, Edmund. 1976. *Oh, What a Blow That Phantom Gave Me!* St. Albans: Paladin Books.

Casey, Edward S. 1996. How to Get from Space to Place in a Fairly Short Stretch of Time: Phenomenological Prolegomena. In *Senses of Place*, Steven Feld and Keith H. Basso (eds). Santa Fe, N.M.: School of American Research, 13–52.

Certeau, Michel de, Luce Giard, and Pierre Mayol. 1998. *The Practice of Everyday Life. Volume 2: Living and Cooking*. Trans. Timothy J. Tomasik. Minneapolis and London: University of Minnesota Press.

Chion, Michel. 1994. *Audio-Vision: Sound on Screen*. Trans. Claudia Gorbman. New York: Columbia University Press.

———. 1999. *The Voice in Cinema*. Trans. Claudia Gorbman. New York: Columbia University Press.

Chopra, Pushpindar Singh (ed). 1996. *The Doon School Sixty Years On*. Dehra Dun: The Doon School Old Boys Society.

Cohn, Bernard S. 1984. *The Peoples of India: From the Picturesque to the Museum of Mankind*. Unpublished manuscript.

Coote, Jeremy. 1992. Marvels of Everyday Vision: The Anthropology of Aesthetics and the Cattle-Keeping Nilotes. In *Anthropology, Art and Aesthetics*, Jeremy Coote and Anthony Shelton (eds). Oxford: Clarendon Press, 245–73.

Coote, Jeremy, and Anthony Shelton (eds). 1992. *Anthropology, Art, and Aesthetics*. Oxford: Clarendon Press.

Crary, Jonathan. 1988. Modernizing Vision. In *Vision and Visuality*, Hal Foster (ed). Seattle: Bay Press, 29–44.

———. 1990. *Techniques of the Observer: On Vision and Modernity in the Nineteenth Century*. Cambridge, Mass.: Massachusetts Institute of Technology Press.

Creed, Barbara. 1995. Horror and the Carnivalesque: The Body-monstrous. In *Fields of Vision: Essays in Film Studies, Visual Anthropology, and Photography*, Leslie Devereaux and Roger Hillman (eds). Berkeley: University of California Press, 127–59.

286 BIBLIOGRAPHY

Crick, Malcolm. 1989. Representations of International Tourism in the Social Sciences: Sun, Sex, Sights, Savings, and Servility. *Annual Review of Anthropology* 18: 307–44.

Danius, Sara. 2001. Orpheus and the Machine: Proust as Theorist of Technological Change, and the Case of Joyce. *Forum for Modern Language Studies* 37(2): 127–40.

———. 2002. *The Senses of Modernism: Technology, Perception, and Aesthetics.* Ithaca, N.Y., and London: Cornell University Press.

Darrah, William C. 1977. *The World of Stereographs.* Gettysburg: W. C. Darrah, Publisher.

Das, Asok Kumar. 1988. The Photographer Prince. *India* (October): 22–32.

David, Philippe. 1978. La carte postale sénégalaise de 1900 à 1960. *Notes Africaines* 157: 3–12.

———. 1986–88. *Inventaire générale des cartes postales Fortier.* 3 vols. Saint-Julien-du-Sault: Fostier.

Davis, Janet. 1993. Spectacles of South Asia at the American Circus, 1890–1940. *Visual Anthropology* 6(2): 121–38.

de Heusch, Luc (ed). 1962. *The Cinema and Social Science: A Survey of Ethnographic and Sociological Films.* Paris: UNESCO Reports and Papers in the Social Sciences 16.

Deleuze, Gilles. 1986. *Cinema: The Movement-Image.* Trans. Hugh Tomlinson and Barbar Habberjam. Minneapolis: University of Minnesota Press

———. 1989. *Cinema: The Time-Image.* Translated by Hugh Tomlinson and Robert Galeta. Minneapolis: University of Minnesota Press.

Desjarlais, Robert R. 1992. *Body and Emotion: The Aesthetics of Illness and Healing in the Nepal Himalayas.* Philadelphia: University of Pennsylvania Press.

Doctorow, E. L. 1989. *Billy Bathgate.* New York: Random House.

Douglas, Mary. 1966. *Purity and Danger: An Analysis of Concepts of Pollution and Taboo.* London: Routledge & Kegan Paul.

———. 1973. *Natural Symbols: Explorations in Cosmology.* 2nd edition. London: Barrie and Jenkins.

Douglas, R. K. 1893. The Social and Religious Ideas of the Chinese, as Illustrated in the Ideographic Characters of the Language. *Journal of the Anthropological Institute of Great Britain and Ireland* 22(3): 159–73.

Doyle, Roddy. 1993. *Paddy Clarke, Ha Ha Ha.* London: Secker & Warburg.

Dyson-Hudson, Neville. 1966. *Karimojong Politics.* Oxford: Clarendon Press.

Eco, Umberto. 1977. De Interpretatione. *Film Quarterly* 30: 8–12.

Edwards, Elizabeth. 1990. Photographic "Types": The Pursuit of Method. *Visual Anthropology* 3(2–3): 235–58.

Edwards, Elizabeth (ed). 1992. *Anthropology and Photography, 1860–1920.* New Haven, Conn., and London: Yale University Press.

Efimova, Alla. 1997. To Touch on the Raw. *Art Journal* (Spring): 72–80.

Eisenstein, Sergei. 1957. *Film Form and The Film Sense.* Trans. Jay Leyda, New York: Meridian Books.

———. 1988. [1924]. The Montage of Film Attractions. In *S. M. Eisenstein, Selected Works, Vol. 1: Writings, 1922–1934*. Ed. Richard Taylor. London: British Film Institute, 39–58.

Epstein, Jean. 1974. *Écrits sur le cinema, 1921–1953*. Volume 1. Paris: Seghers.

Errington, Frederick, and Deborah Gewertz. 1989. Tourism and Anthropology in a Post-Modern World. *Oceania* 60(1): 37–54.

Evans-Pritchard, E. E. 1937. *Witchcraft, Oracles, and Magic Among the Azande*. Oxford: Clarendon Press.

———. 1940. *The Nuer*. Oxford: Clarendon Press.

Fabian, Johannes. 1983. *Time and the Other: How Anthropology Makes Its Object*. New York: Columbia University Press.

———. 1990. *Power and Performance: Ethnographic Explorations Through Proverbial Wisdom and Theater in Shaba, Zaire*. Madison: University of Wisconsin Press.

Feld, Steven. 1982. *Sound and Sentiment: Birds, Weeping, Poetics, and Song in Kaluli Expression*. Philadelphia: University of Pennsylvania Press.

———. 1996. Waterfalls of Song: An Acoustemology of Place Resounding in Bosavi, Papua New Guinea. In *Senses of Place*, Steven Feld & Keith H. Basso (eds). Santa Fe, N.M.: School of American Research, 91–136.

Feld, Steven (ed). 1985. "Chronicle of a Summer." *Studies in Visual Communication* 11(1).

Feld, Steven, and Keith H. Basso (eds). 1996. *Senses of Place*. Santa Fe, N.M: School of American Research.

Forge, Anthony. 1970. Learning to See in New Guinea. In *Socialisation: The Approach from Social Anthropology*, P. Mayer (ed). New York: Tavistock, 269–92.

Forrest, John. 1988. *Lord I'm Coming Home: Everyday Aesthetics in Tidewater North Carolina*. Ithaca, N.Y.: Cornell University Press.

Fortes, Meyer. 1945. *The Dynamics of Clanship Among the Tallensi*. London: Oxford University Press.

Fulchignoni, Enrico. 1981. Entretien de Jean Rouch avec le Professeur Enrico Fulchignoni. In *Jean Rouch: un retrospective*. Paris: Ministère des Affaires Etrangères.

Gardner, Robert. 1957. Anthropology and Film. *Daedalus* 86: 344–52.

Gardner, Robert, and Ákos Östör. 2001. *Making Forest of Bliss: Intention, Circumstance and Chance in Nonfiction Film*. A Conversation between Robert Gardner and Ákos Östör. Cambridge, Mass., and London: Harvard Film Archive.

Geary, Christraud M. 1990. Impressions of the African Past: Interpreting Ethnographic Photographs from Cameroon. *Visual Anthropology* 3(2–3): 289–315.

———. 2002. *In and Out of Focus: Images from Central Africa, 1885–1960*. Washington, D.C.: Smithsonian Institution Press.

Geary, Christraud M., and Virginia-Lee Webb (eds). 1998. *Delivering Views: Distant Cultures in Early Postcards*. Washington, D.C.: Smithsonian Institution Press.

Geertz, Clifford. 1973. Deep Play: Notes on the Balinese Cockfight. In *The Interpretation of Cultures*. New York: Basic Books, 412–53.

Geertz, Clifford. 1983. "From the Native's Point of View": On the Nature of Anthropological Understanding. In *Local Knowledge: Further Essays in Interpretive Anthropology*. New York: Basic Books, 55–70.

———. 1986. Making Experiences, Authoring Selves. In *The Anthropology of Experience*, Victor W. Turner and Edward M. Bruner (eds). Urbana and Chicago: University of Illinois Press, 373–80.

———. 1988. *Works and Lives: The Anthropologist as Author*. Stanford, Calif.: Stanford University Press.

Geffroy, Yannick. 1990. Family Pictures: Their Use in Films. Paper presented at the *5th Regards sur les Sociétés Européennes* seminar, Budapest, 8–15 July.

Gell, Alfred. 1992. The Technology of Enchantment and the Enchantment of Technology. In *Anthropology, Art, and Aesthetics*, Jeremy Coote and Anthony Shelton (eds). Oxford: Clarendon Press, 40–67.

———. 1995. On Coote's "Marvels of Everyday Vision." *Social Analysis* 38: 18–31.

———. 1996. *The Anthropology of Time: Cultural Constructions of Temporal Maps and Images*. New York: New York University Press.

———. 1998. *Art and Agency: An Anthropological Theory*. Oxford: Clarendon Press.

Gillen, F. J. 1968. *Gillen's Diary: The Camp Jottings of F. J. Gillen*. Adelaide: Adelaide Libraries Board of South Australia.

Ginsburg, Faye. 1991. Indigenous Media: Faustian Contract or Global Village? *Cultural Anthropology* 6(1): 92–112.

———. 1994. Culture/Media: A (Mild) Polemic. *Anthropology Today* 10(2): 5–15.

Godard, Jean-Luc. 1972. *Godard on Godard*. Ed. Tom Milne & Jean Narboni. New York: Viking Press.

Goffman, Erving. 1959. *The Presentation of Self in Everyday Life*. Garden City, N.Y.: Doubleday/Anchor.

———. 1962. *Asylums: Essays on the Social Situation of Mental Patients and Other Inmates*. Chicago: Aldine Publishers.

———. 1967. *Interaction Ritual: Essays on Face-to-Face Behavior*. Garden City, N.Y.: Doubleday/Anchor.

Gombrich, E.H. 1960. *Art and Illusion*. Princeton, NJ: Princeton University Press.

———. 1972. The Mask and the Face: The Perception of Physiognomic Likeness. In *Art, Perception, and Reality*, E. H. Gombrich et al. Baltimore: Johns Hopkins University Press.

Greene, Graham. 1932. *Stamboul Train: An Entertainment*. London: Heinemann.

Greene, Graham (ed). 1934. *The Old School: Essays by Divers Hands*. London: Jonathan Cape.

Griffiths, Alison. 1996. Knowledge and Visuality in Turn of the Century Anthropology. *Visual Anthropology Review* 12(2): 18–43.

———. 2002. *Wondrous Difference: Cinema, Anthropology, and Turn-of-the-Century Visual Culture*. New York: Columbia University Press.

Grimshaw, Anna. 1997. The Eye in the Door: Anthropology, Film, and the Exploration of Interior Space. In *Rethinking Visual Anthropology*, Marcus Banks & Howard Morphy (eds). New Haven, Conn., and London: Yale University Press, 36–52.

———. 2001. *The Ethnographer's Eye: Ways of Seeing in Anthropology.* Cambridge: Cambridge University Press.

Groys, Boris. 1992. *The Total Art of Stalinism: Avant-Garde, Aesthetic Dictatorship, and Beyond.* Trans. Charles Rougle. Princeton, N.J.: Princeton University Press.

Gunning, Tom. 1990. The Cinema of Attractions: Early Film, Its Spectator, and the Avant-Garde. In *Early Film: Space—Frame—Narrative*, Tom Gunning (ed). London: British Film Institute, 56–62.

Gutman, Judith Mara. 1982. *Through Indian Eyes.* New York: Oxford University Press.

Haddon, Alfred Cort. 1900. Letter to Walter Baldwin Spencer dated 23 October 1900. Spencer Papers, Pitt Rivers Museum, University of Oxford.

Haggard, H. Rider. 1885. *King Solomon's Mines.* Reprint edition, 1998. New York: Oxford University Press.

Hancock, Mary E. 1989. The Photograph as Ritual Object in Hindu Practice. Paper presented at American Anthropological Association meeting, Washington, D.C., 15–19 November.

Hardin, Kris L. 1993. *The Aesthetics of Action: Continuity and Change in a West African Town.* Washington, D.C.: Smithsonian Institution Press.

Hardy, Forsyth (ed). 1966. *Grierson on Documentary.* London: Faber and Faber.

Hastrup, Kirsten. 1992. Anthropological Visions: Some Notes on Visual and Textual Authority. In *Film as Ethnography*, Peter Ian Crawford & David Turton (eds). Manchester: Manchester University Press, 8–25.

Hattersley, C. W. 1908. *The Baganda at Home.* London: The Religious Tract Society.

Heider, Karl (ed). 1972. *The Dani of West Irian: An Ethnographic Companion to the Film* Dead Birds. Warner Modular Publications.

Heider, Karl G. 1976. *Ethnographic Film.* Austin and London: University of Texas Press.

Herzfeld, Michael. 1985. *The Poetics of Manhood: Context and Identity in a Cretan Mountain Village.* Princeton, N.J.: Princeton University Press.

Hinsley, Curtis M. 1991. The World as Marketplace: Commodification of the Exotic at the World's Columbian Exposition, Chicago, 1893. In *Exhibiting Cultures*, Ivan Karp and Steven D. Lavine (eds). Washington, D.C.: Smithsonian Institution Press, 343–65.

Hockings, Paul (ed). 1975. *Principles of Visual Anthropology.* The Hague and Paris: Mouton Publishers.

———. 1987. Tourism and English National Identity: Corkaguiney and the Nilgiris. In *Dimensions of Social Life: Essays in Honor of David G. Mandelbaum*, Paul Hockings (ed). Berlin: Mouton de Gruyter, 633–51.

———. 1992. The Yellow Bow: Rivers' Use of Photography in *The Todas.* In *Anthropology and Photography, 1860–1920*, Elizabeth Edwards (ed). New Haven, Conn., and London: Yale University Press, 179–86.

———. 1995. *Principles of Visual Anthropology.* 2nd edition. Berlin and New York: Mouton de Gruyter.

Hoffman, Martin L. 2000. *Empathy and Moral Development: Implications for Caring and Justice.* Cambridge: Cambridge University Press.

Holmes, Oliver Wendell. 1859. The Stereoscope and the Stereograph. *The Atlantic Monthly* (June 3): 738–48.

Houtman, Gustaaf. 1988. Interview with Maurice Bloch. *Anthropology Today* 4(1): 18–21.

Howard, Alan, 1988. Hypermedia and the Future of Ethnography. *Cultural Anthropology* 3: 304–15

Howes, David (ed). 1991. *The Varieties of Sensory Experience: A Source Book in the Anthropology of the Senses*. Toronto: University of Toronto Press.

Hughes, Thomas. 1857. *Tom Brown's Schooldays. By an Old Boy*. Cambridge: Macmillan.

im Thurn, E. F. 1893. Anthropological Uses of the Camera. *Journal of the Anthropological Institute* 22 (3): 184–203.

Jacknis, Ira. 1984. Franz Boas and Photography. *Studies in Visual Communication* 10(1): 2–60.

———. 1988. Margaret Mead and Gregory Bateson in Bali: Their Use of Photography and Film. *Cultural Anthropology* 3(2): 160–77.

Jackson, Michael. 1989. *Paths Towards a Clearing: Radical Empiricism and Ethnographic Enquiry*. Bloomington: Indiana University Press.

Jay, Martin. 1988. Scopic Regimes of Modernity. In *Vision and Visuality*, Hal Foster (ed). Seattle: Bay Press, 3–23.

———. 1991. The Disenchantment of the Eye: Surrealism and the Crisis of Ocularcentrism. *Visual Anthropology Review* 7(1): 15–38.

Junod, Henri A. 1912. *The Life of a South African Tribe*. Neuchatel: Imprimerie Attinger Frères.

Kahn, Fritz. 1922–29. *Das Leben des Menschen: Eine Volkstümliche Anatomie, Biologie, Physiologie und Entwicklungsgeschichte des Menschen*. 5 vols. Stuttgart: Kosmos.

Kapferer, Bruce. 1983. *A Celebration of Demons: Exorcism and the Aesthetics of Healing in Sri Lanka*. Bloomington: Indiana University Press.

Keay, John. 2000. *India: A History*. London: HarperCollins.

Kincaid, James R. 1998. *Erotic Innocence: The Culture of Child Molesting*. Durham, N.C., and London: Duke University Press.

Kipling, Rudyard. 1899. *Stalky & Co.* London: Macmillan.

Kracauer, Siegfried. 1960. *Theory of Film: The Redemption of Physical Reality*. New York: Oxford University Press.

Kuhn, Thomas. 1962. *The Structure of Scientific Revolutions*. Chicago: University of Chicago Press

Kümin, Beatrice, and Susanna Kumschick (eds). 2001. *Gruss aus der Ferne: Fremde Welten auf frühen Ansichtskarten*. Zurich: Völkerkundemuseum der Universität Zürich.

Kupfer, Joseph. 1983. *Experience as Art: Aesthetics in Everyday Life*. Albany: State University of New York Press.

Lakoff, George, and Mark Johnson. 1980. *Metaphors We Live By*. Chicago: University of Chicago Press.

———. 1999. *Philosophy in the Flesh: The Embodied Mind and Its Challenge to Western Thought*. New York: Basic Books.

Levitt, Helen. 1989. *A Way of Seeing*. With an essay by James Agee. Durham, N.C., and London: Duke University Press.

Lewis, Gilbert. 1980. *Day of Shining Red*. Cambridge: Cambridge University Press.

———. 1986. The Look of Magic. *Man* (N.S.) 21(3): 414–35.

Lewis, Oscar. 1961. *The Children of Sánchez: Autobiography of a Mexican Family*. New York: Random House.

———. 1964. *Pedro Martínez: A Mexican Peasant and His Family*. New York: Random House.

———. 1967. *La Vida: A Puerto Rican Family in the Culture of Poverty—San Juan and New York*. London: Secker & Warburg.

Lienhardt, Godfrey. 1961. *Divinity and Experience: The Religion of the Dinka*. Oxford: Clarendon Press.

Liotard, André F., Samiuel, and Jean Thévenot. 1950. *Cinéma d'exploration, cinéma au long cours*. Paris: Chavane.

Loizos, Peter. 1993. *Innovation in Ethnographic Film: From Innocence to Self-Consciousness, 1955–1985*. Manchester: Manchester University Press.

Lutz, Catherine A., and Jane L. Collins. 1993. *Reading National Geographic*. Chicago: University of Chicago Press.

MacDougall, David. 1978. Ethnographic Film: Failure and Promise. *Annual Review of Anthropology* 7: 405–25.

———. 1998. *Transcultural Cinema*. Edited with an introduction by Lucien Taylor. Princeton, N.J.: Princeton University Press.

———. 1999. Social Aesthetics and the Doon School. *Visual Anthropology Review* 15(1): 3–20.

———. 2000. Filming Children. In *Bambini/Children/Pizzinos*, catalogue of the Tenth Rassegna Internazionale di Film Etnografici, Paolo Piquereddo (ed). Nuoro, Sardinia: Istituto Superiore Regionale Etnografico, 34–36.

———. 2001a. Renewing Ethnographic Film: Is Digital Video Changing the Genre? *Anthropology Today* 17(3): 15–21.

———. 2001b. Reply to Ruby, Pink, and Wessels. *Anthropology Today* 17(5): 24–25.

Mackendrick, Alexander. 2004. *On Film-making: An Introduction to the Craft of the Director*. London: Faber and Faber.

Malinowski, Bronislaw. 1922. *Argonauts of the Western Pacific*. London: Routledge and Kegan Paul.

———. 1935. *Coral Gardens and Their Magic. Volume II: The Language of Magic and Gardening*. London: George Allen & Unwin.

———. 1967. *A Diary in the Strict Sense of the Term*. Introduction by Raymond Firth. Trans. Norbert Gutterman. Index of Native Terms by Mario Bick. New York: Harcourt, Brace and World.

Marcus, George. 1990. The Modernist Sensibility in Recent Ethnographic Writing and the Cinematic Metaphor of Montage. *Society for Visual Anthropology Review* 6(1): 2–12.

Marcus, George E., and Dick Cushman. 1982. Ethnographies as Texts. *Annual Review of Anthropology* 11: 25–69.

Marcus, George, and Michael M. J. Fischer. 1986. *Anthropology as Cultural Critique*. Chicago: University of Chicago Press.

Marshall, John. 1993. Filming and Learning. In *The Cinema of John Marshall*, Jay Ruby (ed). Chur, Switzerland: Harwood Academic Publishers, 1–133.

Matthews, Gareth B. 1980. *Philosophy and the Young Child*. Cambridge, Mass., and London: Harvard University Press.

McEwan, Ian. 1992. *Black Dogs*. London: Jonathan Cape.

Mead, Margaret. 1930. *Growing Up in New Guinea: A Comparative Study of Primitive Education*. New York: William Morrow.

———. 1975. Visual Anthropology in a Discipline of Words. In *Principles of Visual Anthropology*, Paul Hockings (ed.) The Hague: Mouton, 3–10.

Merleau-Ponty, Maurice. 1964. The Child's Relation with Others. In *The Primacy of Perception*, J. M. Edie (ed.). Evanston, Ill.: Northwestern University Press, 96–155.

Mitchell, W.J.T. 1994. *Picture Theory: Essays on Verbal and Visual Representation*. Chicago and London: University of Chicago Press.

———. 1995. Interdisciplinarity and Visual Culture. *Art Bulletin* 76(4): 540–44.

———. 1996. What Do Pictures Really Want? *October* 77 (Summer): 71–82.

Morin, Edgar. 1956. *Le Cinéma ou l'homme imaginaire: Essai d'anthropologie sociologique*. Paris: Les Éditions de Minuit.

———. 1962. Preface. In *The Cinema and Social Science: A Survey of Ethnographic and Sociological Films*, Luc de Heusch (ed). Paris: UNESCO Reports and Papers in the Social Sciences 16.

Morphy, Howard. 1996. Aesthetics Is a Cross-Cultural Category: For the Motion. In *Key Debates in Anthropology*, Tim Ingold (ed). London and New York: Routledge, 249–93.

Myers, Fred R. 1986. *Pintupi Country, Pintupi Self: Sentiment, Place, and Politics Among Western Desert Aborigines*. Washington, D.C.: Smithsonian Institution Press.

Nichols, Bill. 1981. *Ideology and the Image: Social Representation in the Cinema and Other Media*. Bloomington: Indiana University Press.

———. 1986. Questions of Magnitude. In *Documentary and the Mass Media*, J. Corner (ed). London: Edward Arnold, 107–22.

———. 1991. *Representing Reality: Issues and Concepts in Documentary*. Bloomington: Indiana University Press.

———. 1994. *Blurred Boundaries: Questions of Meaning in Contemporary Culture*. Bloomington: Indiana University Press.

O'Hanlon, Michael. 1989. *Reading the Skin: Adornment, Display, and Society Among the Wahgi*. London: The British Museum.

Okely, Judith. 1996. *Own or Other Culture*. London: Routledge.

Ong, Walter J. 1982. *Orality and Literacy: The Technologizing of the Word*. London and New York: Routledge.

———. 1991. The Shifting Sensorium. In *The Varieties of Sensory Experience: A Sourcebook in the Anthropology of the Senses*, David Howes (ed). Toronto: University of Toronto Press, 25–30.

Östör, Ákos. 1990. Whither Ethnographic Film? *American Anthropologist* 92(3): 715–22.

Oudart, Jean-Pierre. 1977. Cinema and Suture. *Screen* 18(4): 35–47.

Parkes, Fanny. 1850. *Wanderings of a Pilgrim in Search of the Picturesque*. London: Pelham Richardson.

Perez, Gilberto. 1998. *The Material Ghost: Films and Their Medium*. Baltimore: Johns Hopkins University Press.

Peterson, Nicolas. 1985. The Popular Image. In *Seeing the First Australians*, Ian Donaldson and Tamsin Donaldson (eds). London: George Allen & Unwin, 164–80.

———. 1991. The Constructions of Aboriginal Femininity in Early Twentieth Century Photography. In *Aboriginal Australians: Contemporary Perspectives on Their Society and Culture*, S. Koyama (ed). Osaka: National Museum of Ethnology, 59–90.

———. 1997. The Aboriginal Family, Gender, and the State in Turn-of-the-Century Photography. Paper presented at the *Looking Through Photographs* conference held at the Queensland Museum, Brisbane, 8–9 November.

Piault, Marc Henri. 1989. Ritual: A Way Out of Eternity. Paper presented at *Film and Representations of Culture* Conference, Humanities Research Centre, Australian National University, Canberra, 28 September.

———. 2000a. *Anthropologie et cinéma*. Paris: Éditions Nathan/HER.

———. 2000b. From Out of the Mouths of Babes and Sucklings! In *Bambini/Children/Pizzinos*, catalogue of the Tenth Rassegna Internazionale di Film Etnografici, Paolo Piquereddo (ed). Nuoro, Sardinia: Istituto Superiore Regionale Etnografico, 24–30.

Pink, Sarah. 2001. Renewal of Ethnographic Film: The Future of Visual Anthropology? *Anthropology Today* 17(5): 23–24.

Pinney, Christopher. 1990a. Classification and Fantasy in the Photographic Construction of Caste and Tribe. *Visual Anthropology* 3(2–3): 259–88.

———. 1990b. The Quick and the Dead: Images, Time, and Truth. *Visual Anthropology Review* 6(2): 42–54.

———. 1991. Narrative Paradise Lost? Paper presented at the Nordic Anthropological Film Association Conference, Oslo, 21 May.

———. 1992a. The Lexical Spaces of Eye-Spy. In *Film as Ethnography*, Peter Ian Crawford and David Turton (eds). Manchester and New York: Manchester University Press, 26–49.

———. 1992b. The Parallel Histories of Anthropology and Photography. In *Anthropology and Photography 1860–1920*, Elizabeth Edwards (ed). New Haven, Conn., and London: Yale University Press, 74–95.

———. 1992c. Underneath the Banyan Tree: William Crooke and Photographic Depiction of Caste. In *Anthropology and Photography 1860–1920*, Elizabeth Edwards (ed). New Haven, Conn., and London: Yale University Press, 165–73.

———. 1995. "An Authentic Indian 'Kitsch' ": The Aesthetics, Discriminations and Hybridity of Popular Indian Art. *Social Analysis* 38: 88–105.

———. 1997. *Camera Indica: The Social Life of Indian Photographs*. London: Reaktion Books.

———. 2000. Introduction: Public, Popular, and Other Cultures. In *Pleasure and the Nation: The History, Politics, and Consumption of Public Culture in India*, Rachel Dwyer and Christopher Pinney (eds). New Delhi: Oxford University Press, 1–34.

———. 2001. Piercing the Skin of the Idol. In *Beyond Aesthetics: Art and the Technologies of Enchantment*, Christopher Pinney and Nicholas Thomas (eds). Oxford and New York: Berg, 157–79.

Poignant, Roslyn. 1992. Surveying the Field of View: The Making of the RAI Photographic Collection. In *Anthropology and Photography, 1860–1920*, Elizabeth Edwards (ed). New Haven: Yale University Press, 42–73.

Price, Sally, and Jean Jamin. 1988. A Conversation with Michel Leiris. *Current Anthropology* 29(1): 157–74.

Prochaska, David. 1990. The Archive of *Algérie Imaginaire*. *History and Anthropology* 4: 373–420.

———. 1991. Fantasia of the Photothèque: French Postcard Views of Colonial Senegal. *African Arts* 24(4): 40–47, 98.

Proust, Marcel. 1982. *The Guermantes Way*, from *Remembrance of Things Past*, Vol II, trans. C. K. Scott Moncrieff and Terence Kilmartin. New York: Vintage.

Pudovkin, V.I. 1960. *Film Technique and Film Acting*. Trans. and ed. Ivor Montagu. New York: Grove Press.

Randall, Don. 2000. *Kipling's Imperial Boy: Adolescence and Cultural Hybridity*. London: Palgrave.

Rattray, R. S. 1923. *Ashanti*. Oxford: Clarendon Press.

Raum, O. F. 1940. *Chaga Childhood*. London: Oxford University Press.

Riefenstahl, Leni. 1973. *The Last of the Nuba*. New York: Harper & Row.

———. 1976. *People of Kao*. New York: Harper & Row.

Rivers, W.H.R. 1906. *The Todas*. London: Macmillan.

Rock, Irvin (ed). 1990. *The Perceptual World: Readings from* Scientific American *Magazine*. New York: W. H. Freeman and Company.

Rollwagen, Jack R. 1988. The Role of Anthropological Theory in "Ethnographic" Filmmaking. In *Anthropological Filmmaking*, J. R. Rollwagen (ed). Chur, Switzerland: Harwood Academic Publishers, 287–315.

Rosaldo, Renato. 1980. *Ilongot Headhunting, 1883–1974: A Study in Society and History*. Stanford, Calif.: Stanford University Press.

Rosselli, J. 1980. The Self-Image of Effeteness: Physical Education and Rationalism in Nineteenth Century Bengal. *Past and Present* 86: 121–48.

Roth, Paul A. 1989. How Narratives Explain. *Social Research* 56(2): 449–78.

Rouch, Jean. 1975. The Camera and Man. In *Principles of Visual Anthropology*, Paul Hockings (ed). The Hague: Mouton, 83–107.

———. 1985. The Cinema of the Future? *Studies in Visual Communication* 11(1): 30–35.

———. 1995a. The Camera and Man. In *Principles of Visual Anthropology*, Paul Hockings (ed). 2nd edition. Berlin and New York: Mouton de Gruyter, 79–98.

———. 1995b. Our Totemic Ancestors and Crazed Masters. In *Principles of Visual Anthropology*, Paul Hockings (ed). 2nd Edition. Berlin and New York: Mouton de Gruyter, 217–32.

Ruby, Jay. 1975. Is an Ethnographic Film a Filmic Ethnography? *Studies in the Anthropology of Visual Communication* 2(2): 104–1.

———. 1989. The Emperor and His Clothes. SVA Newsletter 5(1): 9–11.

———. 1994. Review of Peter Ian Crawford and David Turton (eds), *Film as Ethnography*, and Peter Loizos, *Innovation in Ethnographic Film. Visual Anthropology Review* 10(1): 165–69.

———. 2000. *Picturing Culture*. Chicago and London: University of Chicago Press.

———. 2001. Digital Video: Responses to David MacDougall. *Anthropology Today* 17(5): 23.

Russell, Bertrand. 1912. *The Problems of Philosophy*. Reprint edition, 1988. Buffalo: Prometheus Books.

Salmond, Anne. 1982. Theoretical Landscapes: On Cross-Cultural Conceptions of Knowledge. In *Semantic Anthropology*, D. Parkin (ed). London: Academic Press, 65–87.

Samier, Eugenie. 1997. Administrative Ritual and Ceremony: Social Aesthetics, Myth, and Language Use in the Rituals of Everyday Organizational Life. *Educational Management & Administration* 25(4): 417–36.

Schieffelin, Edward L. 1976. *The Sorrow of the Lonely and the Burning of the Dancers*. New York: St. Martin's Press.

Scoditti, Giancarlo M. G. 1982. Aesthetics: The Significance of Apprenticeship on Kitawa. *Man* (N.S.) 17: 74–91.

Selfe, Lorna. 1977. *Nadia: A Case of Extraordinary Drawing Ability in an Austistic Child*. London: Academic Press.

Serre, Jacques. 1988. Henri Bobichon (1866–1939). In *Hommes et destines: Dictionnaire biographique d'Outre-mer*. Vol. 8. Académie des Sciences d'Outre-mer. Paris: Editions Montigeon.

Shattuck, Roger. 1980. *The Forbidden Experiment: The Story of the Wild Boy of Aveyron*. New York: Farrar, Straus and Giroux.

Simenon, Georges. 1967 [1952]. *Madame Maigret's Friend*. Trans. Helen Sebba. Harmondsworth: Penguin Books.

Simpson, Anthony. 1998. Memory and Becoming Chosen Other: Fundamentalist Elite-Making in a Zambian Mission School. In *Memory and the Postcolony*, R. Werbner (ed). London: Zed Books, 209–28.

———. 1999. "Jacked-Up Gentlemen": Contested Discourses of Postcolonial Catholic Mission Schooling in Zambia. *Social Analysis* 43(1): 35–52.

Sinha, Mrinalini. 1995. *Colonial Masculinity: The "Manly Englishman" and the "Effeminate Bengali" in the Late Nineteenth Century*. Manchester: Manchester University Press.

Sontag, Susan. 1966. Against Interpretation. In *Against Interpretation, and Other Essays*. New York: Farrar, Straus and Giroux, 1–14.

———. 1977. *On Photography*. New York: Farrar, Straus and Giroux.

———. 1980. Fascinating Fascism. In *Under the Sign of Saturn*. New York: Farrar, Straus and Giroux, 73–105.

———. 2003. *Regarding the Pain of Others*. New York: Farrar, Straus and Giroux.

Sorenson, E. Richard, and Allison Jablonko. 1975. Research Filming of Naturally Occurring Phenomena: Basic Strategies. In *Principles of Visual Anthropology*, Paul Hockings (ed). The Hague: Mouton, 151–63.

Spencer, Paul. 1965. *The Samburu*. London: Routledge & Kegan Paul.

———. 1988. *The Maasai of Matapato*. Bloomington: Indiana University Press.

Sprague, Stephen. 1978. How I See the Yoruba See Themselves. *Studies in the Anthropology of Visual Communication* 5(1): 9–28.

Srivastava, Sanjay. 1998. *Constructing Post-Colonial India: National Character and the Doon School.* London and New York: Routledge.

Stapledon, Olaf W. 1930. *Last and First Men: A Story of the Near and Far Future.* London: Methuen & Co.

Stevenson, Robert Louis. 1910. *Prayers Written in Vailima.* With an introduction by Mrs. Stevenson. Designed, written out, and illuminated by A. Sagorski. London: Chatto & Windus.

Stewart, Kathleen. 1996. *A Space on the Side of the Road: Cultural Poetics in an "Other" America.* Princeton, N.J.: Princeton University Press.

Stewart, Susan. 1984. *On Longing: Narratives of the Miniature, the Gigantic, the Souvenir, the Collection.* Baltimore: Johns Hopkins University Press.

Stoller, Paul. 1989. *The Taste of Ethnographic Things: The Senses in Anthropology.* Philadelphia: University of Pennsylvania Press.

———. 1992. *The Cinematic Griot: The Ethnography of Jean Rouch.* Chicago: University of Chicago Press.

———. 1997. *Sensuous Scholarship.* Philadelphia: University of Pennsylvania Press.

Street, Brian. 1992. British Popular Anthropology: Exhibiting and Photographing the Other. In *Anthropology and Photography,* Elizabeth Edwards (ed). New Haven, Conn., and London: Yale University Press, 122–31.

Sullivan, Gerald. 1999. *Margaret Mead, Gregory Bateson, and the Highland Bali: Fieldwork Photographs of Bayung Gedé, 1936–1939.* Chicago: University of Chicago Press.

Tagg, John. 1988. *The Burden of Representation.* Amherst: The University of Massachusetts Press.

Taussig, Michael T. 1987. *Shamanism, Colonialism, and the Wild Man.* Chicago: University of Chicago Press.

Tayler, Donald. 1992. "Very loveable human beings": The Photography of Everard im Thurn. In *Anthropology and Photography, 1860–1920,* Elizabeth Edwards (ed). New Haven, Conn., and London: Yale University Press, 187–92.

Thapan, Meenakshi. 1991. *Life at School: An Ethnographic Study.* New Delhi: Oxford University Press.

Theweleit, Klaus. 1989. *Male Bodies: Psychoanalyzing the White Terror.* Minneapolis: University of Minnesota Press.

Thornton, Robert J. 1983. Narrative Ethnography in Africa, 1850–1920: The Creation and Capture of an Appropriate Domain for Anthropology. *Man* (N.S.) 18(3): 502–20.

———. 1985. "Imagine yourself set down . . .": Mach, Frazer, Conrad, Malinowski, and the Role of Imagination in Ethnography. *Anthropology Today* 1(5): 7–14.

Todorov, Vladislav. 1995. *Red Square, Black Square: Organon for Revolutionary Imagination.* Albany: State University of New York Press.

Toren, Christina. 1993. Making History: The Significance of Childhood Cognition for a Comparative Anthropology of the Mind. *Man* (N.S.) 28(3): 461–77.

Turner, Victor W. 1957. *Schism and Continuity in an African Society: A Study of Ndembu Village Life.* Manchester: Manchester University Press.

————. 1981. Social Dramas and Stories About Them. In *On Narrative*, W.J.T. Mitchell (ed). Chicago: University of Chicago Press, 137–64.

————. 1986a. *The Anthropology of Performance*. New York: PAJ Productions.

————. 1986b. Dewey, Dilthey, and Drama: An Essay in the Anthropology of Experience. In *The Anthropology of Experience*, Victor W. Turner and Edward M. Bruner (eds). Urbana and Chicago: University of Illinois Press, 33–44.

Twain, Mark. 1885. *The Adventures of Huckleberry Finn (Tom Sawyer's Comrade)*. New York: Charles L. Webster.

Tyler, Stephen A. 1987. *The Unspeakable*. Madison: University of Wisconsin Press.

Vaughan, Dai. 1999. *For Documentary: Twelve Essays*. Berkeley: University of California Press.

Vertov, Dziga. 1984. *Kino-Eye: The Writings of Dziga Vertov*. Ed. Annette Michelson, trans. Kevin O'Brien. Berkeley: University of California Press.

von Bonsdorff, Pauline, and Arto Haapala (eds). 1999. *Aesthetics in the Human Environment*. Jyväskylä: Gummerus Kirjapaino Oy.

Watson, J. Forbes, & J. W. Kaye. 1868–75. *The People of India*. With letterpress by P. M. Taylor. 8 vol. London: India Museum.

Weiner, James. 1991. *The Empty Place: Poetry, Space, and Being Among the Foi of Papua New Guinea*. Bloomington: University of Indiana Press.

White, Hayden. 1978. *Tropics of Discourse: Essays in Cultural Criticism*. Baltimore: Johns Hopkins University Press.

————. 1980. The Value of Narrativity in the Representation of Reality. In *On Narrative*, W.J.T. Mitchell (ed). Chicago: University of Chicago Press, 1–23.

Williams, Linda. 1991. Film Bodies: Gender, Genre, and Excess. *Film Quarterly*, 44(4): 2–13.

————. 1995. Corporealized Observers: Visual Pornographies and the "Carnal Density of Vision." In *Fugitive Images: From Photography to Video*, Patrice Petro (ed). Bloomington and Indianapolis: Indiana University Press, 3–41.

Wober, Mallory. 1966. Sensotypes. *Journal of Social Psychology* 70: 181–89.

————. 1991. The Sensotype Hypothesis. In *The Varieties of Sensory Experience: A Sourcebook in the Anthropology of the Senses*, David Howes (ed). Toronto: University of Toronto Press, 31–42.

Wolpert, Barbara. 2000. The Anthropologist as Photographer: The Visual Construction of Ethnographic Authority. *Visual Anthropology* 13(4): 321–43.

Worth, Sol. 1981. *Studying Visual Communication*. Edited with an introduction by Larry Gross. Philadelphia: University of Pennsylvania Press.

Wright, Christopher. 2003. Supple Bodies: The Papua New Guinea Photographs of Captain Francis R. Barton, 1899–1907. In *Photography's Other Histories*, Christopher Pinney and Nicolas Peterson (eds). Durham, N.C., and London: Duke University Press, 146–69.

Young, Michael W. 1999. *Malinowski's Kiriwina: Fieldwork Photography, 1915–1918*. Chicago: University of Chicago Press.

INDEX